D1125941

BEFORE WALLIS

EDWARD VIII'S OTHER WOMEN

RACHEL TRETHEWEY

For John,
for being with me all the way.

First published 2018

The History Press
The Mill, Brimscombe Port
Stroud, Gloucestershire, GL5 2QG
www.thehistorypress.co.uk

British Library Cataloguing in Publication Data.
A catalogue record for this book is available from the British Library.

ISBN 978 0 7509 8560 4

Typesetting and origination by The History Press
Printed and bound in Great Britain by TJ International Ltd

CONTENTS

FREDA

ACKNOWLEDGEMENTS

From start to finish the writing of this book has only been possible because of the support of many people. The initial idea of looking into the life of Freda Dudley Ward came from the novelist, royal commentator and journalist Christopher Wilson. Since my time as a student journalist Christopher has been a mentor to me and his suggestion of writing about Freda immediately intrigued me. After discussions on the subject with my friend, the novelist and biographer Andrew Wilson, the project grew to include the other women in Edward VIII's life. In most biographies of the Duke of Windsor, Rosemary Leveson-Gower, Freda Dudley Ward and Thelma Furness appear as minor characters. The same stories about them have been repeated many times. I wanted to find out more about the women who captured the future king's heart. I have only been able to do that with the help of their descendants and archivists who have access to their papers.

I would particularly like to thank the Dudley Ward family. Meeting Freda's grandchildren has given me an insight into what she was like because they have inherited her charm, lack of pretension and open-mindedness. Freda's granddaughter Martha Milinaric has been so generous with both her time and hospitality. I spent a magical summer's day at Martha's country house in Somerset, looking through hundreds of letters to Freda, including the collection of love letters from Michael Herbert. Martha showed me her grandmother's photo albums, which capture her life close to the centre of power. Martha and her husband David made my husband and I feel so at home. After an intriguing morning looking at their collection, we had an equally stimulating lunch with the Milinarics. Martha also put me in touch with other members of her family. Freda's grandson Max Reed and his wife Susan were also incredibly welcoming when I visited them in their London home. As I looked through the hundreds of love letters written by the Prince of Wales to Freda, there were welcome visits from the Reeds' two lovely children, Ben and Alice, and their cat, Meg.

Freda's other grandchildren, Ben Laycock and Emma Temple, also talked to me about their grandmother and Ben provided me with some photographs of Freda that show that she remained stylish and fun throughout her long life. Freda's great-nieces, Lady Lucinda Worsthorne and Lady Isabella Naylor-Leyland, and her great-nephew Ned Lambton, Earl of Durham, also talked to me about her and added to the colourful image I was piecing together. Stephanie Hallin at the Feathers Club Association allowed me to see the minutes of the charity, which reveal Freda's dedicated philanthropy. Rosemary Leveson-Gower's family members have also been very kind, sparing the time to tell me about their grandmother. I would particularly like to thank Alexander Ward and Leander Ward for providing me with information about the woman who died long before they were born.

When I first started the project and found out that there were so many letters from Edward, Prince of Wales to Freda Dudley Ward, I wanted to discover who held the copyright. My first starting point was Rupert Godfrey, who edited *Letters from a Prince*, the correspondence from Edward to Freda from March 1918 until January 1921. He was most helpful but warned me that the copyright was 'a thorny issue'. I then contacted the Pasteur Institute in Paris, which is the sole legatee of the Duchess of Windsor. They hold the copyright on all letters written by the Duke and Duchess of Windsor but when I wrote to them they explained that they consider that this only concerns the letters exchanged between the duchess and the duke. They do not claim the copyright on the Dudley Ward letters and told me that I did not need their authorisation to quote from them.

I then contacted the Royal Archives at Windsor. As the copyright on the Duke of Windsor's papers lacked clarity they decided to try to clear up the issue. In the autumn of 2017, Oliver Urquhart Irivine, the Librarian and Assistant Keeper of the Queen's Archives, went to the Family Division of the High Court to formally request a full copy of the Duke of Windsor's will and codicil for research purposes and to fill a gap in the Royal Archives' holding and therefore in their knowledge. In a letter to the court, he explained that their purpose was to ascertain the identity of the current rights holders to the papers of Edward, Duke of Windsor. The president of the Family Division of the High Court, Sir James Munby, decided that the seal on the envelope containing the Duke of Windsor's will and codicil could be broken for the first time, and a copy was made for Mr Urquhart Irivine to see. It was discovered that the Duchess of Windsor was the duke's residual legatee. Therefore, the Royal Archives informed me that the royal family are not claiming copyright on the Duke of Windsor's papers except for the brief period when he was king. Having spoken to the Pasteur Institute and the Royal Archives, I feel that I have done everything within my power to discover who holds the copyright. As the most likely candidates are not claiming it, I am quoting from the Duke of Windsor's papers when he was Prince of Wales in this book. If a valid copyright holder comes forward, they will be credited in any future editions.

I would also like to thank Her Majesty Queen Elizabeth II and the Royal Archives for allowing me to visit Windsor Castle and see Edward, Prince of Wales's diaries and the letters between him and his mother Queen Mary during the First World War. They also showed me correspondence to the prince from Lord Desmond Fitzgerald, Reginald, Viscount Esher and from the prince to Lady Weigall. Another important document I saw at Windsor was the Wigram Memorandum of 1932 recording the Prince of Wales's discussion with his father George V about his attitude to marriage. It was a memorable experience walking up the worn stone steps in the round tower at Windsor and then studying these papers in the timeless, book-lined research room. Archivists Jane Mycock and Julie Crocker went beyond the call of duty in making sure I was able to see all the documents I had requested. Archives manager Bill Stockting explained to me very clearly about the research the Royal Archives had done into the Duke of Windsor's copyright. The material from the Royal Archives in this book is used with the permission of Her Majesty Queen Elizabeth II.

Many other archives have also kindly allowed me to use material from their collections. I would like to thank Dudley Archives and Local History Service for the letters concerning Rosemary Leveson-Gower and her family; Staffordshire Record Office for a letter from Edward, Prince of Wales to Millicent, Duchess of Sutherland and a letter from Millicent, Duchess of Sutherland to Rosemary Leveson-Gower; Wiltshire and Swindon Archives for the Michael Herbert letters; the University of Southampton for letters between Lord Louis Mountbatten and his mother, the Marchioness of Milford Haven; Shropshire Archives for Sir Francis Newdegate's letter to Bridgeman; Hatfield House Archive for Rosemary Ednam's letter to Elizabeth, Marchioness of Salisbury; the Earl of Rosslyn and the National Records of Scotland for letters from the Prince of Wales to Shelila Loughborough; the Churchill Archives Centre, Churchill College, Cambridge University for letters from Freda and Rosemary to Duff Cooper, Freda to Winston Churchill, Brendan Bracken to Winston Churchill, Lord Dudley to Winston Churchill and Winston Churchill to Harold Macmillan; the National Archives for Freda's and Thelma's divorce papers. I would also like to thank Dr Rosie Collins, whose research into the Birkin family in Nottingham for the Radcliffe-on-Trent First World War history project was enlightening. Many thanks too to John Taylor who trawled the Special Branch files to see if a watch was kept on Freda or Thelma.

I have also drawn on many published memoirs, diaries and letters from contemporaries of Edward VIII. Among the most useful and colourful sources were the papers and books of Lady Diana and Duff Cooper. I would like to thank the estate of Lady Diana Cooper and Lord Norwich for granting me permission to quote from all sources in which Lord Norwich owns the rights. Rosemary Leveson-Gower was great friends with Ettie Desborough's daughter, Monica. Viscount Gage has kindly granted me permission to quote from Ettie Desborough's journal with the references to their friendship. I would also like to thank Jerome Thomas, Rosalind Asquith and Roland Asquith and the Random House Group Ltd for granting permission to reproduce quotations from Lady Cynthia Asquith's *Diaries 1915–18* (1968). For the photographs that appear in this book, I would like to thank Martha Milinaric, Ben Laycock, the Mary Evans Picture Library, the National Portrait Gallery and Staffordshire Record Office. I have tried to contact all copyright holders; if there are any I have missed, I will rectify this omission in subsequent editions.

As well as the people who have helped me gather the information I needed to write this book I would also like to thank my agent Heather Holden-Brown and her assistant Cara Armstrong for all their support. Once again, it has also been a pleasure working with my publishers at The History Press. I am very grateful to Laura Perehinec, Chrissy McMorris, Caitlin Kirkman and Katie Beard, who have spurred me on with their enthusiasm; it is great to work with people who are on the same wavelength.

Finally, I would like to thank my family. My husband, John Kiddey, has been there by my side throughout, coming on the research trips and acting as a sounding board for my ideas. Having him with me to share the experience has made it much more fun. My mother, Bridget Day, as always, has been a wonderful listener and adviser. For proofreading I have relied on my sister, Becky Trethewey, while, for making sure my computer worked, my son Christopher has been a great technician.

INTRODUCTION

It is hard to imagine a century later, just how eligible the Prince of Wales, who was to become Edward VIII and then the Duke of Windsor, was. Charismatic, charming and dapper, he caused debutantes to go weak at the knees at the thought of meeting him; and, as he was heir to the throne, future king and emperor, aristocratic mothers were busy with schemes for him to marry their daughters. In dormitories across the country, schoolgirls had photos of him pinned to their walls. Even the tough celebrity journalist Adela Rogers St Johns had a picture of him framed on her dressing table. His face appeared everywhere, in newspapers and magazines, on cigarette cards and Pathé News.[1]

His combination of boyish vulnerability and glamour made him immensely popular and an icon of the age. He was the 'unofficial patron' of the Bright Young Things, totally in tune with the cult of youth of his era.[2] If Edward appeared in 'co-respondent' shoes, a Fair Isle sweater or a loud checked jacket, half the young men across the country would copy him, thinking that it would make them equally irresistible to women.[3]

However, his appeal went deeper than fashion. As James Pope-Hennessy wrote, he personified the longings of the new post-war generation, with their desire for freedom from tradition and convention.[4] He was thoroughly modern, rebelling against his father and rejecting his Victorian values. After the First World War, he recognised the need for a new order in society and wanted to see a land fit for heroes.

No previous member of the royal family had experienced such celebrity. He was like a modern pop star, and everywhere he went he was surrounded by swooning fans. On royal visits girls would scream: 'I touched him, I touched him.' The frenzy that surrounded him was captured in a popular song of the era: 'I've danced with a man, who's danced with a girl, who's danced with the Prince of Wales.'

This book tells the stories of the much-envied women who really got close to the elusive prince. Wallis Simpson was the woman who stole the king's heart and rocked the monarchy, but she was not Edward VIII's first or only love. When the abdication crisis occurred in 1936 it was widely believed that Edward was suffering from an almost pathological obsession with the woman he loved. Only those in his inner circle knew that it was not the first time he had experienced a similar, all-consuming love.[5] Mrs Simpson once told an interviewer that she knew the Prince of Wales had a lot of girls before her, but he said that she was the only one he wanted to marry.[6] As this book will show, that statement might have fitted the legend of the greatest love affair of the twentieth century, but it was not quite true. The assessment made by the prince's private secretary, Sir Alan Lascelles (known as Tommy), seems closer to the reality. He believed that the story of the lonely bachelor who fell deeply in love for the first time with the soulmate for whom he had been waiting all his life was a myth. Tommy had known the prince very well for a long time and he described this romantic interpretation as 'moonshine'. He explained that in 1918 Edward had fallen as deeply in love with Freda Dudley Ward as any man could fall. From then on, he was never not under the influence of one woman or another. There was always a 'grande affaire' going on, alongside a continuous series of 'petites affaires' that occurred in whichever part of the empire the Prince of Wales was in at the time. Lascelles emphasised that Wallis was no 'isolated phenomenon' but just the current woman in an 'arithmetical progression' which had been going on for nearly twenty years.[7]

Wallis Simpson, in her memoir, admitted that it was timing as much as the depth of Edward's feelings for her that led to the abdication. She explained that as Prince of Wales his loneliness could be lessened by 'passing companionships', but as king that would have been difficult. The time had come for him to marry and it was her fate to be the object of his affection at that moment.[8]

This book is about the other women Edward adored before Wallis dominated his life. Once under Wallis's control he never openly admitted the importance of the women he loved before. However, in his memoir, written decades after these affairs, he did hint at his romantic past. He explained that there had been moments of 'tenderness, even enchantment' and without these experiences his life would have been 'almost intolerable'.[9]

Part One of this book seeks to recapture those first enchantments and analyse their pivotal role in shaping the man he became and his later choices. It describes the relationships the prince had with three women. First, Rosemary Leveson-Gower, the girl he wanted to marry; then his long-term married mistress, Freda Dudley Ward; and finally Thelma Furness, his twice-married American lover, who inadvertently paved the way for Wallis. This section looks at these women's lives before the heir to the throne entered their world and transformed it. It then charts the course of their romance up to the point where the prince moved on to his next relationship.

Rosemary would have been the ideal bride: the daughter of a duke, she was not only well connected but also the perfect princess for the post-war era. She had served as a nurse in her mother's hospital in France throughout the war and shared the prince's compassion and respect for the soldiers who had sacrificed so much. She also had a strong personality, which could have steered the often wilful and weak prince in the right direction. Edward had found the perfect partner, but his parents opposed the match. It seems they were worried that the racy family of her mother, Millicent, Duchess of Sutherland, might cause embarrassment. It was a fateful decision; the prince would never seriously court a single woman again.

His next love was Freda Dudley Ward. In many ways, she was the prince's match, both physically and emotionally. They were both petite, fashionable and modern. But beneath her feminine exterior was a strong character. She had the wisdom to guide her lover in the right direction and make him a better person. However, Freda was married, and, unlike Mrs Simpson, she knew that she would never marry the prince.

Edward was obsessively in love with Mrs Dudley Ward for sixteen years. His biographer, Frances Donaldson, claimed Freda might have been with him forever if she had wished to dominate him as much as Wallis wanted to.[10] Research for this book supports this view. It reveals how intense the prince's love for Mrs Simpson's predecessor was. In his letters, he portrayed his affair with Freda as a love affair on an epic scale. Reading the hundreds of letters he wrote to Mrs Dudley Ward for more than a decade, it is clear that no man could have been more besotted. They challenge the legend that Wallis Simpson was the only great love of Edward's life. Even Wallis, in her memoir, admitted that Freda was his first true love.[11] Evidence suggests that he asked Freda to marry him, but – unlike Mrs Simpson – she firmly refused.

One of the reasons that the idea of the legendary love affair grew up around the prince's relationship with Mrs Simpson was because the public was largely unaware of the heir to the throne's romance with Mrs Dudley Ward. Freda was discreet and, although their affair was known about in society circles, it did not appear in the press. This book explores in detail the complicated relationship that developed between Edward and Freda. It shows that not only was Freda married, she also had another long-term lover, Michael Herbert, who was as deeply in love with her as the prince. Throughout the 1920s they were caught in a toxic circle in which neither Freda, Michael nor the prince had the commitment they needed to feel secure nor the strength required to end their affairs. It is probable that this frustrating experience affected Edward's relationship with Wallis Simpson. It seems likely that, having adored Freda and having wanted to marry her, he was not going to make the same mistake again and fail to make a commitment to the woman he now loved. His relationship with Freda may partly explain why he acted so decisively in his relationship with Wallis.

The third woman in this book is Thelma Furness. Although a less serious mistress than Freda, she shared the prince's life for almost five years. She was unlikely to have ever become a permanent partner because she lacked the wisdom and wit of Rosemary, Freda and Wallis. She was also too in awe of Edward and did not have the strength of character to dominate him, which her predecessors and successor did possess. By encouraging the prince's more frivolous side, she prepared the path that led Edward to Mrs Simpson. She will go down in history as the woman who introduced the prince to Wallis. By going on a trip to America and having a fling with Aly Khan, she created a vacancy in the heir to the throne's life that his new mistress enthusiastically filled.

As well as telling the stories of the prince's romances with Rosemary, Freda and Thelma, Part Two examines what happened to these women once their affairs with the prince were over. It seems that returning to normal life after being the centre of attention was not easy for any of them. Although they had other relationships, none of the women found lasting romantic fulfilment after their intense experience with the heir to the throne.

In their later lives, both Freda and Rosemary showed qualities that suggest they would have been admirable partners for the prince. Rosemary was a supportive political wife who also had the potential to become an able politician in her own right. Like her mother, she worked tirelessly for medical charities until a series of tragedies culminated in her premature death.

Once Freda's relationship with the prince was over, she found herself thrown into the glamorous world of the movies. Her second husband Bobby, Marquis de Casa Maury, owned the chic Curzon Cinema, while her eldest daughter, Penelope, became a film star. However, Freda was not just a stylish socialite, she was also a respected charity worker. With the prince's encouragement, she set up the Feathers Clubs to help some of the most deprived people in society. After her relationship with him ended, she continued to work for the charity for more than thirty years. She showed a genuine commitment to social work and in so doing she won the admiration of prime ministers and clients alike. She lived a very full and long life, adored by her daughters, grandchildren and many friends.

Shortly after her affair with the prince ended, Thelma found herself supporting her twin sister Gloria through a custody battle, which had the potential to embarrass the royal family if she had still been involved with the heir to the throne. However, like the other women in this book, Thelma developed more as a person in her own right once she was out of the prince's sphere. She transformed herself from the social butterfly of her youth into a businesswoman. She tried her hand at various ventures with Gloria – some were more successful than others. Although both sisters had other relationships, it seems that their true soulmates were each other. The twins lived together in America until Gloria's death.

The story of the prince's love life is told using the diaries, memoirs, biographies and autobiographies of Edward and many of his family and friends. This book also draws on hundreds of letters which have never been published before. Many of the prince's letters to Freda were published by Rupert Godfrey in 1998 but, as well as these, *Before Wallis* uses information from several hundred more letters written by Edward to his lover which are owned by Freda's grandson, Max Reed. The book also gives a new perspective on what happened in the relationship between Freda and the prince by examining the hundreds of letters written by Freda's other lover, Michael Herbert, which are in Freda's granddaughter Martha Milinaric's collection and Swindon Archives. Unfortunately, Freda's letters to the prince do not survive but we get an idea of her side of the story from an interview she gave to J. Bryan III and Charles J.V. Murphy for their book *The Windsor Story* and from her co-operation in Frances Donaldson and Philip Ziegler's biographies of Edward VIII.

The Royal Archives have kindly allowed me to see the Prince of Wales's diaries, which give a new insight into his early love affairs with Portia Stanley and Marion Coke. They have also permitted me to see the letters between the Prince of Wales and his mother Queen Mary, written during the First World War. They challenge the traditional image of Queen Mary as a cold, distant mother who could not express her affection. These letters show that during the war mother and son developed a warm and loving relationship which was very important to them both.

A crucial source for telling Thelma Furness's story was her joint memoir with her twin sister Gloria, *Double Exposure*. The Duke and Duchess of Windsor also wrote their memoirs. At times, the three accounts contradict each other about the timing of meetings and the denouement of events; where relevant I have pointed out these contradictions. For later events in Thelma's life the autobiographical books of her niece Gloria Vanderbilt have been an enlightening source.

The prince epitomised his era. In the aftermath of the war the younger generation tried to put the horrors they had witnessed behind them in the pursuit of pleasure. The generation gap between the prince's contemporaries and their parents was a chasm. Cynical about conventions, Edward represented a youth culture which rejected the rules of the past. The prince and his friends were determined to have fun, whether that was dancing till the early hours of the morning in nightclubs, playing polo or golfing. This book tries to recreate the atmosphere of the period: the early chapters on Rosemary give an insight into the nihilistic experience of living through the First World War, while later chapters provide a stark contrast as they delve into the decadent world of the jazz age. To capture the spirit of the times, as well as drawing on books about the era, this study draws on hundreds of contemporary newspaper and magazine accounts.

By studying the women before Wallis, this book gives an insight into how Mrs Simpson gained such power over the heir to the throne. It reveals that he had shown similar patterns in his earlier relationships. In each love affair, he behaved like a cross between a little boy lost and a spoilt child. The women who were most successful with him showed a dominant streak which would be even stronger in Mrs Simpson. This book shows that Wallis was certainly not the only woman Edward ever truly loved or wanted to marry. If he had married Rosemary or Freda, either of them would have been a better influence on him than the woman he finally chose. As my research into their lives after Edward reveals, they would both have made good queens. If the Prince of Wales had been allowed to follow his heart earlier, it could have changed the course of history. Biographers have speculated about whether, if Edward VIII had married a different woman, he could have been a 'good king'. When he was young he had great potential. He was charismatic, progressive and compassionate. He also had some fatal flaws as he was wilful, spoilt and insecure.[12] Tommy Lascelles, who saw both sides of his complex character, concluded that as the years went on, the Hyde side of his dual personality would have predominated over the Jekyll. Lascelles wrote to his wife that nothing but the prince's own will could have saved him, and that will was not there.[13]

However, questions still linger. With either Rosemary or Freda by his side, would he have matured in a different way and would his positive side have overwhelmed the negative? With their moderate political opinions and well-developed moral compasses, could he have avoided the political pitfalls he experienced in the 1930s? Could they have given him the vital strength and support to do his duty that Queen Mary gave George V and Queen Elizabeth gave George VI? By re-examining the Prince of Wales's life from the perspective of these women's influence on him, and telling their stories, we are able to explore one of the great 'might have beens' of history.

PART ONE

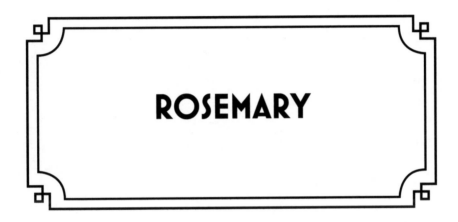

ROSEMARY

I

A WARTIME ROMANCE

n the summer of 1917 a determined young Red Cross nurse was
caring for a young wounded soldier who had been badly affected by
shell shock. He was unable to speak but the nurse and his doctors
were sure that if he could be encouraged to utter just one word then
others would follow. The nurse dedicated herself to his care and sat
with him for hours, telling him stories, pausing before words that were
well known to him, praying that he would supply the blanks. She even
acted out the words and flirted with him in the hope that he would say
that vital first word.

Eventually he spoke: he pointed at his devoted carer and said,
'Darling', to demonstrate his appreciation.[1] Another young man had
been watching this poignant scene. As he observed the animated nurse
nurturing her patient he was deeply moved by her care and felt he had
to get to know her better. This bond, formed in the most harrowing
of circumstances, was a story that was played out in countless similar
scenarios during the First World War. However, this couple was different;
the man who had been watching was Edward, Prince of Wales, and the

nurse who showed such compassion was Rosemary Leveson-Gower, daughter of Cromartie, the 4th Duke of Sutherland and his flamboyant wife Millicent.[2]

It was a meeting of the most eligible bachelor and one of the most alluring aristocrats of the era. He was 23 and she was just a year older. Photographs capture that fateful meeting: the slight, boyish prince, dressed in khaki uniform, looks slightly gauche, standing beside the poised young woman in a white nurse's uniform. He has his head down as though he does not know what to say, while she stares ahead with her hand on her hip looking rather bored. Rosemary's sangfroid had been evident earlier that morning before the prince arrived. The royal visit to Millicent, Dowager Duchess of Sutherland's hospital in France coincided with the arrival of a particularly large number of casualties, which temporarily threw the wards into chaos. Several members of staff began to panic about how an inspection by the king and queen could take place in such conditions. Rosemary remained cool and calm. 'Nonsense,' she said, laughing happily. 'Nothing at all to worry about. The king and queen will see our hospital at its best working at high pressure on a really hectic morning.' Having reassured the rest of the staff, she rushed off to help her mother show the royal party around.[3] Despite her busy schedule, as the photo reveals, it was the prince, not Rosemary, who felt uncomfortable. With a mother's intuition, Queen Mary immediately detected there was an attraction between the young couple. She wrote to her son: 'Have you seen the various photos of you "talking to nurses" with whom you seem on terms of great intimacy?'[4]

Rosemary and the prince already knew each other, as their parents' social circles had overlapped, but it was their wartime experiences that turned acquaintance into something deeper. The prince was already aware of the wonderful work Rosemary and her mother were doing. At the beginning of the war Millicent, Dowager Duchess of Sutherland had left for the continent to set up her military hospital, taking Rosemary with her to help to organise it. They ran their unit, which developed into a British Red Cross hospital, for the rest of the war. It started as a temporary hospital at Malo-les-Bains near Dunkirk, but as the shelling along the coastline increased they moved inland to Bourbourg. Life in 'the hospital in the oat-field' was captured by the French artist Victor

Tardieu, who worked as a volunteer ambulance driver at the hospital for several months. The basic tents were made more attractive by adding coloured awnings borrowed from local hotels along the seafront. Millicent and Rosemary made the atmosphere as pleasant as possible for patients, filling vases made from empty shell cases with poppies picked near the camp and making the most of the sunlight available to boost the soldiers' recovery. In his pictures, Tardieu portrayed the duchess bending over the beds in her pristine white uniform as a ministering angel to the wounded soldiers.[5]

In October 1915 the hospital was moved again to Calais and became part of the British Red Cross. Nursing took place in huts between the sand dunes, a marsh full of yellow irises, and a copse. Thanks to Millicent and Rosemary's dedication it became one of the best-equipped and organised hospitals in France. Special workshops were set up to manufacture splints and other surgical apparatus. The life-saving new Carrel–Dakin technique, which involved the rapid cleaning of wounds with antiseptic, was introduced to minimise infections such as gas gangrene. A barge was used as a floating ambulance to transport casualties from the front line by canal to Calais and the most up-to-date drugs were imported from England, often at Millicent's personal expense.

Before his official visit with his parents in July 1917, the prince had been to the hospital several times to see his friend, Eileen, Duchess of Sutherland, Rosemary's sister-in-law. At this stage, although Eileen was married, Edward was more interested in her than Rosemary. He wrote in his diary: 'Eileen is a dear and far too good for Geordie [her husband, the Duke of Sutherland].'[6] In February 1916 Edward and his friends paid frequent visits to Eileen, Rosemary and Millicent at their villa, which he dubbed 'Sutherland House'. They had dinner, went to the cinema and had lunch together in the mess tent. One afternoon the prince and the two younger women went for a ride on the beach, galloping along the sands at top speed. Two days later they went for a ride in a blizzard and had to take refuge in a farm. The trio had another adventure when they went in search of Rosemary's brother Alastair Leveson-Gower at Le Touquet. After having lunch in a hotel their car got stuck fast in a sand dune and they only managed to move it a few yards at a time using planks by racing the engine and getting people to give it a shove.[7] After one evening out together, the prince wrote: 'Eileen is a dear and so is Lady Rosemary, tho I don't know her so well.'[8]

Just a few weeks later tragedy was to tear the group apart. The prince's friend Lord Desmond Fitzgerald had also enjoyed socialising with Eileen and Rosemary during that hectic month. Desmond was one of the prince's few contemporaries who was allowed to call him 'Eddie'; he was also one of the only people who knew just the right thing to say to Edward when he went into one of his self-pitying moods.[9] While they were both in France they met frequently to walk and talk. In his diary the prince wrote about Desmond joining him for a 'cheery' dinner with Rosemary and Eileen before 'an amusing drive back to "Sutherland House", a fearful squash in the car which no one minded!!'[10]

In March 1916 Lord Desmond, who was commanding the 1st Battalion Irish Guards, was training with his regiment on a sandy beach near Calais. After watching some of the men throw their hand grenades, he encouraged the padre, Father Lane-Fox, to have a go. Lane-Fox pulled out the pin; the five-second time fuse was supposed to be activated as the grenade left his hand, but it turned out to be defective. The bomb exploded immediately, blowing out Father Lane-Fox's right eye and fatally injuring Desmond in the head. He was rushed to the Duchess of Sutherland's hospital where Millicent and her team did what they could to save him, but he died within an hour of the blast.[11] The death of his best friend depressed the prince more than any previous experience in his life. His mother, Queen Mary, was sympathetic, writing to Edward: 'I can't say how much I grieve for you losing such a good kind friend.'[12]

Afterwards, the prince wrote to the Duchess of Sutherland, thanking her for her care of Desmond and for writing to tell him what had happened. He explained: 'It was one of the greatest shocks of my life for Desmond was my greatest friend: and to think of him being killed in such a rotten way [...] of course poor Desmond will be lamented by all who knew him. He was so popular everywhere.' Sensitive to the suffering of others, the prince thought about the effect Desmond's death must have had on Rosemary and Millicent because they had also known him for most of his life and had seen him so recently. He added: 'It must have been very painful for you both poor Desmond dying in your hospital; but to me it is such a relief to feel he did die in the hands of friends!!'[13]

Rosemary had grown used to coping with emotionally challenging situations. Since going with her mother to France, she had taken her war work very seriously. She became a very good surgical nurse and at times worked so hard that she made herself ill. However, as the prince had witnessed, her *joie de vivre* was transformative. One contemporary wrote: 'She was always smiling, always cheerful, whether she was scrubbing floors, rolling bandages, or holding sick bowls. She was beloved for her actual nursing, her cheery presence in the wards and the hundred and one little kindnesses she showed the men.'[14] Rosemary's unstinting work close to the firing line was recognised in January 1917 when she was mentioned in dispatches for distinguished service and devotion to duty. A photograph of her, looking composed and confident in a simple tunic and chunky beads, appeared in *The Tatler* to celebrate her honour.[15]

The prince recognised in Rosemary a kindred spirit. Although, to his lasting frustration, his position as heir to the throne had limited the role he could play in the war, he did everything within his power to get as close to the front line as possible. He wanted to be treated just like his contemporaries and was willing to serve, suffer and if necessary die for his country. In the early days of the war he went to see the Secretary of State for War, Lord Kitchener, and said to him: 'What does it matter if I am killed? I have four brothers.'[16] However, Kitchener explained that the danger was not that he might be killed but that he could be taken prisoner. At this time, Lord Desmond Fitzgerald wrote to his friend saying that he fully realised how disappointed he was not to be able to fight in the war and he was very sorry for him.[17] However, he told the prince that he should not be downhearted because everyone knew how brave he was and how he would much rather be an ordinary person doing ordinary duty.[18]

Undeterred by official opposition, Edward continued his fight to get to France; in November 1914 he was attached to the staff of Field Marshal Sir John French, commander-in-chief of the British Expeditionary Force. His days were taken up with paperwork and delivering dispatches. Exasperated by his non-combatant role and finding that most of the men on the staff were twenty years older than him, he complained that he was the only man without a job. He hated living in relative comfort and safety while his contemporaries were being killed on the front line. His closest friends understood how damaging his lack of a role was to his self-esteem. On the prince's birthday Lord Desmond Fitzgerald wrote to him, commiserating, adding that unfortunately he could not give him the only present he really wanted – to become an ordinary person.[19]

At Givenchy in March 1915 the prince came under shellfire for the first time and saw the horrifying aftermath of a battle. A few months later he was attached to the headquarters of the First Army Corps and from there he often cycled to the front to visit his friends. In September 1915 he was appointed to the staff of Major General Lord Cavan, who commanded the Guards Division. In his new role, the prince experienced danger first hand. After visiting the front line during a lull in the battle of Loos, he had to jump into a trench to avoid an explosion; 50 yards away his car was riddled with shrapnel, killing his driver. That night Edward wrote in his diary: 'It's an absolute tragedy […] I have seen and learnt a lot about war today, having been forward during a fight; how exceptionally bloody it all is!!'[20]

When Sir John French heard what had happened he tried to get the prince transferred to a safer posting, but Edward resisted and remained where he was. The worst danger the prince faced during the war was when he was in an observation post on top of the ruins of Langemarck church. There were two explosions nearby and then the third shell fell even closer. The prince crouched for an hour in a dugout with the Welsh Guards while a French battery shelled them, thinking that they were the enemy.[21] He was frightened but at the same time he felt glad to be sharing the risk experienced by other young men.[22] Although the prince always felt inadequate about his war record, refusing to wear war decorations he felt he had not earned, the public recognised his courage and his desire to share the danger faced by his fellow countrymen. If there was a bad shelling he would always rush to the site and rally the troops or visit the wounded in hospital. Like Rosemary, he made a lasting impact on the soldiers he met, partly because he was so modest and naturally friendly but also because his compassion was genuine. This quality was most clearly illustrated when he visited a hospital for the treatment of English soldiers suffering from facial disfigurement. These patients were extremely sensitive – they were very aware if a visitor recoiled at the sight of them. After the prince had met twenty-seven out of the twenty-eight patients who he knew were being cared for in the unit, he asked to see the final one. The medical officer in charge explained that his case was of 'such a frightful not to say repulsive character' that it had been decided not to include this patient with the rest. The prince firmly replied that he refused to have anyone deprived of his sympathy and that this man had the greatest claim of all to it. He was then immediately taken to the patient's room, where he went straight up to him and kissed him. As Sir Almeric Fitzroy, who recorded this scene, wrote afterwards: 'He who can so bear himself in the dread presence of extreme misery must have a genius for pity.'[23]

The meeting between the Prince of Wales and Rosemary Leveson-Gower seemed to be a case of meeting just the right person at the right time. In so many ways Rosemary fitted the criteria for a post-war future queen. Inevitably the First World War had changed the royal family's attitude about who was suitable as a marriage partner. For centuries, the British royal family had been expected to marry other royalty rather than commoners. Since the Royal Marriages Act of 1772, a formal declaration of the king's consent, signed by him at a special meeting of the Privy Council, was needed before a prince could marry. The last heir to the throne to receive the monarch's consent to wed a subject was James II. Since the time of George I, if any prince in the line of succession chose to do so the marriage was not held to exist officially and so his wife and children had no position. This rule was made law by George III.[24]

In the years leading up to the First World War, Prince Edward's name had been linked to several foreign princesses. When the Kaiser of Germany's only daughter Princess Viktoria Luise visited England with her parents in May 1911 there were rumours of an engagement to the Prince of Wales. However, there was no truth in the gossip. Edward was only 17 at the time and the German princess was just a year older. Although the princess thought he was 'very nice' she felt he looked 'so terribly young, younger than he really was'.[25] A more serious contender for royal bride was Caroline Matilda of Schleswig-Holstein, who was known as Princess May. When the prince visited Gotha during a visit to his German cousins in 1913, he got on very well with her. Although her teeth needed some work done and her nose was rather red, she was tall and very slim. Their initial reaction to each other seemed so promising that her brother-in-law August Wilhelm, who was the son of Kaiser Wilhelm II, wrote to the prince in June 1914 suggesting he should marry Princess May. At just 19 years old Edward was not keen on the idea and, helped by Queen Mary, wrote a tactful reply.[26]

The royal marriage market was changed forever by the war; after the prolonged conflict with Germany, alliances with other European royal dynasties no longer seemed such a good idea. Ironically, in the same month as the royal visit to Rosemary and Millicent's hospital took place, at a meeting of the Privy Council at which George V gave up all his German titles and announced the establishment of the House of Windsor, the king made another momentous decision. He informed the council that he and Queen Mary had decided that their children would be allowed to marry British aristocrats.[27] It was as if the prince's meeting with Rosemary was meant to be; just as centuries of royal precedent was swept away, the ideal bride appeared on the scene.

2

THE PERFECT PARTNER

Rosemary was the perfect partner for the prince: the daughter of a duke, she was one of the most eligible girls of the era. The Sutherland family was certainly a match for royalty. The earldom dated back to 1228 and was linked to Scottish royalty by the marriage of the 5th Earl to Margaret, daughter of Robert the Bruce. The Dukes of Sutherland were treated in their own country as virtually uncrowned kings.[1] Rosemary's grandfather was reputed to be the largest landowner in Europe, owning well over 1,250,000 acres, including the entire county of Sutherland in Scotland and coal mines in England. Throughout the year Rosemary and her two brothers, Alastair and Geordie, moved with their parents between the family's four stately homes, spending Easter at Lilleshall in Shropshire, winter at Trentham in Staffordshire, August at Dunrobin Castle in the north of Scotland and part of the spring and summer at Stafford House in London.

The Sutherlands' extensive possessions had at times made even the royal family envious. When in 1873 the Shah of Persia saw Trentham, which was modelled on an Italian palace, he said to the then Prince of Wales (later Edward VII) that when the prince came to the throne he would have to have the owner of Trentham executed as a possible rival.[2] Stafford House, in the Mall between St James's Palace and Clarence House, was also a residence worthy of a royal owner. It had been built for George IV's brother, the Duke of York, and was held by the Sutherlands on a ninety-nine-year lease from the Crown. It had been designed by the architect Sir Jeffry Wyatville as 'a home fit for a prince'. Filled with period furniture and priceless works of art, it was so palatial that, on visiting Stafford House, Queen Victoria said to her friend, Harriet, Duchess of Sutherland, 'I come from my house to your palace.'[3]

Dunrobin was equally regal; a fairy-tale turreted castle standing high above the Moray Firth, it descended in a series of terraces to the seashore and had been inhabited by the Sutherland family since the eleventh century. During the Victorian era, Rosemary's grandfather had his own railway built from Golspie to Helmsdale. He laid down 17 miles of private line and had his own locomotive that he drove himself, while wearing a red shirt. When Edward VII visited Dunrobin in 1903 he was so taken with the engine that he had a replica of it made for the royal train. As one navvy said when he saw the Duke of Sutherland set off from Dunrobin on his train: 'There, that's what I call a real dook – there he is a-driving his own engine, on his own railway, and a-burning of his own blessed coals.'[4]

The royal family and the Sutherlands had socialised together for generations. Harriet, Duchess of Sutherland, had been Queen Victoria's mistress of the robes. In 1846, she added a new wing to Dunrobin Castle to provide a royal suite for the visit of Queen Victoria and the Prince Consort.[5] In the next generation, Edward VII and Queen Alexandra were good friends of Rosemary's parents and they also stayed at Dunrobin several times. In 1895, Princess May (the future Queen Mary) and Prince George (later George V) visited. Princess May was very kind to the Sutherland children and suggested that they should visit her and her two sons, Edward and Bertie, when they were next in London.[6] When Princess May became Queen Mary, Millicent was one of the four duchesses to carry her canopy at the coronation. A few days later the Sutherlands put on an enormous party at Stafford House for all the foreign royalty and their representatives who were attending the coronation. The traffic in the Mall was so dense that evening that some guests did not arrive until 1 a.m. Among the thousand guests to attend were the Crown Prince and Princess of Germany, the Crown Princess of Sweden and the Prince of Siam. It was one of the most glittering events of the season. Ablaze with lights that illuminated the priceless works of art, Stafford House was full of flowers from the Sutherlands' estate at Lilleshall. The long gallery on the first floor and the great drawing room and octagon room were used for dancing and sitting out, while the ground-floor rooms were supper rooms. The red drawing room, which opened onto the terrace, was reserved for royal guests. As dancing to Gottlieb's band began at 11 p.m. the duchess, dressed in white, and Rosemary, in pink lace layered over a blue dress, were the centre of attention.[7]

Rosemary and the prince had mixed together since their childhood. As they were growing up, they had met occasionally at the children's parties which were among the few times Edward and his siblings socialised with other children. The royal siblings lived a lonely, isolated existence and rarely met children their own age; however, on special occasions they were introduced to carefully selected children. Rosemary was among this elite group. In 1904 Queen Alexandra gave a party for the prince's tenth birthday; dressed in a white sailor suit and broad-brimmed sailor hat, he greeted his guests, including Rosemary, who was wearing a white dress with a pink bow in her hair. They were then treated to a circus before tea.[8] At another party the following year, given by Edward's aunt Princess Victoria for her young niece and nephews, Rosemary was described as one of the 'belles of the day'.[9]

However, although they both came from socially privileged backgrounds, Rosemary and Edward's childhoods could not have been more different. Rosemary had grown up in a warm, close-knit family. According to her brother Geordie, the future Duke of Sutherland, they had the kindest of parents, and as the only daughter Rosemary was doted on by them both. Her father had a special rapport with her. He was a shy, unostentatious man, who was happiest dressed in shabby clothes shooting and deer-stalking on his Scottish estate. As Rosemary grew older, father and daughter would go sailing together on his yacht the *Catania*.[10] Her mother Millicent was very different; outgoing and beautiful, she was a successful society hostess. From an early age Millicent took Rosemary everywhere with her. There are photos of a bonneted Rosemary sitting next to her mother in an early motor car attending the first meeting of the Ladies' Automobile Club, helping at her mother's many charity events and acting as a bridesmaid at weddings.

Rosemary and her brothers were mischievous; the boys were always playing pranks while Rosemary devised escapades of her own. She once joined a procession of soldiers, 'the Blues', as they marched around the streets of Windsor. On another occasion, at a society wedding where she was a young bridesmaid, she sneaked off to drink a glass of champagne when no one was looking.[11] Rosemary showed no interest in academic work; she simply told her governess that she would not bother. She later recalled that her tutor always thought that she was 'quite awful'.[12] Despairing of ever educating her, the harassed governess gave up trying to teach and instead took Rosemary shopping in the afternoons.

With academic achievement not a priority, the Sutherland children enjoyed a relaxed childhood playing games with their friends and many cousins in the spacious gardens of Stafford House or playing ice hockey on the frozen lake at Trentham.[13] Rosemary's closest friend was Monica Grenfell, the daughter of Lord and Lady Desborough. The Desborough and the Sutherland families were great friends. Millicent and Ettie Desborough were both part of the group known as the Souls – a circle where women were prized for their intellect as much as their beauty. At Souls' dinners, the leading politicians and intellectuals of the day discussed profound subjects together. The Desboroughs and the Sutherlands often stayed with each other. The Sutherland boys, Alastair and Geordie, were friends with Ettie's eldest sons Julian and Billy Grenfell. When Monica was in London Rosemary had German lessons with her three times a week, and they went to dance classes, had skating lessons and swam at the Bath Club together.[14] Trying to make learning fun for the girls, Ettie Desborough organised a series of twelve lectures for Rosemary and Monica and their friends on English literature. The essayist Edmund Gosse inaugurated the series with an inspiring speech to the students and at the end of the sessions the girls took an examination. More to Rosemary's taste were the seemingly never-ending holidays. Every summer the two girls paid each other long visits with their governesses at Lilleshall, Dunrobin and the Desboroughs' estate at Taplow.[15]

Making sure her children had a social life to rival her own, Lady Desborough put on elaborate fancy-dress children's parties. At one event, the 180 guests were treated to a ventriloquist act, and live kittens in little hampers were given as leaving presents. Rosemary came dressed as a Sutherland fishergirl and Monica was a snake charmer with silver snakes in her hair. Holidays at Dunrobin were more informal. The girls enjoyed the freedom of bathing every morning before breakfast, then riding all day. Rosemary was a keen horsewoman who was described as 'something of a youthful hoyden' by one newspaper because she rode astride rather than side-saddle, as was expected of young ladies in the Edwardian era.[16]

In contrast to Rosemary's idyllic upbringing, Prince Edward had a less happy childhood. His parents, the future George V and Queen Mary, loved their five sons and one daughter but they both had trouble expressing their affection. According to the queen's lady-in-waiting and lifelong friend Mabell, Countess of Airlie, the problem was that they lacked any understanding of how a child's mind worked and mistook childish behaviour for naughtiness.[17] Queen Mary, who was then the Duchess of York, was not maternal and found it hard to bond with her children when they were small. Finding the demands of a baby distasteful, she handed her eldest son over to a nanny, Mary Peters, who it was later discovered was mentally unstable. The divide between the children's nursery and their parents' domain was rigid. When the prince was brought downstairs once a day to be with his parents at teatime, Nanny Peters would pinch or twist his arm before he saw them so that he appeared sobbing or bawling and was immediately handed back. An orphan and spinster, Nanny Peters became obsessed with her charge. She was so possessive that she did not like anyone else even holding the little prince and therefore she never took a day's leave in three years. The Duchess of York only discovered her son was being abused when the second nanny, Lala Bill, reported it. Nanny Bill had found bruises all over the 3-year-old prince. Miss Peters was then immediately dismissed.

A week later she was in hospital with a nervous breakdown from which she never recovered. As Queen Mary's biographer explains, the potential effects of this early experience on the prince's future relationships with women has been the subject of much discussion. Whether he was sexually as well as physically abused cannot be known but the fact that his first three years were spent in the care of such a mentally unstable woman must have been damaging.[18] From infancy he had a wistful, melancholic look in his large blue eyes. He became an insecure, nervous child, who frequently fidgeted or cried and was shy and hesitant with adults.[19]

Although she found it hard to express her emotions, Queen Mary loved her eldest son very deeply and he always loved her. He relished the hour he and his siblings had alone with their mother in her boudoir before she went down to dinner. As she reclined on a sofa in her negligée, her children sat around her in a circle on little chairs. In this cosy atmosphere, they would laugh and joke together, or she would talk to them about literature, art and history in her soft, steady voice.[20] Practical by nature, she taught her sons and daughter how to embroider and crochet. His mother's boudoir became a place of sanctuary for the young prince. However, ladies-in-waiting and nursery staff were always stationed nearby to remove any child who was naughty. The prince later recalled that he could not remember ever being alone with his mother.[21]

For the duchess, her eldest son was a constant concern. Brought up with an overwhelming reverence for monarchy, she was very aware that she had the responsibility of raising a future king. When he was a teenager she worried about all aspects of his behaviour from his bad spelling to his sudden shyness. She confided in the courtier and politician Reginald, Lord Esher, who advised her to talk to her son on equal terms as though he were an adult. However, her reserved nature made such openness difficult. Esher believed that in her unsentimental way she was very proud of her eldest son, but she was unable to communicate this to him.[22] Reading the letters between Edward and his mother during the First World War, it seems that as he got older their relationship became more relaxed and intimate. In 1916 the prince told his mother that he wrote what he felt to her rather than to his father because he knew 'you understand that I do have feelings of my own and it does me so much good to express them'.[23] Although she found it hard to say what she felt face to face, Queen Mary's letters to her son were very loving. She wrote frequently to her 'Most darling David' and signed off 'lots of love bless you most darling David, Ever your loving Mama'.[24] Her letters are full of family news and show the concern any mother might feel for a beloved son. While he was in France, she worried that he was in danger and she wrote about how much she longed to see him. This developing intimacy was very important to them both. After they had spent time together in 1917, Edward wrote enthusiastically to his mother, 'Tons and tons of love and again millions of thanks for those wonderful talks we had which have made all the difference and you know what I mean!!'[25] Queen Mary replied:

> I quite agree with you that our mutual letters are more intimate, that is natural when mother and son understand each other, which thank God we do – and those long talks were a great blessing to our feelings I know and have cleared up clouds which were gathering on the horizon and have altogether simplified matters.[26]

Edward always blamed his father more than his mother for his cold upbringing. He believed that the Duke of York, the future George V, had a repressive influence on his wife. George had a bad temper and controlling nature and he certainly did not like to be crossed. Running his household as though he was the captain of a ship and his children naval cadets, he was a strict disciplinarian who at times bullied his children by ranting at them. They grew to fear a summons to his library where they might be rebuked for the slightest misdemeanour. He placed an almost obsessive importance on punctuality, deportment and dress. Like his wife, he was undemonstrative. Prince Edward could recall only one time in his childhood when his father embraced him.[27]

As his children grew older the duke alternated between saying he wanted to be their best friend and criticising their every action. His 'awkward jocularity' made them squirm while his angry outbursts intimidated them.[28] Even once they became adults he wanted to control their lives. George V had difficult relationships with all his sons, but the greatest clash was between Prince Edward and his father. As heir to the throne much was expected of the Prince of Wales, but Edward was a very different character from his father and he rebelled against his rigid regime.[29] This rebellion affected every aspect of the prince's life. Recent writers consider that the prince verged on anorexia; his distorted body image meant that he dreaded becoming fat, so he ate very little and exercised excessively.[30] Concerned about his son's erratic habits, his father encouraged him to take less exercise, eat more, rest more and smoke less. Edward ignored his advice. As the years went by he would increasingly define himself by always being the complete opposite to his father.

Both Queen Mary and King George brought their children up to believe that they were not different from or better than anyone else – meaning the well born.[31] However, as Edward soon learnt, because he was the heir to the throne people always treated him differently.[32] From an early age, he hated anything that set him apart; he did not want to be a prince on a pedestal, but rather to be treated like an ordinary man.[33] The women who appealed to him most treated him as a man, not a monarch in waiting. He needed a partner who saw herself as an equal and not a subject.

3

THE GIRL OF GIRLS

I f the Prince of Wales was not going to marry royalty, wedding the
daughter of the Duke of Sutherland would be the next best thing.
However, it was not just her aristocratic background that made
Rosemary such an alluring prospect for the prince. It was her personality. After meeting Rosemary again in July 1917, it was clear that
she had made a lasting impression on Edward and he wanted to get to
know her better. A few weeks after the royal visit, the prince went to
see Rosemary at her mother's hospital. They walked on the beach, went
to the cinema in Calais and dined at a hotel. According to Edward they
had 'great fun' together.[1] By September he was discussing her with his
mother. He confided that he thought Rosemary was 'very attractive
though very cold!!!!'[2] In fact this was the perfect combination to attract
the prince and, rather than being negative, the fact that he considered
her 'cold' was an essential element of her appeal. As thousands of pretty
girls threw themselves at him, in awe of his position and treating him as
a demi-god, the fact that Rosemary did not seem in the least impressed
by him made her a challenge. As was to be repeated in his later relation-

ships with Freda Dudley Ward and Wallis Simpson, he was attracted to women who could be cool towards him.

It seems Queen Mary did not approve of Rosemary because in his next letter Edward was keen to play down his interest in the duke's daughter. He wrote: 'When I told you I thought "R" looking attractive at Calais the other day I didn't mean I was really struck and you need have no fear of my having any designs on her!! Of course when one hasn't seen a lady for weeks and weeks as I hadn't that Sunday, any nice-looking girl looks attractive and rather strikes one at the time; "mais ca passe".'[3] However, it seems that Edward was protesting too much and, as usual, writing what his recipient wanted to hear. Rosemary's elusive quality intrigued the prince and no doubt he realised that he would have to work hard to win her over. Other eligible bachelors had tried before and failed. Everyone who knew Rosemary agreed that she was special: known as 'the girl of girls', many men fell in love with her.[4] Attractive rather than conventionally beautiful, she was 5ft 6in tall and very slim, with wavy blonde hair, large blue eyes, a slightly turned-up nose and a radiant smile. She spoke in a distinctive husky voice.[5] Lady Cynthia Asquith, who looked very much like Rosemary and was often mistaken for her, described her 'snub face and slap-dash voice – very in-loveable'.[6] Lady Diana Manners, who saw Rosemary as a rival, wrote that 'she had lank primrose-coloured hair, a raucous voice, a laugh that quickened the sad to gaiety, a wide mouth and a general look of bedraggled apple blossom'.[7]

It was Rosemary's sense of fun and her distinctive laugh that were most appealing. Her mother's friend, the author J.M. Barrie, recalled how, as she was approaching womanhood, he used to take her to plays but he had to take her out halfway through as, if something appealed to her sense of the absurd, she would not be able to stop laughing. Even when she was fishing near her Scottish home, she would burst out laughing, alerting her intended victims and preventing her from landing many fish.[8] The author of *Peter Pan* was so charmed by his young friend that he based the heroine in the play *Mary Rose* on her.[9] Her friend Lady Victor Paget described Rosemary as 'the most enchanting personality of anyone I ever knew'.[10] In some ways Rosemary was unworldly. One journalist described her as 'entrancingly absent-minded, there were moments when her spirit seemed to have wandered off into another world and she would suddenly come back to earth with a laugh at her inattention'.[11]

In 1909 Rosemary went to finishing schools in Dresden and then Paris. In Germany, she was taught to play the piano by one of the best teachers, Herr Pachmann. However, she showed no more aptitude for music than she had for academic study. Herr Pachmann asked her to play a piece to him and when she had finished he took her music and threw it on the floor, declaring that she was the worst pianist he had ever heard and nothing on earth would induce him to teach her.[12] After finishing school, Rosemary 'came out' in society. Her great friend Monica Grenfell also made her debut in the season of 1911. Before the parties began the girls went to Paris together to get their 'coming out' trousseau and to experiment with the latest Parisian hairstyles. Monica was given extravagant coming-out presents, including a long, Renaissance necklace of pearls and emeralds and a string of pearls that had belonged to the French Empress Marie Louise. On seeing the gifts, Rosemary said, with her characteristic sense of humour, that Monica was certain to be murdered for her jewels. She added: 'Look at me, with nothing but my handsome set of Sutherland cairngorms.'[13]

Photographed in a white lace dress, with curls escaping from a lace mob cap, a serious-looking Rosemary was dubbed 'the debutante of the season' by society newspapers.[14] *The Tatler* described her as being like her mother and aunts, 'a daring and distinctive personality'.[15] She was soon caught up in the social maelstrom, attending balls in London and house parties in stately homes across the country. Monica described those happy, carefree pre-war days. She wrote that they 'shared all the happiness as a band of close friends, united by affection and laughter and we rushed to meet all the fun'.[16] The Prince of Wales's great friend Lord Desmond Fitzgerald was part of this close-knit circle and mooted as a possible husband for Monica, while Monica's brother Billy Grenfell was one of Rosemary's early admirers. He wrote to his mother that she was 'looking delicious' and added that after spending most of the day with her and another girl he had 'nearly lost my reason to all those delectable girls'.[17] However, it was John Manners, Marquess of Granby, the son of the Duke and Duchess of Rutland, who fell most deeply in love with

Rosemary. The Rutlands and the Sutherlands had known each other for years. Stafford House and the Rutlands' London home looked out on to Green Park where the children used to meet with their nannies.[18]

When Rosemary came out John Manners became her most serious suitor. She was photographed in a cardigan and tweeds at a shooting party at Belvoir Castle, the Rutlands' estate. However, Rosemary was not an easy conquest. Lady Diana wrote: 'She was boy-shy (what a ghastly expression) and accepted his proposal of marriage and unending adoration with hesitation, almost reluctance.' In January 1913, an imminent engagement was rumoured in the newspapers, jewels had been bought and everyone was very happy, but then Rosemary became ill and had to undergo an operation for appendicitis. During her convalescence she confessed to her mother that she wanted to end her engagement. Millicent, who was described by Lady Diana as 'a true Edwardian schemer and large-scale liar for the public good', sent for John and told him, with tears in her eyes, that the doctors, having peered into all parts of his beloved bride, said that she was biologically 'infantile and quite undeveloped and would never have any children'. As John loved Rosemary so much, he said that he was still willing to marry her. However, Rosemary had made up her mind and broke off the engagement, plunging her ex-fiancé into depression for several years after losing her.[19]

For Rosemary romance was placed firmly on the back burner once the First World War began. Nothing would ever be the same again for her or her friends. So many of the vibrant youthful circle who had socialised together in those pre-war days were killed that those who survived clung to each other in a search for solace. When Monica's eldest brother, Julian Grenfell, was killed in the spring of 1915, Rosemary immediately rushed to see her great friend. She drove over to the hospital where Monica was nursing and persuaded her to come to her mother's hospital for a break, promising that she could be given a lift back in an ambulance which had to come to Boulogne the next day. Monica wrote that she was 'enchanted' to be with her friend because she loved Rosemary more than anybody outside her own family circle. After working together on the wards at Millicent's hospital, the girls had tea in a shop in Boulogne. When they saw two hungry children gazing wistfully through the tea shop window Rosemary invited them in and gave them the two best cakes available.

It was a lovely summer afternoon and the girls then drove through the countryside. As they looked up they saw two specks in the sky which were aeroplanes flying close together. A second later a bomb was dropped in the canal next to the road just a short distance in front of them and mud and water splattered across their route. Another bomb then dropped in the field to their right. Monica and Rosemary had been lucky to survive; shaken but not daunted by their experience, they returned to the hospital. That evening the girls had dinner at a long table in a tent with Millicent and the other nurses and doctors. Afterwards, they stayed up late talking by candlelight in the small cottage where Rosemary had a bedroom. The next day Rosemary was on duty alone in her ward during the afternoon, so Monica joined her to help. Monica wrote that her friend was obviously adored by the patients. Rosemary had been told to rearrange the beds and lockers in the ward and while doing this the girls bumped into a cluster of crutches which fell around a badly injured patient. Luckily, none of the crutches touched him and both he and the other patients were cheered up by the incident. Later that afternoon, Monica returned in the ambulance to her own hospital. Two days later she heard that her second brother Billy had also been killed.[20]

Whenever Rosemary was back in England she visited her friends' bereaved mother, Ettie Desborough. In December 1916 Ettie and Monica organised a house party at Panshanger, one of the Desboroughs' homes. It was their first attempt to socialise since their double loss; mother and daughter had gathered together a few of the friends they loved dearly who were home on leave. All the carefully selected guests were close enough to the family to understand what a heroic effort it required from Ettie to make the weekend a success.[21] At the house party Rosemary had a flirtation with the charming pursuer of beautiful women, Duff Cooper, who was in a relationship with John Manners's sister Lady Diana. As Rosemary and Diana had a similar type of blonde beauty, Duff was attracted to both aristocratic young women. His love affair with Diana was very serious, but at the house party he was enchanted by Rosemary. She was on leave from nursing in France after a record-long term working at her mother's hospital. The surgeons had grown so accustomed to having her help that they told her very earnestly that they could not do without her. However, Millicent knew Rosemary needed respite from the unrelenting pace and had insisted she went to England.[22]

At Panshanger, Duff and Rosemary played tennis together then in the evening she helped with some of the old party games they used to play before the war. That night Duff wrote in his diary that he had been unfaithful to Diana in his thoughts about Rosemary and the flirtation made him question how much he loved his girlfriend.[23] When Duff returned to London, Diana was suspicious and questioned him about her rival. He admitted that he had been attracted to Rosemary but denied that he was in love with her.[24] However, when he saw Rosemary again a few weeks later he felt such a strong attraction to her that he found he could not speak to her at all. He drank a great deal to try to get up courage but still he could not do it. Afterwards he came home and wrote a 'silly' letter to her. A few days later Rosemary sent a rather abrupt reply. When he saw her again at a dinner party she complained that she had not liked the letter he had written to her. However, before she was due to return to France, Duff persuaded her to dine with him and a group of friends. Duff described Rosemary as looking 'lovelier than ever' but he did not make any progress with her and instead got drunk and ended the evening having a terrible quarrel with Diana.[25]

It seems Rosemary was enjoying the flirtation but did not take it seriously. Her mother wrote to her: 'Darling child, Your letter made me laugh [...] you will have to tear yourself away from the fleshpots and come out here Sunday 28th January.'[26] However, Rosemary's return to France was delayed because she was still run down and suffering from a liver complaint. Her mother insisted that she should go to the spa at Harrogate for a three-week cure where she could have massages and rebuild her strength. As soon as she was better, Rosemary returned to France to take over running the hospital and to give her mother a much-needed break.

In December 1917, Duff and Rosemary were thrown together again at another of Ettie Desborough's house parties. Duff thought Rosemary was looking 'most beautiful' but, as in her relationship with the Prince of Wales, it was not just a physical attraction. Duff and

Rosemary went for a short walk together before tea. Walking down an avenue of stark, leafless trees as the sun set on a cold, bleak winter afternoon, they discussed their friends who had been killed in the war. During the house party, the reality of what the tragedy of the war meant at home in Britain was reinforced for Rosemary. She had spent so much of her childhood at the Desboroughs' homes, growing up with Monica but also with Julian and Billy, who were now dead. The house must have felt full of ghosts that wintry weekend. One death of their friends followed so closely upon another that, as Duff wrote, they had not had time 'to find new words for our new sorrow'. [27] Duff's and Rosemary's depressed moods matched, and they found that they shared each other's 'rather gloomy hopeless views'. [28] When they talked about a future life Rosemary told Duff that increasingly she was coming to believe in complete annihilation. After their talk, Duff wrote in his diary: 'If I could love anybody besides Diana I think it would be her.'[29]

Evidently Rosemary had enjoyed Duff's company too, because at the end of the month she invited him to stay at Calcot, a house taken by her uncle and aunt, Lord and Lady Rosslyn. There were only four people there: a mutual friend, Michael Herbert, cousin of the Earl of Pembroke, Duff, Rosemary and Lady Rosslyn. After dinner, they sat up until one in the morning playing 'Truth' by firelight. Duff admitted to his diary that he found himself falling in love with Rosemary again and feeling jealous of Michael Herbert, who sat beside her. The next day Michael left after lunch and the remaining three went for a walk with five dogs and a pet goat. After tea Rosemary and Duff had a long talk; he told her that he loved her, but she said that he mustn't. She was very fond of him but could not be in love with him. [30] Although they had found consolation in each other's company, the flirtation between Rosemary and Duff came to nothing, perhaps because the prince was courting her at the same time. Duff soon returned to a jealous Diana.

The prince, who was known as David to his close friends and family, had also had other relationships before Rosemary. He had been a late developer. His assistant private secretary, Tommy Lascelles, suggested that for some physiological reason his normal mental development had stopped when he reached adolescence. The outward symptom of this was that he needed to shave less often than most men. [31] However, once he discovered the pleasures, both romantic and sexual, offered by the opposite sex he showed a voracious appetite for encounters of both kinds.

His first romantic attachment was to Marion, Viscountess Coke, who was married to Tom, the son of the Earl of Leicester. The couple had four children. Twelve years the prince's senior, Marion was the type of experienced quasi-maternal figure who would often appeal to him. Small and lively, with a good sense of humour, she was the prototype of the women the prince would be attracted to for the rest of his life.[32] The flirtation began early in 1915 during one of the prince's periods of leave from active service with the Grenadier Guards in France. She was the first in a long line of female confidantes who mothered him and proved themselves willing to listen to his self-centred monologues. By November 1915, the prince wrote in his diary that they had had 'a most delightful talk; she is a dear!!'[33] Soon Edward was writing frequently to Lady Coke about his frustrations at not being able to fight on the front line. No doubt the older woman was flattered by the attentions of the world's most eligible bachelor. When her younger son was born at the end of 1915, she called him David, the name by which the prince was known to his closest friends, and the prince stood as sponsor for the new baby. As in his later relationship with Freda Dudley Ward, Edward showed a genuine interest in Lady Coke's children. He used to visit them in the nursery and play with them. It seems that at first Marion's husband, Tom, was happy about his wife's friendship with the Prince of Wales as he attended events with them and the trio played golf together. However, as the prince's attentions became more intrusive Tom was less sanguine.

As was to become the pattern in Edward's love life until he met Wallis, he always had at least two women in his life at the same time. While he was flirting with Marion Coke he was also courting the Honourable Sybil Cadogan, one of the daughters of Viscount Chelsea. Sybil, who was known as 'Portia' to her friends, was the first young single woman who could have been a potential bride. Unlike so many of his later girlfriends she was acceptable to the royal family. As she was a close friend of Edward's sister, Princess Mary, she was invited to stay by the king and queen at Windsor Castle. They liked her so much that soon there was a charming bedroom set aside for her. The prince first got to know her during one of these visits in the spring of 1915. They played golf and enjoyed intense conversations. By the end of her stay the prince wrote: 'She seems to get sweeter every day: I'm slightly in love there is no doubt!!!'[34]

After meeting a few times in London, due to his commitments in France, Edward did not see Portia for eight months. When they met again in January 1916 he wrote in his diary that she was 'most adorable' and looked 'more attractive and beautiful than ever!!'[35] During his leave, the prince saw her most days and nights. They went to the theatre together with mutual friends and dined and danced the night away.[36] However, the best part of the 'stunt' for him came at the end of the evening when they drove around St James's Park half a dozen times. 'It was divine,' he enthused in his diary, 'and we sang and ragged and finally deposited her at Chelsea House at 12.00!! It naturally took a long time to say "good-night" and we didn't get back till 12.30 after the best night I have had since the war began!!'[37] On one occasion, he pretended to walk home after saying goodnight but returned to be let in by her to her parents' Chelsea house. They then stayed up talking and playing the gramophone until after 1.30 a.m.

Edward was soon, rather self-consciously, confessing to his diary: 'I'm madly in love with her!! Oh! If only ---!! But I must be careful even in my diary [...] She is a perfect darling and no mistake.'[38] A few weeks later, they talked for ages and 'fixed up certain things!!' Forever taking his emotional temperature and analysing his feelings, he added: 'I am so desperately in love that I don't know what to do!! Qu'elle vie!!!!'[39] Many society observers thought they would marry, but although in worldly terms it would have been a suitable match, physically Portia was not the prince's type. He was always attracted to very slim, physically fragile women while Portia was sturdy. It seems that their bond was more romantic than sexual. Reflecting the chaste nature of their relationship, the prince thought it worthy of note in his diary to record when he held 'an angelic hand'.[40] As in all his relationships, talking to Portia was an important part of her appeal. When they were together they 'talked about every sort of thing: better not to mention what!!'[41] When apart, he enjoyed 'long yarns' with her on the telephone. Once his leave was over and he was back in France, he wrote to her late at night.[42] In his letters, Edward called Portia 'my angel' and he recorded with delight receiving a 'heavenly letter from HER'.[43]

However, by the beginning of 1917, Edward seemed to be more interested in Marion Coke than Portia Stanley. He admitted to his diary that Lady Coke attracted him 'more and more'.[44] During his leave he would visit Marion at her Devonshire Street townhouse in the afternoon then spend the evening with Portia at Chelsea House, before having a late-night assignation with Lady Coke. Marion Coke's sister acted as chaperone on these occasions; they would meet at her house and then dance until the early hours of the morning. Edward wrote in his diary: 'Marion and I sat out a good deal and talked; she is such a little darling and I'm afraid I love her!!'[45] Just before the prince went back to France, after one of their late-night dancing sessions, Edward took 'sweet little Marion' home, and he noted, 'She bid me a tender farewell tho we didn't kiss.'[46] It seems that Lady Coke was careful not to compromise her marriage too much. Although she saw the prince frequently their relationship was more about talking than sex. When Edward was back in England in March, the prince wrote about coming back to her house and having 'a yarn'; he added, 'Wish to hell it could have been more than a yarn, as I've got a letch on Marion and love her!!!!'[47]

Perhaps, knowing Lady Coke was always in the background, Portia realised that the prince was not the type of husband she wanted. In June 1917, when Portia sent a telegram to her parents telling them, 'Engaged to Edward', they presumed that her engagement was to the prince. In fact, she had ended her relationship with the heir to the throne and had agreed to marry his university friend Edward, Lord Stanley. The prince wrote in his diary: 'How depressed I am!! I suppose its Portia having gone West.' It seems that Queen Mary talked to him and may have reassured him that there was no rush to get married because he added: 'Of course that talk with Mama has cheered me up and taken a big weight off my mind.'[48] There seems to have been no hard feelings on either side. Queen Mary attended Portia's wedding and wrote to Edward about it. He wished the newlyweds well, writing to his mother: 'She is charming and Edward is a very lucky fellow and I'm sure they'll be very happy.'[49] A year later the prince became godfather to their first child. His behaviour suggests that despite his earlier protestations in his diary, his feelings for

Portia had never been particularly deep. However, her exit from his life left a vacancy which was soon to be filled by Rosemary.

At this point the prince seemed in no hurry to get married. As he heard about a flurry of his friends walking down the aisle, he wrote to his mother: 'One's wedding must be a fearful ordeal, but I suppose I shall have to go through with it one day.'[50] At home and abroad, the prince was never short of female company. Alongside his official girlfriends was a secret world of other conquests. He quickly began to distinguish between girls he could marry and women he could sleep with. If the single aristocrats he courted had consummated their relationship with him they would have ruined their future marriage prospects. Prostitutes and courtesans were soon to provide an outlet for his growing sexual appetite. The prince had been physically slow to mature and at first showed little interest in sex. As late as May 1916 (shortly before his 22nd birthday) he was telling a friend that although he understood sexual hunger he did not actually experience it himself. When he visited a brothel in Calais and saw some naked prostitutes in erotic poses, he was revolted by the sight. However, his attitude changed towards the end of 1916 when his equerries Joey Legh and Claud Hamilton took him to Amiens and introduced him to an experienced French prostitute called Paulette. She was permanently attached to an officer of the Royal Flying Corps, but he loaned her to the prince for a few evenings.[51] Apparently, the encounter was a success. Although any material referring to it is cut out of his diary, Edward later told his elderly confidant Lord Esher that she had brushed aside all his shyness.[52] Over the next few months he saw Paulette occasionally in Amiens and wrote about her affectionately in his diary, calling her 'my little Paulette' and describing her as 'a heavenly little woman of her kind'.[53] It seems that he treated her more like a girlfriend than a prostitute. They would dine in a hotel and then enjoy singing and dancing together before Paulette 'dragged' him off for more entertainment elsewhere.[54] He described sitting on a seat talking to her by moonlight, and even considered taking her on a trip to Calais.[55] Sometimes he would drive to Amiens to try to find her only to discover to his disappointment that she was with her 'ami'.[56]

From now on sex became a major preoccupation for the prince. Soon after the fling with Paulette, he began having an affair with a Parisian courtesan called Marguerite Alibert. Known as 'Maggy' or 'Maggie Meller', this *demi-mondaine* was very popular at the time, counting among her clients Bendor, Duke of Westminster, a womanising friend of the prince. Having worked in a high-class brothel as a teenager, Maggy was an expert in the arts of love.[57] According to her biographer, she enjoyed a reputation as a dominatrix.[58] As fiery as she was experienced, Maggy described herself as being 'a terrible she-devil'.[59] By the time the prince met her she had come a long way from her humble roots; she now held court in her own salon in an elegant Parisian apartment. Petite and chic, she was dressed by the leading couturier Paquin. Maggy embodied many of the elements that Edward found alluring. Intoxicated with this newfound intimacy, he wrote indiscreet love letters to his 'bébé'. Including as they did comments about the conduct of the war, and mocking his father, these letters were to leave him open to blackmail once their affair was over.[60]

At the same time as the prince had begun to show an interest in Rosemary on his visit to her hospital in July 1917, he was clandestinely meeting Maggy. While Edward was staying with Queen Mary and escorting her to casualty clearing stations, hospitals, ammunition dumps and railway depots, his mistress was waiting for him at the Hotel Normandy in Deauville. After receiving enthusiastic receptions from troops and French civilians wherever he went with his mother, for four consecutive days the prince drove to Deauville in his open Rolls-Royce to see his lover. To cover his tracks, he made sure he was back with his parents by 7 a.m. the next day. It seems this affair continued until the end of the war. Experiencing a regular sex life for the first time, after one interlude with his mistress the prince wrote in his diary: 'It's fearful what a change in my habits "48 hours of the married life in Paris" has wrought.'[61] However, although he always blurred the lines between suitable and unsuitable women, frequently being more attracted to the latter, he knew that his relationship with Maggy had no long-term future and it was just an exhilarating fling. With his boundless energy, it seems that the prince was often in love, or lust, with more than one woman at a time. Like many of his contemporaries, he saw no inconsistency in the fact that while he was considering marrying Rosemary, he was sleeping with more sexually available women.

4

BAD BLOOD

In the autumn of 1917 the prince went with XIV Army Corps to Italy to support the Italian army as German troops came to the aid of their Austrian allies. It was felt that Edward's presence would raise the morale of the troops. However, in early 1918 he was given six weeks' home leave, ostensibly to make a tour of the defence plants. In fact, most of his time was spent socialising and during his leave Rosemary and Edward's relationship became the talk of society. The prince wrote to a friend about their time together, describing a delightful week at Windsor during which he rode every morning and played golf in the afternoon. He explained that he had seen a great deal of a woman he only identified by her initial 'R' but who seems likely to have been Rosemary. He described her as 'charming', adding that when he came home on leave he enjoyed being with good-looking women again. After his stay at Windsor the prince motored up to London to see friends.[1]

To his parents' disgust, he was soon partying every night at debutante balls. King George V and Queen Mary thought his behaviour was misguided while so many of his contemporaries were still fighting for their king and country abroad. However, Edward refused to be reined in and his presence helped to create a heightened atmosphere of anticipation. Cynthia Asquith described 'the wild excitement fluttering all the girls over the Prince of Wales'. Every aristocratic mother wanted to ensnare the prince for her daughter. Cynthia Asquith called it the 'dash for the throne'. She explained: 'No girl is allowed to leave London during the three weeks of his leave and every mother's heart beats high.'[2]

Most determined was the Duchess of Rutland. Although Edward was three years younger than her daughter, Lady Diana Manners, her mother thought she would make a perfect queen and that this should be her ambition. However, Diana had other plans and was appalled at the thought. She had no rapport with the prince and she was already deeply involved with Duff Cooper. During Edward's interlude in London, the Duchess of Rutland was furious with Diana because the prince did not dance with her at Irene Lawley's ball.[3]

The Countess of Strathmore, mother of Lady Elizabeth Bowes-Lyon, also seemed in with a chance. Lady Elizabeth wrote to a friend that she sat next to the Prince of Wales at a dinner and then had the first dance with him. During the evening, she had two more dances with him.[4] However, out of all the matchmaking mothers it seemed that the Duchess of Sutherland was the one most likely to succeed. Cynthia Asquith added: 'So far he dances most with Rosemary and also motors with her in the daytime.'[5]

Over those hectic months since they had met again at the Duchess of Sutherland's hospital, the well-matched couple had grown increasingly fond of each other. Rosemary, like the women who were to come after her, soon realised the strange dynamic that appealed to the prince in his relationships with women. In March 1918, when an Australian socialite, Sheila Loughborough, who was married to Rosemary's cousin, Lord Loughborough, asked her how she should treat the Prince of Wales and his brother, Rosemary told her to curtsy low, call them sir and treat them like dirt.[6]

According to Lady Victor Paget, who was a close friend of Rosemary's, a few months into their relationship the prince proposed. At first, Rosemary had been firmly against accepting him; she was a very independent young woman, and as a duke's daughter with her own trust fund of £100,000 left to her in her father's will, she had no need of additional social status or wealth. Apparently the idea of becoming queen appalled her. However, the prince kept asking her and gradually she was won over. She told her friend that she was very fond of the future king, but she was also very aware of his weaknesses, knowing that he was childish and irresponsible. Equally aware of her own strengths, she decided to accept his proposal because she thought that she could 'make something of him'.[7]

Friends thought an announcement was imminent, but before an engagement was made public Edward's parents made a fateful mistake by opposing the marriage. Their reaction was known among a small circle at court. Although she did not name Rosemary, Lady Hardinge of Penshurst – whose husband was assistant private secretary to George V – wrote in her memoirs that the prince had wished to marry a lady from 'a good English family' but there was opposition. She claimed that at this time it was still felt that Edward should marry a royal princess and the woman he wished to marry was reluctant to become queen. She wondered how the history of the monarchy in the twentieth century would have turned out if Edward had been allowed to have his way in those early days.[8] The prince himself later explained what had happened in a letter to Freda Dudley Ward. He wrote: 'TOI knows how I used to feel about her [Rosemary], that she was the only girl I felt I ever could marry and I knew it was "defendu" [forbidden] by my family!!'[9] It seems his parents' grounds had nothing to do with Rosemary as an individual. In fact, they liked her very much and considered her to be a good moral influence on their son. However, according to Philip Ziegler, Queen Mary wrote to her son that although Rosemary was attractive there was 'a taint' in the blood of her mother's family. It seems her comment related to an alleged strain of madness in the St Clair-Erskine family, which was widely gossiped about at the time.[10]

Certainly, Millicent Sutherland's relatives had a racy past and many of them were eccentric. As a friend of the family, Sir Robert Bruce Lockhart, wrote, they had 'charm, originality, extravagance and weakness'.[11] The Duchess of Sutherland was the daughter of the 4th Earl of Rosslyn. Millicent, her sisters and half-sisters were Victorian beauties who over the years attracted many admirers and much scandal.

Queen Victoria had wanted Millicent's half-sister, Frances Maynard, who was known as 'Daisy', to marry her haemophiliac son Prince Leopold. However, the headstrong heiress rejected the offer and married instead Francis Greville, Lord Brooke, heir to the Earl of Warwick. As Countess of Warwick, Daisy became the mistress of Leopold's brother, Bertie, the future Edward VII. He doted on her and called her his 'little wife'. For almost a decade she dominated his Marlborough House circle. However, Daisy had a reputation for being indiscreet and she soon became known as a 'babbling brook'.[12]

After Edward VII's death Daisy antagonised King George and Queen Mary by threatening to publish the late king's love letters to her. Needing money, she resorted to blackmail, getting a go-between to meet King George's private secretary, Lord Stamfordham, to find out if the royal family could be persuaded to pay between £85,000 and £125,000 for the suppression of the letters. She then sent an ultimatum claiming that unless the money was paid her manuscript memoirs, including the letters, would be sold in America for £200,000. King George was not amused; his main motivation was to prevent his mother, Queen Alexandra, from being hurt by revelations about her husband's infidelities. Relying on the law of copyright, which meant that although the letters were the property of Daisy, the copyright was vested in George V, as heir of the author, the king's private secretary and solicitor served Daisy with an interim injunction, which stopped her from making her royal letters public.[13] However, Daisy's agent, Frank Harris – a seedy former newspaper editor who had been a friend of Oscar Wilde – had already left for America with some of her letters. In July 1915 an action was brought in the King's Bench Division against Daisy, her husband and Harris, using the Defence of the Realm Act, which allowed the arrest of anyone engaged in activities likely to be detrimental to the nation's war effort. On 5 July the action was suspended provided that the letters were handed over by Daisy to be destroyed.[14]

Equally controversial were Daisy's politics: she was an ardent socialist who criticised the wealthy and championed the poor. Nicknamed by Margot Asquith, the Liberal Prime Minister's wife, 'Comrade Warwick', in 1904 Daisy became a leading light in the Social Democratic Federation, which favoured direct action and aimed to bring about a revolutionary change in society and the end of capitalism.[15] Eight years later she joined a new group called the British Socialist Party, which included trade unionists and socialist intellectuals. During the industrial unrest of 1912 she supported the workers. Dressed in a large hat with ostrich feathers and a long black silk cloak, she spoke for the strikers and offered to pay for the cost of housing 1,000 strikers' children while the strike lasted.[16] When the Russian Revolution took place in 1917, Daisy declared, 'Vive L'Internationale!' She hoped that it might lead to the end of monarchies across Europe.[17] As Rosemary and the prince's courtship took place just months after the revolution, it would be understandable if such sentiments did little to endear Rosemary's family to her potential in-laws. As Queen Mary wrote to Edward in 1917: 'Altogether that Russian business is a tragedy.'[18]

Rosemary's mother Millicent was also a flamboyant figure. After her husband died in 1913 she had shocked society by marrying Major Percy Desmond Fitzgerald very quickly afterwards; such impetuous behaviour was considered indecorous for a matron of 47. In fact, Millicent had been having an affair with the dashing but unreliable Irish major for about a decade before her husband died. She had even travelled to Algiers and Morocco with him under a false name.[19] However, by the time they married all passion was spent between them. During the war, they rarely saw each other and by the time of Rosemary's courtship with the prince they were separated and on the brink of divorce. In an era when divorce was still rare and frowned upon at court, it seems likely that it would have been considered unsuitable for the daughter of a divorced woman to become Princess of Wales.[20]

If the behaviour of Millicent and her sister threatened future controversy, Rosemary's uncle, Harry, the 5th Earl of Rosslyn, was an even greater potential embarrassment. Once he inherited the earldom and a large fortune, he began a thirty-six-year-long gambling spree. Three months after his father's death he attended the Newmarket thoroughbred sales in his late father's fur coat with a long cigarette holder in his mouth and spent £6,000 on one horse and several thousand more on others. Within six years he had gambled away most of his £50,000 inheritance. In 1893 he faced financial ruin after betting £15,000 on his favourite racehorse, called Buccaneer, who, unfortunately, crossed the finish line fourth. The earl was forced to sell his stable of racehorses and the family home and silver. However, even this experience did not stop him from gambling. Within four years he was declared bankrupt and banned from taking his seat in the House of Lords.[21] He continued to pay regular visits to the gaming tables of the south of France and so infamous was his addiction to casinos that it was said that the popular song, 'The Man Who broke the Bank at Monte Carlo', was written about him. The earl was open about his fatal flaw, calling his memoir *My Gamble with Life.*

Like Millicent, he had also made some unsuitable decisions in his love life. He was divorced twice. In 1890, he married Violet de Grey Vyner, and the couple had a son and daughter together, but his gambling and infidelity broke up the marriage. Looking for a new career and wife, Rosslyn became an actor, forming a company of players called 'Lord Rosslyn's Theatrical Performances', which toured the country. After launching himself on the New York stage, in 1905 he married an American actress, Georgina 'Anna' Robinson. Their relationship did not last long as the earl accused his bride of being 'a drug fiend and addicted to drink' while she described him as a philandering wastrel.[22] In 1908 he married for the third time, an actress named Vera Bayley who was known as 'Tommy'. She was eighteen years younger than her husband; the couple had two more sons and a daughter, but the earl continued gambling and drinking.

Evidently there were quite a few challenging characters in Rosemary's family. However, if strict moral standards were applied to the relatives of most aristocratic brides they would have been found wanting. According to Lady Victor Paget, once Rosemary heard of the king and queen's opposition she retreated with dignity. From that time on, she always gave the impression that she had never wanted to marry the Prince of Wales. However, privately her family pride was deeply wounded.[23] In agreeing to accept the prince's proposal she had not been driven by ambition but duty: her motivation had been based on knowing that she had the strength of character and qualities which could have made Edward a better king. It seems that Millicent Sutherland was also very offended. There was to be no more correspondence or meetings between her and the king and queen for more than a decade.

By discouraging the prince from marrying Rosemary, King George V and Queen Mary missed an excellent opportunity to update the royal family for the twentieth century. After the Russian Revolution in 1917, followed by an epidemic of rebellions and abdications which ousted monarchs across Europe, Edward realised that to keep the British throne secure his family needed to keep in the closest possible touch with the people. He promised his father that this need would always be at the forefront of his mind.[24] The prince felt that he understood the changed post-war society far better than his father. His service in France had allowed him to get to know his future subjects from all classes and he was sure that he knew their hopes and aspirations. He believed that they were heroes who deserved a better society and if they were not given it they would reject their rulers.[25]

Interestingly, Edward found an ally in his mother. After one of their long talks, Queen Mary wrote to him saying that she was glad to discover that he felt about '"the cause" as I do'. She added: 'We shall have to work very hard to set self completely on one side, but one is ready to do just anything when it is for the sake of our people and country. It will be just everything having you to work with and to feel I can explain my views to you.'[26] Like the prince, she also had doubts about her husband's ability to adapt. She wrote to her son: 'There will be so much to do and I sadly fear Papa does not yet realise how many changes this war will have brought about.'[27] Showing a political astuteness that she could not express in public, she told Edward that she hoped the government would 'hurry up and get the much needed reforms (which the working class need) passed'. She added that if they did this it would 'take the wind out of the sails of the extremists and I trust they will be wise enough to realise this'.[28] The prince wrote back to her saying that he was glad that they both understood the 'general situation' and that they had 'to work for all the changes that are so absolutely necessary for the future'. He added: 'We've got some funny or rather serious times before us, but they've got to be faced and in the right and modern way and "to hell" with precedents!! They won't wash nowadays!!'[29]

Rosemary could have helped the prince modernise the monarchy as, despite her immensely privileged background, she had been brought up by her mother to have the common touch. Millicent Sutherland had a strong social conscience and she had proved herself willing to take on vested interests. As the daughter of a notable social reformer, if Rosemary had married the prince it is likely that she would have appealed more to ordinary people than many less compassionate aristocrats in the more democratic post-war era. As Millicent's granddaughter, the Countess of Sutherland, wrote, the Duchess of Sutherland had a 'deep sense of the equality of all human beings'.[30] Her sister Lady Angela Forbes explained that her good looks and social position allowed her to ignore convention. In her houses 'penniless artists, pensioned governesses or Presbyterian parsons' might find themselves sitting next to members of the royal family or Cabinet ministers.[31]

Known as 'the Democratic Duchess', Millicent had always found it easy to build a natural and unstilted relationship with working-class people. Before the war, the Duchess of Sutherland had been so involved in fighting a range of social injustices that she became known by her opponents as 'Meddlesome Millie'. In the Potteries, near Trentham, she campaigned against the lead poisoning that was damaging local people's health. The novelist Arnold Bennett caricatured her as an interfering lady bountiful, the Countess of Chell or 'Interfering Iris'. In his novels, the character based on Millie frequently annoyed the conservative councillors of the Five Towns. However, although the Duchess of Sutherland was mocked by some, her crusade was successful, leading to new regulations which saved the lives of many pottery workers.[32]

Another of her projects was to start a 'Cripples' Guild' to help disabled children. In 1898, she opened a home at Hanchurch to provide a fortnight's summer holiday for these children. The scheme was then extended to visiting disabled children in their own homes to provide medical treatment and surgical appliances. The project kept growing and eventually developed into an orthopaedic hospital at Hartshill, Stoke-on-Trent, which helped children with disabilities. Millicent wanted to make the most of disabled children's talents. To enable them to earn their own living, she set up a workshop where instructors trained them in a trade or craft. By 1902 more than 100 boys and girls were being taught. The project transformed lives; one young disabled lad who had been living on the streets of Stoke, where he sold newspapers, was trained to be a skilled craftsman making silver vases.[33] There were many other success stories, and their high-quality art-metalwork was sold locally and at a shop in New Bond Street, London, set up by the duchess.[34]

Millie also helped her husband's tenants in Sutherland with practical schemes that aimed to give them economic independence. One of the works she was most proud of was the opening of a technical school at Golspie that provided free education and boarding accommodation for about fifty crofters' sons aged 12 to 16. The boys were given a good elementary education and taught practical skills, including running their own farm and market garden and repairing the buildings. The school allowed boys whose parents were unable to finance them to serve apprenticeships to trades, on the understanding that repayment would be made by them once they were earning enough to do so.

Millie was determined to make a real difference in the lives of local people. Another of her projects was to reinvigorate the old traditional craft of handloom weaving by reorganising the industry in a more businesslike way, as the Sutherland Home Industries. She held annual sales of the crofters' tweeds in the palatial gardens at Stafford House, where handmade goods were sold to their society friends on stalls manned by the duchess and Rosemary.[35] Businesslike and determined, Millicent encouraged her circle to spend by telling them: 'The success or failure of the scheme means life or death to these poor people.'[36]

Since childhood, Rosemary had been involved in her mother's many campaigns. From the age of 6 she was enlisted as a saleswoman for Scottish tweeds at Stafford House. When she was at Dunrobin her mother insisted that Rosemary was dressed in Scottish homespun cloths and thick knickerbockers. By the time she was a young woman, Rosemary shared much of the work with her mother. Under the headline, 'Hardly in Homespun at the Homespun at Home,' the *Sketch* published a photo of Rosemary wearing a fashionable picture hat with a large feather, an elegant gown and immaculate white gloves selling goods made by the Cripples' Guild in one of her mother's many sales.[37] The charity work was an ideal apprenticeship for a future queen. As Rosemary's brother Geordie, Duke of Sutherland, wrote in his autobiography, with their mother playing the dual role of society hostess and social reformer they 'gained an early insight into the two extremes of life, and I think that, if only sub-consciously, that was very good for us.

As witnesses to much of her welfare work, we grew to understand the meaning of poverty as well as wealth and instinctively began to share her interests.'[38]

The culmination of Millicent's public service was during the war. If the prince had been allowed to marry Rosemary, her work with her mother in France could have inspired popularity which would have more than compensated for any whiff of scandal. When war broke out Millicent had been among the first to establish an ambulance unit in Belgium. She left England on 8 August 1914 and three weeks after hostilities began she and her team of eight British nurses and a surgeon were nursing at a convent in Namur, a border town. Soon soldiers with injuries worse than she could possibly have imagined were arriving. However, she immediately rose to the occasion.

As the Germans advanced, Namur was attacked. Millicent and her nurses were cut off and captured. There was no electricity or gas supplies and her team had to work using hand lanterns. Throughout the crisis, the duchess remained calm. She buried her revolver under an apple tree and then confidently negotiated with the enemy. Millicent and her team were soon released once German officers realised how well connected and determined the duchess was. Learning that she had entertained both the Kaiser and the Crown Prince of Germany before the war, they allowed Millicent and her staff to make their way to Holland where they were repatriated. Undeterred by this dangerous six-week interlude, the duchess was determined to continue her war work. After a brief break in England she travelled to France to set up her military hospital, taking Rosemary with her.

At her hospital, the duchess once again showed her courage under fire. Whenever there was an air-raid warning or shelling Millicent would pull on a pair of trousers, put a tin helmet on her head and start a round of the wards.[39] Accompanied by the nurses, she would try to keep morale up.[40] Millicent was in her element. She made a lasting impression as she gracefully moved from bed to bed in her immaculate white nurse's uniform. She was an inspiring figure for both her patients and nurses. During the four years of the war the Duchess of Sutherland's hospital treated about 8,000 men; in recognition of the scale of her work during the conflict, she was awarded the Belgian Royal Red Cross, the

French Croix de Guerre and the British Royal Red Cross.[41] With a war record like that, the Leveson-Gowers were just the type of family the heir to the throne should have been marrying into. The British public would have been able to identify with a hard-working nurse more than most previous royal brides.

The prince did not fight his parents' opposition to Rosemary as strongly as he was to assert himself in later love affairs, first with Freda Dudley Ward and then Wallis Simpson. Perhaps this was because his fondness for Rosemary was just not deep enough. Over the previous years, Edward had constantly been infatuated with different women. His passion for Rosemary had been short lived and on the rebound from Portia's rejection. He must also have known that she had doubts about their relationship and was not totally in love with him. As a mother who desired her son's happiness, perhaps Queen Mary was concerned not only about 'a taint' in Rosemary's blood but that the young couple's affection for each other was not strong enough to survive the rigours of a royal marriage.

Throughout his relationship with Rosemary, the prince was feeling particularly close to his mother, so he would have valued her opinion. Immediately after the royal visit to Millicent Sutherland's hospital in July 1917, Queen Mary wrote to her son about the 'wonderful time' they had spent together in France. She added: 'How nice it was our being together for so many days and having those interesting drives which will always stand out in my memory […] I confess I felt very low at parting from you at Calais and hated saying "good-bye".'[42] Edward felt the same, replying: 'What a joy it was to me to be with you so long and I loved our long drives and talks together.'[43] Edward's diaries and letters at this time frequently mention confidential talks with Queen Mary about various aspects of his life.[44] After Edward's relationship with Rosemary had ended and when the prince was returning to France, Queen Mary wrote to Edward in April 1918: 'It was a great grief taking leave of you after our delightful seven weeks together and we really did manage to see something of each other and to have some nice talks.'[45] Having felt deprived of his mother's affection as a child, Edward would have recognised the importance of such intimacy and would not have wished to jeopardise it.

By not embracing Rosemary as their future daughter-in-law, the king and queen missed an opportunity that would not come again. It is possible that the younger woman could have done for Prince Edward what Queen Mary did for George V. Throughout his reign she had given him the unstinting support and a domestic life that made the burden of ruling tolerable. Rosemary and Edward also had the potential to build a partnership on firm foundations. In the photographs of Queen Mary and Rosemary on that fateful day in July 1917, when they met at Millicent Sutherland's hospital, there is a similarity in the two women's self-contained poise: both exude a calm, inner confidence which the Prince of Wales lacked. Rosemary was a match for the queen, and she could have been an ally in turning the Prince of Wales into a man fit to be king.

Rosemary's war service meant that the prince was not only attracted to her; he also respected her deeply. The war had been a profound experience for both Edward and Rosemary and led to a strong bond between them. Although the prince had not been allowed to run the same risks as his contemporaries, he had been there with them and seen for himself the horror of the experience. He believed his education had been widened by the war because, unlike previous Princes of Wales, he had lived under all kinds of conditions with men from different classes.[46] It left him with a lasting loyalty and respect for the veterans of the war. As someone who had nursed in France, Rosemary understood and shared the prince's feelings. If Edward had married Rosemary their relationship would have been based on the most fundamental value of compassion. Both young people had this quality, as was shown in Rosemary's nursing of the shell-shocked young man which was mirrored in the stories of the prince's genuine tenderness to the wounded. This sensitive, caring quality was the best element of Edward's nature and with a woman like Rosemary by his side it could have been brought even more to the fore and might have suppressed his selfish side. As one journalist wrote about her:

Her sense was like a radiant ozone in which nothing falsely silly could live. She killed all pretence and all shams, all wrong kind of nonsense; with her sun-like humour, but never with a hard body blow or a sharp upper cut. She had sense and sensibility. She was as sensitive to beauty and feeling and sorrow as she was responsive to fun and to all the shades of the ludicrous.[47]

The same correspondent compared her to Shakespeare's heroines Rosalind, Beatrice and Portia for her 'blend of gravity, sympathy, grace and wit'.[48]

By overruling their son's choice of bride, as well as eliminating an ideal future consort, the king and queen antagonised him. According to Lady Victor Paget, the prince was 'bitter and furious' about it.[49] Lady Hardinge, who knew the prince and the court well, thought that the thwarting of his marriage plans, following so soon after his frustrations at not being able to take the role he desired in the war, 'crystallised the Prince of Wales's rebellious attitude towards established authority'.[50] He had found a model modern queen and he had not been allowed to marry her. His parents' opposition to the match was to have fateful repercussions. Rosemary was the last aristocratic single girl he seriously considered as a possible wife; from now on his lovers would be married women.

FREDA

5

THE LOVER

The prince did not pine for Rosemary Leveson-Gower for long; suggesting the fickleness of his feelings, he immediately transferred his affections. In March 1918 a chance encounter was to change the life of a young woman called Freda Dudley Ward forever. Disenchanted with her marriage, she was out for the evening with a male friend, 'Buster' Dominguez (a Latin American diplomat in London), when she got caught up in a Zeppelin raid. As the alarm sounded she took refuge in the doorway of a house in Belgrave Square. A party was happening inside and the hostess, Maud Kerr-Smiley (the sister of Wallis Simpson's husband Ernest), invited Freda to join them. One of those present that night was the Prince of Wales, and as soon as he met this uninvited guest he was smitten. He was attracted by her vivacious manner and her slender figure. They first met in the semi-darkness of the cellar where all the guests were taking shelter. The prince came up to Freda and started an animated conversation. Once the air raid was over, the party continued upstairs. They danced until 3 a.m., then the prince took Freda back to her mother-in-law's house in Lowndes Square. He begged to come in for just a minute, but Freda refused.

The prince was not the only man to fall under Freda's spell. Edward's biographer Frances Donaldson claimed she was one of the most attractive women of her generation.[1] Her contemporary, Lady Diana Cooper, described her as 'a dream of beauty', while Shane Leslie called her 'an angelic waif'.[2] Petite and pretty with dark curly hair and sparkly, periwinkle blue eyes, she was very feminine and exuded sex appeal and warmth. An acquaintance, the novelist Barbara Cartland, described her as 'irresistible' to men. She gave the impression of needing a man's protection; she seemed so physically fragile that she could not face the world without his strength. Yet beneath the vulnerable exterior, she was a very strong woman who had great integrity and was 'spiritually courageous'.[3]

Freda was a vivacious storyteller who turned mundane events into amusing adventures. Perhaps her most distinctive characteristic was her high-pitched voice, which some people described as squeaky, but others found oddly alluring.[4] It was not just men who loved Freda; she made friends wherever she went and kept them for the rest of her life. Frances Donaldson, who first met Freda when Frances was 7 or 8 years old, said that her good manners and kindness were particularly noticeable in an era when arrogance was the fashion.[5] Freda was classless, which meant that she talked to members of staff in the same informal way as she chatted to her best friends.[6] No doubt this was part of her appeal for the prince as it was such a contrast to the rigid hierarchy and formality of court life. Like Freda, the prince won over people from all sections of society. Once a young beautician came to give him a manicure. On her first visit, she was so nervous that she upset all her instruments; Edward got down on his hands and knees and helped her to pick them up. He then asked her about herself and laughed with her, which put her totally at ease. His sensitivity to her situation made her his fan for life.[7]

Both Freda and Edward were thoroughly modern in their outlook. They refused to be bound by the conventions of the past. Born Winifred Birkin in 1894, Freda was the eldest of the three daughters and one son of a wealthy Nottingham lace manufacturer, Colonel Charles Birkin, and his American wife, Claire Lloyd Howe. The colonel's father, Sir Thomas Isaac Birkin, was known as the 'lace king'; he had been a successful industrialist who ran lace factories that employed many people.[8] When Colonel Birkin took over the business, he was a very strict, patriarchal figure. His great-grandaughter says that he was rather like Soames in the *Forsyte Saga*.[9] In contrast Freda's mother, Claire, was fun-loving and lively. Born in New York, she was the daughter of a wealthy moneybroker, Alexander Howe; she spent most of her childhood in Paris and travelled extensively.[10] A good singer, she was nicknamed 'Pearly' in the family because of her exquisite teeth. After Freda was born Claire suffered a series of miscarriages, which meant that her two other daughters, Violet and Vera, and her one son, Charles, were born with gaps of several years between them. As the years went by she became increasingly frustrated in her marriage. She fell in love with a tennis player but as divorce was not an option she stayed with her stern husband.[11] Claire always had a theatrical streak which she passed on to her children and later her grandchildren. During their childhood, they were all encouraged to take part in elaborate amateur dramatics staged by Mrs Birkin.

The Birkins were a large and important family in Nottingham and the various branches of the clan often gathered together for massive Sunday lunches at Charles and Claire's imposing three-storey mansion, Lamcote House in Radcliffe-on-Trent. Freda hated these stuffy occasions and longed for a freer life.[12] Although Freda and her siblings had a conventional upbringing, there was an unconventional and daring streak running through the family. Freda's brother became a successful writer of horror stories and two of her first cousins became racing drivers.

As Freda came from middle-class rather than aristocratic stock, when she first came out in society, Lady Cynthia Mosley, daughter of the Marquess of Curzon, snobbishly recalled that 'nobody knew her. She was terribly dressed.' However, Freda was soon enjoying the attentions of what she described as 'a barrage' of men. To give her an air of sophistication, a friend of Freda's, Ali Mackintosh, took her under his wing and taught her how to dress elegantly.[13] The young woman from Nottingham was great company and had a wonderful sense of humour. Adding to her attractions, underlying her sense of fun were common sense and wisdom. Perhaps the quality which made her most appealing to men – particularly rather insecure ones – was her ability to build them up and make them feel good about themselves. When talking to someone, she would focus completely on them and not want to talk about herself but about them. She really listened and gave advice that was worth taking. With his complex insecurities and lack of self-esteem, Freda was just what the prince needed, but there was a major problem: she was not free.

In 1913, shortly before her 19th birthday, Freda had married William Dudley Ward. The couple met sailing across the Atlantic. A few months before the voyage, Freda had been expelled from the private girls' boarding school Heathfield for climbing over the school wall with some friends to go to the races at nearby Ascot. In disgrace with her parents, she had been taken on a trip to America to see Claire's relatives. Under her father's critical eye, she was not allowed to go to any parties or have fun. However, even under close surveillance she managed to attract male attention. In September 1912 the Birkins sailed from New York to Southampton on the Cunard liner *Mauretania*; Freda was sitting on deck reading a trashy novel when three young politicians kept passing her on their walking circuit. They soon started chatting to her. They were the up-and-coming MPs Tommy Agar-Robartes, F.E. Smith and William Dudley Ward. One of them seized her book, claiming it was unsuitable reading for a pretty girl her age, and threw it overboard.[14]

William was immediately attracted by this spirited young woman and on their return to England he started courting her. Although he was sixteen years older than her, William was a fit and handsome man in his prime. After going to school at Eton he went to Trinity College, Cambridge. He became a notable athlete, rowing for the university and captaining the winning team in the 1899 and 1900 boat races. A university newspaper described him at the time: 'His hair is red, his complexion is pink, and he is smooth, plump and pleasing.' He was notoriously laid back about punctuality and keeping engagements. Apparently, he also had a liking for the 'flesh-pots' of Cambridge and was known, occasionally, to turn up for rowing training still dressed in white tie and tails. He had many nicknames, including 'the Terra Cotta Baby' and 'the Cheaper', but he was known to his friends as 'Duddie'.[15]

After he met Freda the couple enjoyed a whirlwind romance, and within a few months she agreed to marry the much older politician. Their wedding was held at St Margaret's Church, Westminster, in July 1913. Society and politics were well represented in the congregation. Looking very youthful, Freda wore a white tulle dress embroidered with silver and a train of tulle lined with silver tissue. Her delicate veil was secured by a small wreath of orange blossom. After the ceremony, a reception was held at Claridge's and then the couple went on honeymoon to the United States and Canada, sailing once again on the *Mauretania*, the ship on which they first met.[16]

Her marriage put Freda at the heart of London society; on his father's side Dudley Ward was a nephew of the Earl of Dudley. His mother Violet's family were equally well connected and closely linked to the court. Her brother, Reginald, the second Viscount Esher, was a respected courtier and politician to whom Queen Mary frequently turned for advice about her eldest son. Duddie's sister Eugenie was also married to a courtier, Sir Bryan Godfrey-Faussett, who was one of the king's equerries. His youngest sister, Enid, was a great friend of Princess Mary.

By the time William married Freda, he was a rising star in politics. In 1906, he had become the Liberal MP for Southampton. Described by a friend as 'kind, jolly and vague', he was well liked in parliament[17] and gained a reputation for his witty speeches. While he was contesting Southampton, a heckler asked him if he was in favour of marriage with a deceased wife's sister. 'Yes,' he replied, sweetly, 'if it is not to be made compulsory.'[18] From 1909 he was treasurer of the royal household and a Liberal whip. When he first appeared in parliament in his new role as treasurer, wearing his uniform, which was 'all gold lace and gorgeousness', etiquette demanded that he should retire from the House walking backwards. He did it with the agility of an athlete and won the approval of a critical audience.[19] He was described by one newspaper as 'the handsomest Treasurer of the Household ever seen in official uniform'.[20]

In the first years of their marriage the Dudley Wards had two daughters. Penelope (known as 'Pempie') was born on 4 August 1914, on the first day of the First World War. Angela (known as 'Angie') arrived two years later, on 25 May 1916. During the war Duddie was commissioned as a lieutenant commander in the Royal Navy Volunteer Reserve, which involved secret intelligence work as well as his political duties. At first Freda tried to be a dutiful political wife, attending events in the constituency. In 1915, she opened a bazaar in aid of 'the poorer country churches'. In her short speech she thanked the stallholders, saying that it was a good thing to do during the war as it 'helped them to forget a little of their worry, for was it not true that the busier one was the quicker did time fly'. The local vicar was evidently enchanted by her naïve style as he commented on the 'delightful lilt and graciousness of her speech'.[21] At a dinner for servicemen in 1916 she distributed 'woolly comforts' from under a Christmas tree. As well as winning admirers in her husband's constituency, Freda was beginning to be noticed in society. In *The Tatler* that year there was a full-page photograph of her, wearing a floaty gauze dress and posing seductively on a chair, under the headline: 'The Wife of a Very Distinguished Wet Bob Who is Doing his Bit Afloat with the Fleet.'[22]

However, by the time Freda met the prince her marriage was already under strain. In 1917 Duddie was made vice-chamberlain to the royal household. In his new role he reported regularly to the king about what was happening in parliament. His increased responsibilities meant that he was often away from home. With her husband spending late nights in parliament, Freda was bored and soon found new ways of amusing herself.

Her marriage did not prevent her relationship with the prince developing rapidly. After their first encounter, Edward wrote to 'Mrs Dudley Ward' at Lowndes Square proposing another meeting. This caused some confusion as Freda was staying with her mother-in-law at the time. The older woman opened the letter and thought that the prince wanted to visit her. Mrs Dudley Ward Senior invited Edward to tea, which was not quite the assignation he had hoped for.[23] However, this was only a temporary setback and nothing would deter the prince from being with Freda. At first, he felt self-conscious and shy with her, but Freda's easy manner soon broke down any barriers. For Freda, having the most eligible bachelor in the world chasing after her must have been intoxicating. His charm was legendary. Lady Hardinge, who was married to George V's assistant private secretary, analysed his charisma. She claimed that it was a not a natural charm but a force at his command which he could switch on or off at will. If he was in a room full of people he would be the centre of attention, not just because he was the Prince of Wales, but because of his personality. It was as if he had cast a spell over people, and if he wished he could change the whole atmosphere on a whim.[24] With the full force of his charm turned on Freda it would have been hard to resist.

The besotted couple found ways to be together almost every day. Their relationship soon became the talk of society. Physically they were well matched. Edward was a little taller than Freda, but both were fashionably svelte: the prince weighed just over 9 stone, while she was 2 stone lighter.[25] On 12 March 1918 Cynthia Asquith wrote:

Saw the Prince of Wales dancing round with Mrs Dudley Ward, a pretty little fluff with whom he is said to be rather in love. He is a dapper little fellow – too small – but really a pretty face. He looked as pleased as Punch and chatted away the whole time. I have never seen a man talk so fluently while dancing. He obviously means to have fun.[26]

After the parties were over they would drive around for ages in taxis as he longed to spend every hour of the day with her.

When not in London Freda stayed at Kilbees Farm, Winkfield, near Windsor. Kilbees was owned by one of her husband's sisters, Mrs Charles Seymour. The farm was 350 years old and had once been a hunting lodge of James I. It was a charming house with low, beamed ceilings and it had much carved and panelled oak. An ancient kitchen had been turned into a smoking room.[27] It was much easier for the couple to meet there undetected than at Lowndes Square. From when they first met, Edward felt that they knew and understood each other. They had much in common in tastes and ideas; both were fashionable not just in the clothes they wore but in their attitudes. They were soon lovers, and within weeks of meeting the prince referred to a Sunday afternoon and evening at the farm which was 'our best stunt […] but may it often be repeated is all I can pray for!!' He claimed he would never forget it.[28] Edward's passion for his married mistress was all-consuming. If they were apart he would phone her four or five times a night and he would be bereft if she was not in.

As the Germans made a final push towards the Channel in March 1918 all leave was immediately cancelled and soldiers who were in Britain were ordered back to their units. One evening at Buckingham Palace, King George looked up from studying his war maps and said to his son: 'Good God! Are you still here? Why aren't you back with your Corps?' In fact, the prince had asked the War Office to transfer him to

France and he was waiting to see if his request was to be granted. The king took matters into his own hands, saying that he could not have his son seen around London when the British army had its 'back to the wall'. Edward was sent back to join Lord Cavan in Italy immediately.[29]

Once in Italy at the end of March, the prince bombarded Freda with dozens of letters written to 'My Angel' and signed with 'tons and tons of love from your E'.[30] Many were written late at night, as he sat in his room trying to recreate her essence by putting some drops of her scent, 'Royal Briar', on his handkerchief. He would look at her photograph, which was kept in a little leather frame by his bed when it was not in his pocket, and kiss it. He told her that thinking of her made him feel 'fearfully naughty'.[31] To conjure up their time together he would smoke a cigarette and play their special tunes 'Have a Heart' and 'The Little Cottage' on his gramophone. It was as though he could only go to sleep once he had jotted down his every thought and experience and shared it with her. His letters were often in pencil and full of spelling and grammatical errors. At first the notes were littered with swear words, but it seems that Freda told him off, so he tried to stop using bad language in correspondence with her.[32] However, he continued to send her puerile jokes and rhymes which he thought might amuse her.

The prince told his mistress that her letters were the only joy of his dull existence, but it seems that Freda was not so single-minded. She was working with a Voluntary Aid Detachment, nursing at a hospital in Ascot and then in Windsor. There was a photo of the Prince of Wales hung up in the ward where she worked scrubbing floors, and she looked at it occasionally. While Edward was away she had a brief fling with Captain Reginald Seymour, great-grandson of the Marquess of Hertford. The prince knew Captain Seymour as he had been an equerry to George V since 1916 and he regularly attended the royal family. Born in 1878, like her husband, he was much older than Freda.[33] Major Seymour realised that he took a 'back seat' when the prince was in England and that it was going to be just 'a short little love affair' but 'a very sweet one'.[34] He wrote to Freda: 'How was your young man? Do you like him making love to you better than me? [...] I fully accept my position of No. 2.'[35]

Freda was equally worldly-wise, and she did not show any concern when the prince admitted to flirtations with other women. While in

Rome in May 1918 he attended a party where he misbehaved with some attractive VADs. As was to become his habit, he half confessed to Freda about these incidents but played them down, perhaps partly to salve his conscience while making her jealous or 'thulky' (as they called it in their baby talk). He promised never to lie to her again and told her: 'I just "grovel" at my idol's feet asking forgiveness.'[36] Freda replied coolly, describing these incidents as his 'medicine' and adding: 'Les petits amusements ne contes pas.'[37] Getting surprisingly close to the truth, she also teased him about what sort of French school he had been to and what he had learnt. He told her about the French courtesan, Maggy Alibert, who he now called 'IT' as she had begun to blackmail him. He wanted to get his indiscreet letters back and he admitted that he had been a fool to write to her, although he excused himself by saying he had been very young at the time.[38]

As well as illicit encounters, there were rumours of official alliances for the prince. While he was in Rome there were stories in the newspapers that he was going to marry an Italian royal, Princess Yolande of Savoy, eldest daughter of King Victor Emmanuel III of Italy. Freda asked her lover directly whether the gossip was true. Edward denied it and was characteristically ungallant about his suggested bride, telling Freda that Yolande had 'a face like a bottom!!'[39] However, in another letter he acknowledged that he would have to marry one day, although he did not intend to do so for years. He added that he would have told her if he had got engaged.[40] It is evident that even at the height of their relationship both lovers understood that they would never be able to marry. It was a situation that they accepted at the time, but as the years went by this inability to make a permanent commitment was to haunt them both. Although there were always other women for the prince and men for Freda, they could just about cope with the complexities of their relationship provided they knew that they came first in the other's life.

Freda felt secure in Edward's affections because she knew that she had a powerful hold over him. Her power was emotional as much as sexual; increasingly she was not just the prince's lover, she was his confidante and he relied on her for advice. His letters refer to the pleasures of talking to her more often than they mention their sexual encounters. He described her as a real friend to whom he could say anything he felt.

He became depressed and anxious if he could not unburden his soul to her regularly. Reflecting how isolated he had been, he told her that he felt he knew her better than he had known anybody before.[41] Believing that they had been predestined to meet, he sent her photographs from his childhood saying he had always been waiting for her to enter his life.[42] Although he still suffered from fits of depression and periodically hinted that he would kill himself if he did not have her, he told her that these moods were now only superficial because she made him happier deep down than he had ever been before.

His letters show how immature and needy he was and how he turned to her as an emotional prop. He often wrote in baby talk as though he was trying to capture a lost childhood. He wrote: 'What babies we both are sweetheart, but I do love it so and it does us both so much good.'[43] In fact, Freda was the grown-up in their partnership, and that was a large part of her appeal. In letters to his 'precious darling little Mummie' he called himself her 'v. v. own little David'.[44] Long before Wallis Simpson, he found dominant women attractive. Explaining to Freda what he needed in a relationship, he wrote:

> You know you ought to be really foul to me sometimes sweetie and curse and be cruel; it would do me worlds of good and bring me to my right senses!! I think I'm the kind of man who needs a certain amount of cruelty without which he gets abominably spoilt and soft!! I feel that's what's the matter with me.[45]

In later letters, there are hints that he liked to be dominated by women. In one he asked her to come up to London 'to give me that hiding'.[46] In another he wrote: 'I do need you so so badly to chase me into bed with a big big stick.'[47] However, even in this letter it was clear that he was looking for a mother figure at least as much as a dominatrix, because he added that he also needed someone to look after him in his day-to-day life and do things like 'chase him' to the dentist.[48]

Freda had a deep understanding of her lover's psychology. Edward soon trusted his mistress enough to be totally honest with her about every aspect of his existence. He complained to her about the stifling formality of court life, his dislike of official duties and even his doubts about whether he ever wanted to be king. Part of him believed that the days for kings and princes was over and the concept of monarchy was out of date.[49] If he could have chosen a career for himself, it would have been to remain in the army. Instead he had to take on the role of heir apparent and to prepare for when he would become king.[50] He discussed with her what it took to be a good king. He said he would have to be a figurehead and 'a wooden man', doing nothing that would upset the prime minister, the court or the Archbishop of Canterbury. He would have to go to church and mind his manners. As a modern man he did not want that sort of life.[51] However, his promise to his father that he would do everything he could to save the monarchy was genuine. He feared Bolshevism and believed that there could be revolution in Britain. To prevent it he dedicated himself to trying to find out about social problems first hand through his visits to deprived areas and to then do something about them. He told Freda that he was going to 'slave' for the cause of monarchy more for the sake of the country and the empire than his family.[52]

After his return on leave to England in August 1918, the couple spent much of their time together. While he was staying with his family at Windsor Castle Freda was nearby at Kilbees Farm. Describing Windsor as 'this prison', he would sometimes escape late at night and cycle over to his mistress's 'little cottage', then creep back into the castle in the early hours.[53] He believed that the monarchy needed to be modernised. In 1918 he wrote to Freda: 'Oh!! That court life, beloved one, that's what's going to hasten the end of it if it isn't vastly modified; people can't and won't stand it nowadays and how well do I understand it and abhor all that sort of rot!!'[54]

The court at Windsor was particularly formal and rigid in its routine. The same elderly guests were invited to stay every year. There was rarely any 'new blood' to enliven the conversation or introduce some original ideas.[55] It seems that this stagnant circle was more the king's than the queen's choice. Queen Mary had written to Edward during the war expressing her desire for more stimulation, writing: 'Anything for a change of ideas say I and to relieve the monotony of our present, dull routine.'[56] However, as usual Queen Mary gave in to her husband, trying to keep him happy and putting her own needs second to his wishes. At times, the formality at Windsor was stifling. If the king's sons were present they were expected to remain standing after George V left the room because Queen Mary did. Then, beginning with the Prince of Wales and following in age order, they would go up in turn to face the queen as she stood in the middle of the room and bow to her before withdrawing.[57]

Yet behind the scenes and away from her husband, Queen Mary was trying to build a more natural relationship with her eldest son. The account of Edward's visit to Windsor in the letters between the queen and the prince show that he was feeling close to his mother. After the prince's stay Queen Mary wrote to him that it had been 'such a pleasure' having him at 'this beloved old Castle'.[58] Edward replied: 'I simply loathed leaving you at Windsor on Monday, where I spent such a delightful fortnight with you and I loved our talks!!'[59] Over the next few months, Edward's alliance with his mother became even stronger. The prince wrote to her: 'It's so wonderful to feel that we really can talk things over now and vital and "intime" things and I can assure you darling Mama, that this makes all the difference to me; we understand each other so well now.'[60] Queen Mary was delighted, replying:

> Surely no mother ever received so warm a tribute of praise from her son as that contained in your dearest of letters […] I am deeply touched and grateful at what you so kindly say about our delightful talks, yes, I think I do understand and can enter into other people's feelings which is the great thing – I enjoyed our talks above everything.[61]

Edward's relationship with his father was never as harmonious. Clothes always led to clashes between the king and prince, and nowhere was the gulf between them about fashion more apparent than at Windsor. George V was very strict about dress codes and uniforms. For dinner, the ladies wore full evening dress with white gloves and splendid jewels while the king and the Prince of Wales were dressed in the 'Windsor uniform'. This dress code had been introduced by George III and was a dark-blue tailcoat with red collar and cuffs worn with breeches or trousers and a white tie and waistcoat. These outdated outfits were just the type of clothes which Edward hated wearing.

While his son rejected pompous ceremonial costumes, the king was equally scathing about modern fashions, particularly if they suggested a degree of female emancipation. He detested the 'new woman' or the emancipated flapper. Painted fingernails, women smoking in public, drinking cocktails or wearing frivolous hats were among his pet hates.[62] His conservative prejudices ruled Queen Mary's style of dressing. She was never allowed to wear a colour he disliked or short skirts, even though she had very shapely legs.[63] George V particularly loathed women wearing trousers and if he ever saw female tourists at Windsor wearing them he would make derogatory remarks.[64] He also thoroughly disapproved of the prince's informal style and accused him of being the worst-dressed man in London. One day a palace official heard George V rowing with his son. He shouted at him: 'You dress like a cad. You act like a cad. You are a cad. Get out!'[65] As he was now an adult, Edward resented his father's interference. He loved all the things the king loathed. Freda encouraged him to stand up to his father and live his life in his own way.[66]

In September 1918 Freda and her husband were invited to dine at Windsor by the king and queen because of William Dudley Ward's position as vice-chamberlain. Edward was not there and at this stage his parents had no idea about their charming guest's role in their son's life. Apparently, the king was captivated by Freda and he became quite animated in her company. Edward had hoped that Freda would have had a chance to talk to his sister Mary, who was very close to him, but they were unable to have a private chat.

Although Queen Mary believed her son was confiding in her at this time, the prince did not tell her about what was going on in his love life. His relationship with Freda remained a secret he kept from her. However, Edward wanted his brothers and sister to meet the woman who was already so important to him. When the prince returned to England, he and Freda formed a foursome with Edward's brother Bertie and Freda's friend Sheila Loughborough. Sheila was unhappily married to Rosemary's cousin, Lord Loughborough, who – like his father, the Earl of Rosslyn – gambled and drank too much. Freda and Sheila became good friends; they were both about the same age and young mothers who were in failing marriages. The two couples called themselves the '4 Dos' and they formed a secret club. Edward said what babies they all were together and, reflecting this, they had a teddy bear as their mascot. The foursome had a great deal of fun together. Freda and Edward's relationship was always the more intense and they saw themselves as the 'bear leaders' of the gang.[67] Although Edward never mentioned Freda directly in his memoir written many years later, he did describe the effect she had on his life at this moment. He wrote how grateful those men who had come back from active service were to be alive and that life had never seemed more desirable. Everything he did seemed 'invested with a sort of magical charm'.[68]

There were dances every night in Mayfair and Chelsea. Sometimes the prince received as many as four invitations for parties the same evening. If one did not amuse him he would move on to another. Among the most enjoyable events were the small dances Freda put on in her house for their closest friends. As in his earlier flirtations, the prince loved to dance. Gossip columnists noted how 'perfectly' he partnered Freda.[69] When the Charleston arrived in London from the United States they had lessons at the Café de Paris from Santos Casini, a well-known dance instructor, who demonstrated the steps of the new dance on the roof of a taxi moving down Regent Street. In the morning or afternoon, Freda and Edward enjoyed having the whole polished parquet floor to themselves. The dance was described as 'neurotic' and 'vulgar' by some critics, but that did not deter the fun-loving couple from wanting to perfect it.[70]

After dinner or a show, or once a party had finished, they would move on to a nightclub with their friends. They went to Ciro's, Quaglino's and the Kit Kat but their favourite was the Embassy. Described as 'the Buckingham Palace of Nightclubs', the Embassy was in a basement in Old Bond Street. The club came alive after 9 p.m. Walking through the club's swing doors, guests entered a long, mirrored room where they would be greeted by the imposing, grey-haired maître d'hôtel, Luigi. Famous for his discretion and snobbery, Luigi knew just where to place his guests whether they were aristocrats, writers, actors or politicians, wives or mistresses. With a well-chosen word for regular guests and an assured familiarity with the famous, he made his clientele feel part of an exclusive club. It was said that at the Embassy Club you could get anything from a Player's cigarette to a white elephant within three minutes of asking for it.[71]

Once comfortably seated at the sofas and tables, guests would dine, drink gin and tonic and waft Turkish cigarette smoke into the heady atmosphere. The club's famous black cat, Embassy Jackson, would walk along the backs of the sofas, gracing the chosen few with his presence.[72] After the theatre, the club would get so busy that tables were jammed over every inch of the floor. Night after night, people fought for the last remaining tables, the less-favoured customers perched on small chairs in overcrowded corners.[73] Just enough space was left for dancing on the dancefloor in the centre of the room. At one end, on a balcony, was the bandstand.[74] The band leader was Ambrose. Standing on the balcony, poised to play his violin, he often looked rather bored as he surveyed his audience.[75] His ennui contrasted with the excitement which pulsed through the room. The crush added to the thrill; you never knew who you might meet at the Embassy – one night you could be dancing next to the American actress Tallulah Bankhead, and on another, sipping cocktails at a table opposite Winston Churchill. For social climbers, the club offered outstanding opportunities to break into society. Much nodding and waving went on across the room and guests regularly transferred from one table to another.[76]

During the season Freda and Edward were at the Embassy almost every Thursday night. Once the prince walked in with his elegant entourage a ripple of anticipation would pass through the room. Edward and Freda gathered a close-knit circle of friends around them; the chosen few included Shelia Loughborough, the Colin Buists, the Brownlows, Ali Mackintosh, Rosemary and her husband Eric Ednam and Poppy Baring. The prince avoided the scions of the great aristocratic families, preferring to choose his own friends. He regarded many of the 'old guard' as stuffy while they thought he was 'rather vulgar'.[77] The women in the prince's set were slim and glamorous, while the men were rich and some were flashy. They all liked to party and, occasionally, for a change of scene, they would go to the Kit Kat or the Café de Paris, to watch a cabaret performed by the black musicians Layton and Johnson. After the nightclubs closed, the prince would take the musical duo back to York House to entertain him and his friends for another hour. The West Indian singer Leslie Hutchinson was another great favourite and after he had performed at the Café de Paris, he also entertained the prince's parties with the latest songs. The strains of 'These Foolish Things' could often be heard at York House into the early hours of the morning.[78]

6

'FREDIE MUMMIE'

Although they had great fun together, the prince's relationship with Freda was never just about partying. Edward rarely felt at home in his parents' palaces, and Freda provided the domesticity he craved. He wanted them both to have their own homes in London where they could meet and have some privacy. He told his mother's friend and lady-in-waiting, Mabell, Countess of Airlie, that he did not want to marry for a long time, but at 25 he could not live under the same roof as his parents. He needed to be free to lead his own life. He also told the countess that he had stopped spending half an hour before dinner with his mother. As Lady Airlie knew, this time had been very precious to them both. She begged Edward not to stop making these visits to his mother but Queen Mary's role as confidante was over; she had been usurped by Freda.[1]

The prince persuaded the king and queen to let him move out of Buckingham Palace into York House, which was part of the redbrick Tudor St James's Palace. When the prince first arrived in his new home it was a 'rabbit warren' of asymmetrical rooms filled with hideous

Victorian furniture.[2] Freda helped to create an atmosphere of informal intimacy at York House. She introduced chintzes and lighter panelling. The walls of the sitting room were decorated with survey maps of the world on which the British Empire was marked red. Instead of eating in the formal dining room Freda and the prince would dine on a table in front of the sitting-room fire.[3] When friends came around she would sit at his feet leaning against his legs.

When Freda was not there Edward was lonely rattling around in seventy-five rooms. From 1919, when Freda moved into a grand, Grade I John Nash house in Cumberland Terrace, the prince spent more time there than in his own home. He usually arrived at 5 p.m. and stayed to dinner or until it was time for his evening engagement. He would then return to her house later that night. He told her that he only felt at home in her house.[4] As Freda got to know his brothers better, they would also drop in and tell her their troubles. Prince George became great friends with Freda.[5]

Freda's husband, Duddie, seems to have accepted his wife's relationship with the heir to the throne. There is a photograph of Freda standing between her husband and her lover in the early 1920s; she looks completely composed and in control, casually holding a cigarette in her hand, while the two men look slightly less comfortable. At first Freda and Edward hoped that Duddie did not suspect anything, but as time went on it was inevitable that he became aware of what was going on. For generations, Duddie's family had served the Crown, and now, as his wife did so in a less conventional way, he chose not to rock the boat. His attitude made the affair possible. It is hard to know William Dudley Ward's motivation, but it is likely that he would not have wanted the scandal involved in divorcing his wife and the detrimental effect this would have had on his political career and on his daughters. Instead, he and his wife led increasingly separate lives. Freda still attended some constituency events and family weddings with him, but in London they did their own thing.

Although the prince demanded much of his mistress's time and energy, he was away for long periods. Always sensible and balanced, Freda developed a very full life of her own. She still sometimes had to play the role of political wife and during the general election of

December 1918 she supported Duddie, helping him to campaign in his Southampton constituency. She visited the slums and reported back to the prince about her experience of working people's homes and her impressions of their general spirits and conditions. She was a good influence on Edward politically. As one biographer has said, she was 'not the kind of woman a playboy Prince was supposed to want as his playmate'.[6] She preferred thinking people to the cocktail set and was very interested in politics. One friend described her as one of the brightest women he had ever known; she had strong opinions and was willing to express them.[7] Her husband's uncle, Lord Esher, wrote to the prince about a lunch he hosted with the Liberal politician Philip Sassoon, the Labour MP and trade union leader Frank Hodges and Herbert Smith, a leader of the Miners' Federation. When Freda joined them Lord Esher described how she held her own in the ensuing highly political conversation. She was totally at ease with the politicians and debated animatedly with them.[8]

The prince was also political but, as he explained in his memoir, he was expected to remain not only above party and faction but be apolitical. He found this particularly difficult because he had an independent and questioning mind.[9] Like most of his class, he feared a Labour government, but he believed that the injustices in society should be redressed and he was particularly concerned about poor housing and unemployed ex-servicemen. In 1913, 1.2 per cent of the workforce had been unemployed; by 1920 the figure was 9.8 per cent.[10] From 1919 the prince toured the country visiting slums in South Wales and Glasgow, gaining a greater understanding of industry and working men than any of his predecessors. He was no radical crusader, but he did believe in moderate reform. On his Duchy of Cornwall estates, in both the West Country and London, he improved the working conditions and housing for his tenants. Politically, he sympathised most with Lloyd George and the radical wing of the government.[11] According to Lloyd George's private secretary and mistress, Frances Stevenson, the prince and prime minister were fond of each other.[12] It seems that Freda and her husband had similar political views. Duddie was a close ally of Lloyd George; the prime minister was the godfather of their youngest daughter, Angie. Although Duddie was not popular in his constituency as he was rarely there due to his additional responsibilities in parliament and at court, he was re-elected.

Freda was only a part-time wife, but she was a full-time mother. She was devoted to her two girls and they came first for her. There are dozens of photographs of her pretty daughters, dressed identically in various imaginative outfits. From an early age, they appeared in society magazines with their mother. In *The Tatler* in 1920, there was a full-page photograph of Freda leaning over the back of a chair with her angelic daughters, a mass of ringlets and frills, on either side of her.[13] The girls were usually dressed in matching outfits or fancy dress. At a midsummer fete in aid of infants and welfare funds at Ham House, Richmond, Angie appeared as a butterfly with lopsided wings while Pempie pirouetted around as an ethereal fairy.[14]

However, the girls were never just designer accessories to Freda's image. In contrast to many of their contemporaries, in the Dudley Wards' house there was no divide between the nursery and the drawing room. The girls were included in their mother's busy social life and she took them with her whenever possible. In 1921 Pempie was photographed with her mother outside Number 12 Downing Street when Freda was visiting her friend Philip Sassoon, the prime minister's parliamentary private secretary.[15] It was a case of 'love me, love my daughters'.[16] Freda even put on a new type of 'half-and-half' party to entertain her girls and their friends. These occasions were officially children's parties but ones 'which grow up a little towards their close and offer just as much for adults as infants'. When Freda gave one of these parties at Philip Sassoon's Park Lane house, society mothers and their offspring flooded in. A band played upstairs and the girls, dressed as gipsies and dairymaids, danced with their schoolboy partners, who then took them down to tea in the dining room with 'a most gallant and sophisticated air'. The children were then given balloons and gifts. As one gossip columnist commented, they were 'half babyish' with their balloons but then, as they remembered that they were at a party, they flirted with their feather fans 'with the air of grown-up minxdom which is so amusing'.[17] At the end of the party many young men arrived, including the Prince of Wales. They drank cocktails with the glamorous mothers, who then left the children with their nannies before going off for the evening to their more adult parties.

Early in her relationship, Freda introduced her girls to the prince.[18] Edward genuinely adored her children and enjoyed playing with them. He wrote to Sheila Loughborough: 'I am so fond of those two babies and they are so sweet to me and we all have such fun together sometimes the four of us!!'[19] Pempie and Angie saw so much of their mother's lover that he was soon treated as an honorary uncle whom they called 'Little Prince'. He contrasted their close relationship with Freda with his own childhood. He told Angie how lucky she was to have a loving mother.[20] Rather than resenting Freda's bond with her daughters, he relished it. He would come to see the girls when Freda was away and sit with them cutting out patterns and pictures until their bedtime at 7 p.m. He invited them to see a Charlie Chaplin film he was screening and wrote an affectionate letter to Pempie when she had a fever and was unable to come. When they developed flu and then whooping cough he shared Freda's worries about them and wished that he could join her in her vigil by their bedsides. He never forgot their birthdays. Freda's younger daughter Angie became very close to the prince. As she grew older he took her on outings and had her to stay without her mother.

When they were together, Edward and Freda created a happy environment for the girls. They never rowed; Freda told an interviewer that he was the gentlest, kindest, most thoughtful man imaginable.[21] Angie recalled how the heir to the throne always gave in to her mother; if she made a proposal to him he would reply, 'Anything to please, anything to please.'[22] Freda explained that if she asked him for anything he was very generous and would give it to her immediately. However, unlike Wallis, she never exploited his generosity. He brought her gifts back from his tours and sent her sentimental presents, but there is no record of him giving her priceless jewellery. Freda used her power over him more for other people's benefit than her own. She once asked him to bail out a friend of hers who was heavily in debt for several thousand pounds. The prince immediately wrote out a cheque without asking any questions.[23]

Soon much of London society and the government knew about Freda and Edward's trysts. However, the affair was kept secret from the public; there was not a whisper of it in the newspapers and only the couple's closest friends knew how serious the relationship really was. The prince and Freda were seen playing golf, going to the races and staying at country house parties together. They behaved as if they were a married couple. Edward turned down invitations to parties if Freda was not invited. They most enjoyed socialising in small groups with other couples. When the prince's equerry, Piers 'Joey' Legh, and his girlfriend, Sarah Shaughnessy, were invited to tea with them at Freda's house, Sarah commented on how natural and happy they seemed together.[24] Lady Diana and Duff Cooper also socialised with them. After an amusing lunch party at the house of artist Sir John Lavery and his wife Hazel, Duff noted that Freda seemed only to want to put the prince at his ease and for him to appear at his best. He described her manner towards and about him as 'perfect'.[25] Winston Churchill also met the couple at a dance in Lavery's studio. After telling his wife, Clementine, about stepping on the prince's toe while dancing and making him yelp, he added that 'the little lady', as he called Freda, was 'very much to the fore'.[26]

When rumours reached the king and queen about their son's relationship with a married woman they tried to find out more. Their old friend, Lord Esher, who was Duddie's uncle, was invited to Balmoral, but he refused. Lord Esher was very fond of Freda and always told her to be discreet like Edward VII's mistress Mrs Keppel.[27] He thought that the king knew nothing about the affair, but Queen Mary wanted to know all about Freda. Lord Esher told a friend that he was not willing to be pumped for information and did not want to put his nose into 'what some day will prove a hornet's nest'.[28]

When his parents eventually asked the prince about his new relationship, he denied it, saying that he did not know Freda better than anyone else. When they later discovered the truth they were horrified. The king snobbishly dubbed Freda 'the lace-maker's daughter'. When Freda's friends heard about this comment they made a joke of it and started calling her 'Miss Loom', after the weaver's daughter in the card game Happy Families.[29] Freda knew that the king and queen regarded her as 'a scarlet woman'. She believed that they were always pushing the prince to marry someone of his own rank.[30]

In fact, Freda's family deserved to be respected. While Rosemary Leveson-Gower had the perfect aristocratic pedigree, Freda Dudley Ward had a model middle-class background. The Birkins represented the backbone of post-war British society. Freda's parents were highly regarded in Nottingham. Her father had fought bravely in the war; in August 1914, he had raised the 1st/7th Battalion (Robin Hoods), The Sherwood Foresters. Although he was aged 50 and did not need to volunteer, he became their commanding officer and went with them to France. When he led his men into action at the Battle of Hooge in July 1915 his skull was fractured by an explosion, and he was brought home to England in a hospital ship. For a year afterwards, he suffered from the effects of concussion. His injury was to affect him for the rest of his life, leaving him with frequent headaches.[31]

Freda's mother Claire was also very involved in the war effort, working tirelessly as president of the American, French and Belgian Red Cross committees that were formed in Nottingham. She was commandant of a Voluntary Aid Detachment and she turned Lamcote House into an auxiliary hospital for officers. She also acted as a Red Cross searcher, helping families trace men who had been reported missing. Her war work was recognised when she was awarded the Médaille de la Reconnaissance française, the Medaille de la Reine Elisabeth of Belgium and the American Red Cross Medal.

The *Nottingham Journal* claimed that if local people were asked, 'Who is the best-known lady in Nottinghamshire?', nine out of ten would reply: 'Mrs Charles Birkin, of course.'[32] After the war, Claire became the stalwart supporter of every good cause in the area. She became president of the Women's Institute and president of the Nottinghamshire Cancer Campaign. She was very warm and inclusive, and her charity fundraising events involved people from all sections of the community. Lamcote House was used to host fetes for her favourite charities, while her family and friends were persuaded to take part in the amateur dramatics she staged.[33] Claire was a confident woman with strong opinions. During the 1920s she was very active in the local Conservative association, becoming president of the City of Nottingham Women's Conservative Association.[34] She was such a good public speaker that it was suggested she might stand for parliament.

Freda had learnt a great deal from her dynamic mother, and even when she was the darling of London society she spent a great deal of time with her family in Nottingham. She often stayed at her parents' Lamcote House. She drew on her society connections to help her mother's charity work. One year, Freda, her two daughters and her sisters starred alongside the actress Gladys Cooper in a matinee Mrs Birkin put on at the Empire Theatre, Nottingham, in aid of the Widows' and Orphans' Fund of the National Union of Journalists.[35] Another year, Freda and her friends appeared in a series of tableaux arranged as Dresden porcelain figures from the Victoria and Albert Museum. Freda posed as 'Summer', one of the Four Seasons.[36] Flushed with their theatrical success, Claire formed 'Mrs Birkin's Players'. They put on plays Freda had adapted from children's books in the village hall at Radcliffe-on-Trent. Pempie and Angie took the lead roles in front of an audience of children from the village school. The performances raised money for 'Miss Penelope Dudley Ward's fund for the Children's Hospital, Vincent Square, London'.[37]

Although Freda pretended to her parents that she was just friends with the heir to the throne, they soon recognised the reality. It seems that her father disapproved of his daughter's adulterous relationship as much as the royal parents did. Edward complained that he was not invited to lunch at Lamcote when he was picking Freda up. At first, it was hoped by both sets of parents that the prince's long trips abroad would undermine the relationship. After the popularity Edward achieved during the war, Prime Minister David Lloyd George saw him as one of the country's greatest assets in securing the loyalty of the empire. It was at the prime minister's suggestion that throughout the 1920s the heir to the throne was sent on a series of tours to thank the countries of the dominions and colonies for their contribution to the war and build a bond between those countries and their future king. In August 1919 Edward went to Canada for three months. Initially, Freda had considered being there at the same time as him because Duddie had business interests in Canada. She consulted Sarah Shaughnessy, the girlfriend of the prince's equerry Joey Legh, about it. Freda told Sarah how unkind people were gossiping about her relationship with Edward. Sarah advised her not to go to Canada as it would fuel further gossip, so Freda reluctantly decided to stay in England.[38]

Before their tearful goodbye, Freda and the prince exchanged spider mascots; Edward had a 'Mrs Thpider' seal on his watch-chain while Freda kept 'Mr Thpider'. As Edward set sail on HMS *Renown* he wrote to his lover to tell her that both he and Mrs Thpider were crying inside. Once in Canada Edward was mobbed wherever he went. His boyish vulnerability and charm made a tremendous impression. As he spoke in his slightly cockney accent, he seemed eager to please and friendly.[39] He symbolised youth and hope for the future. During the trip, his right hand became so bruised from endless handshaking that he had to use his left. Girls threw themselves at him; 14-year-olds would jump on his car and ask for a kiss, while others would wait for hours to give him flowers or chocolates. Newspapers noted with whom he danced and how many times. However, Edward assured his lover that he was not attracted to anyone but her. This was not the whole truth; he had a flirtation with Sarah Shaughnessy, who was in Canada visiting her family. At first their conversations were about Freda, but soon the prince was dancing with Sarah most evenings. He paid her so much attention that their friends on the trip thought he might propose. Sarah was an American and the daughter-in-law of a British peer. As she had been widowed in the war she was free to marry. Edward's other equerry, Claud Hamilton, and Sarah's friend Lady Joan Mulholland thought such a match would be a good thing and 'save the British Empire'. They agreed to do their best to make it happen, but they admitted there were two difficulties standing in the way: Freda and Joey.[40] Inevitably, nothing came of the plan; in 1920 Sarah married Joey Legh.[41] As usual, the prince told Freda half the story. He played down just how much he danced with Sarah and how attractive he found her, instead emphasising that he only thought of her as a link to Freda. Although they could not marry, Edward assured his mistress that he considered himself to be a 'married man' and she was his 'little wife'.[42]

Most of the time the prince was exhilarated by the public reaction, but there were moments when he was over-tired and became depressed. Most exhausting were his visits to hospitals, where he insisted on speaking to every ex-soldier he came across. His compassion was genuine and it drained him emotionally.[43] When he met the widows and parents of soldiers who had been killed in the war, they looked into his face and saw sympathy and understanding. He took time to speak to each person individually and that made a great impression on them.[44]

However, although he was so good at his role, he believed that he was living an unnatural life for a 25-year-old. Describing his position as if it was just a job, in one letter to Freda he wrote that he felt like resigning.[45] Although he appeared so natural, his official duties were done at a great personal cost to himself. He found public speaking stressful. Meeting so many people who had such high expectations of him was a constant strain, particularly as he had no partner by his side to share the experience. He wanted Freda there to comfort him and boost his self-esteem. He felt that he was putting on an act. Reflecting the duality of his personality, he believed that there was the real him, known only to those closest to him, and the public persona who was adored by the public. As time went on the gap between the image and the reality became a chasm. In his letters to Freda he exposed his vulnerabilities and lack of self-esteem. He could not reconcile how he felt about himself with the hero worship he received and it made him feel a fraud. He wanted his private life to be his own affair and totally separate from his public one; he could never accept that the two were inextricably intertwined. When he said to Freda that he had had enough of 'princing' and wanted to be an ordinary person with a life of his own, as always, she was honest with him. She told him that he could not be an ordinary person because he was born to be king and whether he liked it or not, that fate was awaiting him. He could not escape it.[46]

Overall the Canadian trip was a great success. The Canadians had taken him into their hearts and he had inspired genuine affection, which was due to his appealing personality more than his position. This personal triumph increased Edward's self-confidence. He had enjoyed the informality of Canadian life and he told Freda that he had become 'the completest democrat'.[47] He bought a ranch in Alberta and, in a foretaste of what was to happen with Wallis, he fantasised about leaving England and giving up his responsibilities to settle there with Freda. He wrote that if she would move to Canada he would never want to return to England. He explained: 'I've got thoroughly bitten with Canada and its possibilities, it's the place for a man, particularly after the great war, and if I wasn't P. of W. well, guess I'd stay here quite a while!! But alas I am P. of W!!'[48] In another letter he wrote that if he resigned he would be 'free to live or die according to how hard I worked though I should have you all to myself sweetheart and should only then be really happy and contented'.[49]

Another, more dangerous fantasy was that they would commit suicide together. The prince wrote in one letter to Freda that, like her, he wanted to die young, adding 'how marvellously divine if only WE could die together; there's absolutely nothing I could wish for more though perhaps you don't quite feel like that darling one and why should you? But I'm just dippy to die with YOU even if we can't live together.'[50] His flippant sentiments about such an extreme action reflected a fascination with death that was common among Edward's generation. Some men who had seen the carnage of the First World War and survived it felt a sense of emptiness in the post-war era. In their rebellion against their parents' generation, they exalted youth and feared growing old. Suicide became a 1920s malaise as growing numbers of young people considered self-destruction. In Paris there was even a suicide club, which drew lots once a year to see which of their members would take his life. For this group, committing suicide was seen as the bravest, purest expression of contempt for the futility of life. Edward's idea of suicide with his lover was also not unique. After harbouring the fantasy for many years, the wealthy publisher and socialite of the jazz age Harry Crosby committed suicide with one of his girlfriends in 1929.[51]

After a brief return to England, in March 1920 Edward was sent abroad again for a seven-month tour of Australia and New Zealand. This time he took his cousin Lord Louis Mountbatten with him. Louis was six years younger than the prince, but he became his closest companion and confidant. Lord Louis recalled that when he collected the prince from Freda's house, Edward cried like a baby all the way to Victoria Station. He worried about the other men who would pursue her while he was away and told her that he felt totally tied to her. Separation only made Edward's love stronger and being apart from his supportive lover reduced him to a nervous wreck. He turned his cabin on HMS *Renown* into a shrine to her by sticking up all her photographs. He lived for the arrival of her letters; his staff dreaded the days when no letters came from her to lift his spirits.

Separated from the flesh-and-blood Freda, he idolised her; she became his Madonna or goddess whom he worshipped. As later with

Wallis, the prince was a romantic who portrayed his relationship with Freda as the greatest love affair of all time. He was ecstatic when she wrote to him that she adored him 'as people loved once long ago, as they love no more and as they will never love again!!' He said that she had exactly expressed his own feelings. He described their love as 'sacred and holy'.[52] He told her that he was obsessed with the thought of marrying her but, unlike with Wallis, he did nothing to precipitate it. Instead, he believed that fate and time would bring them together forever one day and that something would happen which would allow them to belong to each other legitimately. He promised: 'Mon amour I swear I'll never never marry any other woman but YOU!!!!'[53]

During his Australian tour, it seems that the prince hoped that Freda was pregnant with his child. He had first hinted that he would like to have a baby with her the previous year. When nothing came of his hopes he was deeply disappointed. Biographers suggest that Edward may have been sterile due to a serious attack of mumps he suffered while at Dartmouth Naval College in 1911.[54] The difference between Freda and the prince's later love, Wallis Simpson, was that his earlier mistress always knew the rules of the game. Although at times he talked about wanting her to have his child and be with her forever, she knew that he could never marry her and be king.

Edward believed that Freda was good for him. He claimed that she had set him high standards that he tried to live up to in both his private and public life. She had made him more of a man and less of a boy. He wrote to her that if only they could live together, 'I would become of some use perhaps and have a will of my own and be strong!'[55] He admitted that he was not strong by nature and relied on other people to bolster him up. Many of the people closest to the prince, including Louis Mountbatten, thought Freda was a good influence. During the Australian tour Lord Louis wrote to his mother, the Marchioness of Milford Haven, about how 'stiff and unnatural' the king and queen's letters to Edward were. Lord Louis was very close to his own mother and he felt that his cousin did not know what it was like to have a real, comforting mother like her. He added:

He's only had one 'mother', though he'd be the last person in the world to admit it, and that is his great friend Freda Dudley Ward, who is so nice, and about whom you have probably heard – Oh, such wicked lies. She's absolutely been a mother to him and he has brought all his troubles to her and she has comforted and advised him, and all along he has been blind, in his love, to what the world was saying.[56]

Lord Louis Mountbatten's comments were rather unfair to Queen Mary. She had tried her best to be a supportive and loving mother to her son. At times her reserved nature had stood in the way of establishing the rapport the prince desired, but at other periods, for instance at the end of the war, their relationship had been close. Edward was such an emotionally needy character that it was hard for any woman, whether his mother or lover, to fulfil his unrealistic expectations of what an intimate relationship involved for any prolonged length of time. As his latest confidant, it seems that Lord Louis was relying on Edward's self-pitying version of events.

In Australia, as in Canada, the prince was mobbed by crowds. Australian ex-servicemen were particularly enthusiastic. They all wanted to touch him: they would drag him out of his car and pass him from one to another, shoulder high, in the streets or shake his hand and slap him on the back until he was bruised.[57] There was a freshness about him. He seemed sensitive and his capacity to be moved by what he saw melted the hearts of people who were usually critical of monarchy. His eyes would fill with tears if he was told a sad story or saw deprivation.[58]

While he continued to charm the public, Edward was increasingly difficult in private. His spoilt behaviour was hard for his staff to handle. His equerry Joey Legh complained that he often lost his temper and behaved like 'a naughty school-boy'.[59] Even his close friend Lord Louis Mountbatten found it difficult to keep the prince cheerful. Lord Louis believed his cousin was a sad and lonely person, prone to deep depression. Edward told Lord Louis that he would give anything to change places with him.[60] He particularly disliked the formal dinners, receptions, parades and balls he had to attend. Knowing that his every dance partner would be recorded in the newspapers, the prince made sure that he sent edited versions of his encounters to Freda. He asked her not to be 'thulky' because he found it nauseating dancing with other women and wanted only her. However, as usual he was not completely truthful. While in Australia he had an intense flirtation with Mollee Little, a friend of Sheila Loughborough, whose sensuous, dark looks reminded the prince of Sheila. They enjoyed dancing together and laughed constantly. According to Joey Legh, Mollee was considered rather 'vulgar' as she wore low, backless dresses. She was not asked to official parties in Sydney society.[61] However, the prince was so keen on her that he made sure she was invited. He pretended to Freda that Louis Mountbatten was 'smitten' with her but he was the one who was infatuated. He admitted to Freda that he liked her to be a bit jealous; it seems to have been part of the dynamic of their relationship that they told each other about the other people who were attracted to them.

While Edward was in Australia Sir Francis Newdegate, Governor of Western Australia, observed the heir to the throne. He liked the prince and he admired his manners and friendliness. Edward was kind and considerate to everyone, whatever section of society they came from; the governor's housemaid said he was so affable she could not believe he was royalty. He noted that Edward liked to talk to 'a sprightly elderly woman of the world'. Earlier in his tour, while he was in Adelaide, he made friends with Grace, Lady Weigall, who was the wife of Sir Archibald Weigall, the Governor of South Australia. The wealthy daughter of the furniture magnate Sir John Blundell Maples, Lady Weigall was a lively woman in her 40s whom Sir Francis described as 'painted and enamelled, covered with jewels and a bit vulgar'.[62] She was just the type of older woman the prince liked, and he was soon turning to her as a mother figure. The governor's wife would stay up late with him, listening sympathetically while he poured his heart out to her. They became so friendly that Lady Weigall gave up her sitting room to him and sent a message saying that he could use it for any purpose he liked and have 'fairies' there.[63] After his visit to Adelaide, Edward wrote effusively to his new friend thanking her for 'all your sweetness to a very worn out little boy who really was beginning to think the whole show to [sic] big for him and too much to go thro' with'.[64]

The other woman who continued to make his time in Australia tolerable was Mollee. Sir Francis Newdegate wondered if the prince's relationship with her was serious. He thought Mollee was very attractive and that she could hold her own anywhere in a way no other

Australian girl could. The governor added: 'He might do much worse.' With a considerable degree of insight, Sir Francis wrote to a friend that he wished the prince would get married to 'some real nice woman, but to keep him she would have to be very strong and clever'.[65]

With the prince away for such a long time his parents hoped to break up Freda and Edward's relationship. Lord Esher was once again asked to Balmoral and this time he accepted the invitation. During his stay, he was teased about 'Princess Freda' and the royals complained about her friends. However, he made a good case for her and tried to suggest ways of putting the illicit relationship on a more satisfactory basis.[66] Lord Esher wrote to the prince afterwards about his visit, telling him that the queen was very kind to him. She was good company and very understanding. He told Edward that his mother cared 'tremendously' for him.[67]

The prince considered Lord Esher to be a good friend to him. The older man also championed Freda and Edward's relationship when he met the Archbishop of York, Cosmo Lang. Esher wrote to the prince that the archbishop had been 'well-primed' about the affair, probably by the king's private secretary, Lord Stamfordham. During their meeting, there was talk about marriage; however, to Esher's surprise the prelate said some very sensible things. Archbishop Lang realised that the prince might have a worse friend than Freda. By the end of their conversation, Esher believed that he had made the archbishop see that there might be something 'rather chic' about having a bachelor king.[68] More than a decade later, when Cosmo Lang was in his next position as Archbishop of Canterbury, he found himself at the centre of the abdication crisis. Dealing with Mrs Simpson and Edward's determination to marry her, no doubt he thought that he had been right to consider that the prince could be in a relationship with someone far worse than Mrs Dudley Ward.

While Edward was away in Australia the king persuaded Bertie to end his fling with Sheila Loughborough, rewarding him with the title Duke of York for his obedience. Bertie told his brother that the king had also spoken to him about Edward's relationship with Freda. When he heard what had happened, Edward was furious, writing to his lover: 'If HM [His Majesty] thinks he's going to alter me by insulting you he's making just about the biggest mistake of his silly useless life.'[69] The prince was right to be concerned. Freda became convinced that their relationship was doomed. A very private person, she found all the gossip about her upsetting and she feared that it might be detrimental for her daughters. Seeing no future for her relationship with the prince, she tried to end it by telling him that they must make the greatest sacrifice of their lives and give up their love. The prince was shattered by her suggestion. Feeling isolated and tired, thousands of miles away from her, he went to bed and cried. He told her that whatever happened, he loved, adored and worshipped her 'as no man has ever loved adored or worshipped before or ever will again'.[70]

As with Wallis during the abdication crisis, Edward just would not let Freda go, and bit by bit he eroded her resolve. He used every form of emotional blackmail he could muster. He told her that if they split up he could not go on with the tour. He explained to her that she would never know how much pain her letter had caused him. He said that he did not know how he could carry on without her wonderful influence and advice. He made her delay any decision until he was back in London when they could discuss it properly. He refused to be intimidated by his parents and the court into ending their relationship and said they should only change things for their own sakes or for Freda's girls. He asked what Duddie thought about the situation, adding that if he 'produced that big stick' it would be different, but he had not done that yet and seemed unlikely to do so. Perhaps suggesting that he would consider ending the sexual side of their relationship provided he could continue to see Freda as his greatest friend and confidante, he wrote in terms that would give Freudians a field day: 'From now onwards I'll twy [sic] to teach myself to look on you only as Fredie Mummie though it's going to be the hardest task of my life; [...] but I swear I will twy [sic], though a chap can love his mummie.'[71]

The prince became so depressed after Freda's letter that members of his staff guessed what had happened. Joey Legh wrote to his fiancée, Sarah, that Edward had sent endless cables in code. He noted that he had never seen the prince so upset before. He wrongly suspected that Duddie had been sent for by the royal family and told that the whole affair must stop.[72] The only person Edward confided in was his closest friend on the tour, Lord Louis Mountbatten. Lord Louis wrote to his mother: 'She [Freda], sensible creature that she is, is trying to shift the friendship to a more platonic and casual footing (but please don't tell anyone) and he is rather miserable, but is beginning to see that it is best so.'[73] He also observed that Edward was overworked on the tour. Even Lord Louis got very tired and at times did not know what he was doing. He added that the Australians worshipped the prince. From 8 a.m. to 1 a.m. up to a thousand people had stood around the gates of Government House in Adelaide in the hope of catching a glimpse of him. Feeling insecure in his relationship with Freda, all this pressure was too much, and the prince found it hard to complete his tour. The press reported that he rambled in his speeches. He seemed close to a breakdown. His parents and the government were so concerned that they postponed Edward's trip to India and Japan, which had been planned for later that year.

Once the prince returned to England he seemed to slot back into his old relationship with Freda. From autumn 1920 until the autumn of 1921 he had a whole year in England before his next tour. During part of this time, his parents decided that he needed a break from official duties after overworking on the Australian tour. They wanted him to rest, eat well, sleep well and enjoy country pursuits, but Edward had other ideas.[74] He wanted to spend as much time as possible with Freda. While he had been abroad she had sold her Cumberland Terrace house for £10,000, making a profit of £6,000 on it in just over a year. However, Edward was sad to see the house go as he had seen it as 'our house'.

Having faced losing his lover, Edward became more abject in their relationship than ever. Friends noticed how dependent he was on Freda. Duff Cooper described seeing them together at a party; the prince hardly left his mistress's side. Duff had heard that Edward had told Freda he loved her so much that she must either give in to him or break off their relationship completely as he could no longer bear the situation.[75] After a small dance at Freda's, Winston Churchill wrote in a similar vein. He told his wife that 'the Little Prince' was there 'idolising as usual'. He added that people were getting quite bored with his behaviour and thought that 'a door should be open or shut'.[76]

In his letters, the prince called himself Freda's 'little slave' or 'parpee' (puppy). He suffered from bouts of depression and told his mistress that only she could save him by letting him pour out his heart to her. He knew when he was being pathetic and if he became too self-critical and despondent Freda tried to shake him out of it by telling him not to be 'dismal David'. After endless soul-baring sessions she told her lover that she had never known any other man as well or as intimately as she knew him.[77] With her, he felt that he experienced the same kind of man–woman relationship that other young men who were not royal were able to have. She treated him as an ordinary person. Unlike the many sycophants around him, she only laughed at his jokes if she really thought they were funny and she disagreed with him if his opinion differed from hers.[78]

Any plans for their relationship to be on a platonic footing seem to have been forgotten once they met again. They arranged trysts while Duddie was away from the Dudley Wards' rented home, Nether Woodcote at Epsom. Despite Freda's attempt to cool their relationship, it was as if nothing had changed. Edward was soon saying that although he did not want anything awful to happen to Duddie he still believed that one day they would be able to be together.

In his definitive biography of Edward VIII, Philip Ziegler speculates whether, if Freda had been widowed, she would have been able to marry the prince. He points out that the king and queen would have opposed the marriage, partly because she was middle class but also because she had been married before, which would have posed the problem of semi-royal stepchildren. However, the king genuinely wanted his son to find happiness and security so there was a chance that the determination of the prince, coupled with Freda's charm, would have won him over.[79] It might also eventually have been supported by the government. In 1920, Prime Minister Lloyd George advised the king that the country would not tolerate an alliance with a foreigner. The government now openly preferred the prince to marry into the English or Scottish nobility.[80] It would have been hypocritical for Lloyd George to oppose the match between Edward and Freda if she had been widowed. The prime minister was a married man having an affair with his much younger private secretary, Frances Stevenson; he married her after his wife's death.

As Philip Ziegler writes, Queen Freda would have been a surprising choice for the British public, but the Prince of Wales was so popular, it is likely that the majority of people would have supported him.[81] In fact, it might have further boosted his democratic image. As one commentator, Hannen Swaffer, asked in January 1921: 'Why is the Prince of Wales the most popular man who ever lived?' The answer was because 'he is one of us. He has made our Royalty the truest Republican force in the world. He has anglicised "Ich Dien" and made it "I serve".' The article in *The Graphic* emphasised that to live up to his image it was important who the prince married. For modernisers, a break with the past would have been welcome. Using the xenophobic terms of the times, Hannen Swaffer added: 'Flunkeydom would marry him to a foreign princess. But Prince Charming's Cinderella will be found by our English fireside. Not for him a Dago or a Hun. Like the prince himself, his princess will be One of Us.'[82] No one had better credentials as 'One of Us' than Freda Dudley Ward.

7

THE TOXIC CIRCLE

For the first few years of their relationship it seems that Freda was in love with the prince, but as time went on it was clear that he was more in love with her than she was with him. There was a slavish quality to his adoration that prevented it being completely reciprocated.[1] While he behaved so abjectly it was impossible to build an adult relationship between equals. Clear-sighted and shrewd, Freda realised that there was no long-term future for them and so, throughout their long liaison, she neither gave nor demanded exclusivity.

For most of their relationship she was involved in an equally intense affair with Michael Herbert, a wealthy banker who was a cousin of the Earl of Pembroke. His father had been the youngest ever British ambassador to Washington; his mother, Leila Wilson, was the daughter of Richard Wilson, a New York banker. The family was very well connected and one of Leila's sisters married Cornelius Vanderbilt. When Michael was only a child his father died of tuberculosis at the age of 46. He and his brother Sidney returned to England to be brought up with their cousins at Wilton House; the two boys were very close and throughout their lives they were devoted to each other. After Eton and Oxford, Michael fought bravely during the First World War. He joined the Royal Wiltshire Yeomanry but later transferred to 'The Blues', where he served as an infantryman, a machine gunner and a road builder. He had a premonition that he would be killed, but – unlike so many of his contemporaries – he survived.[2]

After the conflict, he had a meteoric rise in the City. For nearly two years he worked very hard in a chartered accountant's office. He gained such a good reputation with his employers that while he was only in his 20s he was made a partner in the banking house of Morgan Grenfell and Company. He was well liked by both his partners and employees. He claimed that a business career was a form of national service and he was always keen to argue that a man could serve his country as well in the City of London as in any other occupation.[3] His future looked full of promise; his brother Sidney was the Conservative MP for Scarborough and Whitby, and it was rumoured that Michael might follow him into politics.[4] Michael often supported his brother during campaigns. The two young men were so inseparable that the Liberal candidate in the constituency compared them to the 'Dolly Sisters', the famous female identical twin entertainers.[5]

Dark-haired, handsome and slight, Michael was an eligible bachelor. He was fun to be with and had an infectious smile. According to one observer, when he laughed he threw back his head with 'a careless gesture that seemed almost to issue a challenge while it won your heart'.[6] He moved in the same circles as the prince and he was a friend of Rosemary Leveson-Gower, and Diana and Duff Cooper. He could be very charming but not everyone admired him; Diana's mother, the Duchess of Rutland, thought that he was rude and always lounging around.[7] Others accused him of 'oiliness'.[8]

Throughout the 1920s Freda managed to juggle her two lovers. Michael's letters to her are as copious and obsessive as the prince's; they are so similar in tone that it suggests there were psychological similarities between the two men. Both were much weaker than Freda and they looked to her for the wisdom and strength they lacked. It seems that her maternal nature as much as her charm and sex appeal attracted both men. Freda and Michael's relationship began in 1918 and for more than a decade Freda seesawed between her two lovers. At times, the prince was in the ascendant; at other times Michael was. It was a frustrating situation for all three participants and without the full commitment of marriage no one could feel secure. Both men knew about the other and they felt an intense rivalry. The prince said that he loathed Michael with a hatred that passed 'all understanding'. He wrote to Freda: 'Gud! That man makes me angry, sweetheart, and I long to tell him off properly, though I'm not big enough!!'[9] Michael felt equally aggrieved at having to share his lover.

While the prince was in England Freda prioritised his needs. Before Edward went on tour again to India in the autumn of 1921, Freda moved into her new London home in Portland Place. It was a relief to her to have a house of her own again after a year of staying in other people's houses. A talented interior designer, she spent much time and money doing it up to create a stylish and original home where they could spend time together. Knowing time was short before Edward went away, they preferred quiet evenings in to partying.

In September, they spent a happy fortnight together at Dunrobin, Rosemary's childhood home, as guests of Geordie, Duke of Sutherland. Although they were part of a large house party and Duddie was among the guests, they managed to get plenty of time alone together. Freda had arrived two days before the prince and he asked her to study the plan of the castle so that at night they would be able to creep along the corridors to each other's bedrooms for secret assignations. While her husband went shooting or fishing with Geordie, Freda and Edward went off on their own in his car. One evening they went out in a boat on Loch Chrine with a ghillie. The prince looked back on their stay at Dunrobin as an idyllic time and he relived every second when they were apart.

However, Michael was driven to distraction by jealousy knowing that the woman he loved was with his rival. He wrote that he was 'tortured' by thoughts of what she was getting up to at Dunrobin:

I hate and hate that place and the more I think of it the more I loathe it – it is getting an obsession [...] Darling, it is such an eternity till I shall see you again, it depresses me terribly and more when I think of how very very quickly you forget that you really love me.[10]

He agonised about whether he could trust her and if she was faithful to him. He bombarded her with letters which were slightly more erotic that the prince's. He wrote: 'Ah Fredie, I do so want you; to hold you and kiss you and tell you that I love you from the crest of your permanent waves to the soles of your shoes.'[11] His attraction to her was very physical. He wrote: 'I love it so when you come into a room where I am and it never ceases to give me a little thrill all down my spine and to make my heart beat faster.'[12] But the bond went far deeper than that, he explained: 'I fear you have a little way of growing into one so that one remembers your moods and your gestures all the time.'[13]

While she was at Dunrobin, Michael felt that she was drifting away from him again, but he told her that their separation had just stiffened his resolution to get her somehow. He expressed almost identical sentiments as the prince did, telling her:

> I am so certain that you are the one person for me my beloved, and that you are my great chance of happiness that I can't and won't even consider the possibility of our being permanently separated. – I know that we could and will be so divinely happy together if only we can find a solution.[14]

While Edward was away in India for eight months Michael had Freda more to himself, although there was still her husband in the background. They had some perfect days together by the sea. Michael described the 'sheer joy' of it and told her, 'I shall remember it always because I felt more than I have ever felt that we were grandly alone and divinely self-sufficient one to another.'[15] Unlike the prince, Michael thought about the risks she was taking, as a married woman having an affair. He told her that he was so frightened of hurting her one day. He explained that this was 'the trouble of illicit love, there is always the risk of that – please tell me that you have thought it out and counted the risk and that it is worth it. I do want to bring you only happiness my Fredie, you are too sweet for pain from a rather worthless fellow like me.'[16]

However, it was more likely that Freda was going to hurt Michael than the other way around. She still had another equally adoring lover and showed no signs of making a choice between them. Before the prince left, Freda gave him a platinum wristwatch and they exchanged identical crosses engraved with 'Dieu te garde'. He wore her presents all the time to feel close to her while they were apart. Edward resented being thousands of miles away from Freda for so long. He wrote to their mutual friend, Sheila Loughborough: 'I do loathe it and hated leaving her far more than even last year and that was bad enough. These long separations are really too cruel for words.'[17]

He found it particularly difficult being apart from Freda because his cousin and companion, Lord Louis Mountbatten, had just got engaged to the beautiful heiress, Edwina Ashley. They were able to be together in Delhi while he could not be with his love. He wrote to Freda:

> I shall loathe Delhi with Edwina there when you have so much more right to be there than she has [...] However much they love they can't possibly love each other a fraction as much as we do can they Fredie? I'm sure its foul of me but I do resent Dickie being happy at Delhi when I can't be.[18]

Edward's sister Princess Mary also got engaged to Henry Lascelles, heir to the Earl of Harewood, while he was away. Edward had always been close to his only sister and he hoped that she would be happy with her older fiancé. Although he was pleased she was escaping life at 'Buckhouse prison', he could not help feeling envious of her because he could not formalise his relationship with the woman he loved.[19]

The prince's tour of India was controversial from the start. In 1919 new constitutional measures should have improved Anglo-Indian relations. However, the introduction of trial without jury for people accused of political crimes and the massacre at Amritsar, in April 1919, when troops of the British Indian Army fired machine guns into a crowd of unarmed protesters, left a deep sense of distrust.[20] In 1920 Gandhi and the Congress organisation had formed a temporary alliance with the Muslim community and begun a movement of non-co-operation. At one point, there was a threat that there would be a complete boycott of the prince's tour.[21] The king and his advisers had told Edward that his informal style, which had worked in Canada and Australia, would not work in India.

Gandhi and the Congress party discouraged ordinary Indians from going to see him. At Allahabad, the streets were empty and a ceremony at the university was boycotted by the students. At first the prince felt that his trip was a waste of time and not doing any good. There were threats of violence against him, and the police rarely let him drive through native quarters. However, although it put him at personal risk, Edward insisted upon going among ordinary people.[22] In Mumbai, he drove through the busiest parts of the city. As he left the amphitheatre, where he had delivered his speech, thousands of Indians prostrated themselves before the chair he had sat in and kissed the dust his car had driven over. As people crowded around his car he was not frightened. He insisted on standing up in his car so that they could see him, and he told his guards not to push them back. At Poona, crowds who could not get close enough to touch him threw silver and gold coins in front of him so that his feet might tread on them.[23]

As on his earlier tours, the prince had a hectic schedule. While he charmed many of the Indians he met he managed to alienate many of his own countrymen.[24] He hated the 'pompous' round of garden parties, banquets and parades and at times he looked bored and offended his hosts. He was very critical of the native rulers. He wrote to Freda that he felt contempt and loathing for 'these servile, cringing and insincere native potentates'.[25] He also dreaded the many dances because of 'the bitches' he had to dance with.[26] When not performing official duties there was some light relief. He enjoyed the polo and exercised to excess to relieve the strain he felt on tour. After going to bed at 2 a.m. he was up at 7 a.m. to ride four gallops on the course, then he schooled his polo ponies for an hour followed by three games of squash. He ate as little food as possible and had only biscuits for lunch. Always obsessive about his weight, he wrote to Freda with pride that after all the riding and recreation he was down to 9 stone.[27]

When the prince returned to England he received an enthusiastic welcome home. In London, cheering crowds lined his route. Freda, Duddie and her daughters had gone to a gala lunch at the Berkeley Hotel to celebrate his return. Every window and balcony of the hotel had red, white and blue canopies and they were filled with people who had attended the lunch. Guests were given a basketful of rosebuds to rain down on the prince as he passed by in his carriage, escorted by the Life Guards. As he reached the Berkeley a loud cheer greeted him. After so many months away from her, Edward at last saw Freda again standing in one of the windows, looking lovely in a black dress and a wide-brimmed hat with her two little girls excitedly waving flags. When he caught sight of her, Edward looked up, smiled and bowed.[28]

Once the prince was back, Michael had to share Freda again. In 1922, she took her daughters to a seaside villa called Westward Ho in Frinton for the summer. It was a fashionable place to be. It was dubbed 'our Deauville', and *The Sketch* described it as 'the jolliest little place on earth'.[29] The town became famous for its tennis tournament that attracted many well-known amateurs. Before the summer season began Freda had tennis lessons with a professional to prepare for the challenge. Freda's friends Lady Victor Paget and Clemmie Churchill were at Frinton too with their children. The families relaxed, playing tennis, golfing and swimming in the sea. Pempie and Angie spent hours on the beach with their friends playing leapfrog and having donkey rides.[30]

When Duddie was not in Frinton both Freda's lovers visited her as often as possible. While Freda was out of London, Michael and Edward would sometimes meet by chance at Buck's Club. They just about managed to be civil, but each listened carefully to the other's guarded conversation for any hints that they were seeing their mutual mistress. They got on better when they found themselves together at a dance at Wilton House without Freda. They agreed that parties were no fun without her and they stood looking at the dancing and laughing a good deal. The prince admitted that he had never really talked to Michael properly before and he found that he was very amusing and great fun.[31]

The prince had been assigned a private detective, which made assignations with Freda more difficult. Whenever Edward went anywhere by road a car with a detective in it had to follow him. He resented 'this foul shadowing business' but had to put up with it for his protection.[32] There was an Irish threat between 9 and 14 August 1922 because Reginald Dunne and Joseph O'Sullivan were to be hanged in Wandsworth Prison that week. The two ex-servicemen had shot the influential Ulster Unionist Field Marshal Sir Henry Wilson on his doorstep in London on 22 June, acting on the orders of the Irish leader Michael Collins.

Reggie Dunne was a friend of Collins and second-in-command in the London IRA.[33] In such a tense political situation, the prince was told to keep out of London as much as possible that summer. He spent much of his time in Rugby playing polo while Freda was in Frinton. He knew that his 'whining' and 'grousing' were 'foul' for Freda but his letters continued to be full of self-pity and hints that he would like to give up being the Prince of Wales. He wrote to her: 'Oh! Mine's a "lovely" life now isn't it Fredie darling; I so often think of chucking in the sponge especially lately but the knowledge that you love me my precious beloved sweet-heart does keep me going so marvellously and makes my foul life worth living.'[34]

Freda did not only have her two lovers making demands, she also had a duty to her husband. During the November 1922 general election, Freda once again went down to his Southampton constituency to campaign for Duddie, who was standing as a National or Lloyd George Liberal. The Liberal party had split when Lloyd George and some of his colleagues decided to set up their own party, the National Liberal Party, which formed a coalition government with the Conservatives. However, in October 1922 Lloyd George resigned as prime minister because the Conservatives had withdrawn from the coalition. Duddie regretted the end of the coalition government and the split in the Liberal party and hoped that it would unite, but he remained loyal to his old friend Lloyd George. Sensing there was a good chance of taking the seat, Labour and Conservative activists made a special effort to defeat him. Duddie fought back, criticising 'the old reactionary conservatives' who belonged to a party 'which for centuries had opposed all democratic reform and wanted to see things as they were, and not as they ought to be'.[35] He told his constituents that he stood for the improvement of trade and increased employment, for strict economy and sound finance. He added that he believed in industrial co-operation and not industrial warfare.[36] However, his progressive pleas fell on deaf ears. His constituents had complained about his absences from the constituency for years. His parliamentary duties and trips to Canada meant that he rarely visited Southampton. During the campaign, he was heckled by electors for failing to keep in touch. On election day they finally voted him out.[37] Duddie was not the only Liberal MP to lose his seat; the general election was disastrous for both Liberal parties, with only sixty-two Liberals and fifty-three National Liberals elected.

No longer a member of parliament, Duddie had to find a new focus for his life. In the Dissolution Honours he was made a privy councillor. In 1923 he became a member of the Council of the British Olympic Association, which made an appeal to raise £40,000 to give athletes a fair chance in the International Games that were to be held in Paris the following year.[38] Duddie's defeat also affected Freda and her lovers, because her husband spent increasingly long periods away from home in Canada promoting a scheme for trade between the two countries.[39]

The pressure on Edward to find a suitable bride and get married increased as his friends and siblings got married. In April 1923 his brother Bertie married Lady Elizabeth Bowes-Lyon. At first the newspapers had made a mistake and announced that the Prince of Wales was engaged to Lady Elizabeth. Her friends all teased her, bowing and calling her 'Ma'am'. The diarist Henry 'Chips' Channon explained that although it couldn't be true, everyone would have been delighted if it was.[40] The palace had to issue an official denial. The following week the Duke of York proposed and was accepted. Bertie was the first English prince to marry a commoner with consent since 1660.[41] Emphasising how close the Dudley Wards were to royal circles, Freda attended the wedding at Westminster Abbey with her husband.

Edward got on very well with his new sister-in-law, who brought warmth and fun into the royal family. The Duchess of York enjoyed his company too. The newly married couple occasionally joined the Prince of Wales's glamorous set. Elizabeth wrote in her diary about driving up from Windsor with Bertie to spend the evening with Freda and Edward at the Embassy Club. Many years later she wrote to her daughter, Queen Elizabeth, about going back to dances at York House after the theatre and the excitement of being partnered by the American star Fred Astaire.[42] However, although the prince was pleased to see his brother settled it must have been hard for him to know that he could not make the same commitment to his great love.

Marriage to Freda seemed as unlikely as ever. His mistress was more concerned about convention and what his family thought than Edward was, and she encouraged him to be discreet and not do anything silly.

Many years later, she told one interviewer that she never tried to marry the prince and did not even want it, although he asked her to marry him often.[43] The prince's letters suggest that he was prepared to take the same steps with her that he later took at the abdication for love of Wallis Simpson. He wrote to Freda that the only thing he wanted in the world was 'to be with you always' and that it would break his heart if she stopped loving him. He promised 'to just nip off with you at any moment and to any place in the world if you will make up your mind to do so – if you knew how very deeply and truly I loved you to the exclusion of all else in the world – you could not be unhappy and doubtful'.[44] One of the prince's closest confidants, Lord Brownlow, confirmed that Edward proposed to Mrs Dudley Ward and she said 'No' because she recognised the royal rules about divorce.[45] Freda always told her lover that the idea of marrying or running away was ridiculous. As she was already married there would have to be a divorce, and his parents and the Church would never have allowed it. She kept telling him that she would not let him do such a stupid thing and eventually she persuaded him.[46]

Michael also wanted to marry Freda. He could not stand sharing her with the prince forever. He told her that if she was unfaithful to him, 'I shall strangle you and drown myself – it's awful how I love you'.[47] He begged her to do something about the situation soon instead of wasting so many years of their lives and spending so much time apart. In 1922 there was talk of the Dudley Wards divorcing, which worried the prince as he feared Freda would then marry his rival.[48] However, Freda eventually decided against it because she feared that she would lose custody of her daughters. Until the Matrimonial Causes Act of 1937, divorces in England were rare; there were fewer than 5,000 a year.[49] In an era when there was still such a stigma attached to divorce, there was also a chance that Michael might have lost his position as a partner at Morgan Grenfell if he married a divorcee. J.P. Morgan Junior (known as Jack), the financier John Pierpoint's son, was scrupulously Protestant and morally conservative. He ruled that staff at the Morgan bank were not permitted to divorce.[50] Michael assured Freda that he would not mind if he lost his job and that they would still have plenty of money, but she would not take the risk.

8

INTERNATIONAL AFFAIRS

Until Wallis, fidelity was not a word in Edward's vocabulary. Knowing Michael was always in the background, the prince also had additional affairs, often with women who were in Freda's circle. It was rumoured that he had a fling with Freda's youngest sister, Vera. The two women were quite similar to look at, but Vera was not quite as slim and fine featured as her older sibling. Freda often had her sister to stay with her in London, so Edward saw her frequently. When they were together as a trio they had great fun, but the prince admitted that he was 'kept quite busy keeping your noses in joint!!!'[1] Edward and Vera became friends and she wrote to him when he went to India. When he could not get Freda on the phone he would have long chats with her sister as a second-best substitute. Before Vera married, Freda and the prince had semi-seriously discussed the possibility of her sister becoming his wife. Although he dismissed the option, he admitted to loving Vera a little bit because she was Freda's sister.[2]

Another of the prince's flings was with Freda's and Rosemary's friend Lady Victor Paget (Bridget). Bridget's father, Baron Colebroke, was one of Edward VII's lords-in-waiting and the family had lived at Royal Lodge, Windsor, for several years.[3] During the war, Edward had often socialised with Bridget when he was on leave because she was in the same circle as Portia Stanley and Rosemary Leveson-Gower. In March 1916 the prince noted in his diary that Bridget was 'quite attractive' and played the piano 'beautifully'.[4] A few months later in May he wrote that she was 'a lovely dancer' and had taught him several foxtrot steps and the Viennese waltz, but at this time he preferred Portia.[5] In 1922 Bridget married Lord Victor Paget, brother of Lord Anglesey. However, shortly after her marriage she was once again flirting with the prince. Like so many of the prince's girlfriends, Bridget had a fashionably boyish figure and dressed very well. Edward assured Freda that he had only danced with her and they never saw each other in the daytime. He claimed that she meant nothing to him but her 'sordid and melancholy view of life' rather suited his.[6] However, Bridget later admitted to being one of the prince's mistresses.[7] It seems Freda was not possessive about sharing Edward, provided she remained the number one woman in his life. It also seems that it was important to her that she was kept informed and thus, to a degree, in control of the situation. She knew that women threw themselves at the prince. As she told an interviewer, every woman who saw 'that sad little face felt she had just the shoulder for him to cry on'.[8]

However, Freda was not so sanguine about all his relationships. The first serious threat to her position came in 1923 when the prince became involved with Audrey Dudley Coats. Born Audrey James, she was the daughter of the American industrialist Willie James and his exuberant wife, Evie. There were rumours that Audrey's mother was the illegitimate daughter of Edward VII or that she was his mistress. Whatever the truth, the then king was a regular visitor at the James's large estate, West Dene, near Chichester. When Audrey was born Edward VII became her godfather.[9]

According to her brother, Edward James, Audrey was not a very kind little girl. She teased him mercilessly. When she was about 10 years old and he was 4, she would kick his castle down in the nursery. She had been her father's favourite child until Edward was born but, as the only son, he replaced her in Mr James's affections. Her brother claimed that she had 'an extraordinary animosity' towards him for the rest of his life.[10]

After her father's death, Audrey was left £4,000 a year which enabled her, by the age of 17, to keep two fully staffed houses. Before his marriage, Lord Louis Mountbatten had been in love with Audrey. They were on the brink of getting engaged when the prince took Lord Louis on tour with him to Australia. Lord Louis wrote ecstatically to his mother about Audrey's grey eyes, clear complexion and 'most kissable mouth'. Apparently, all the men in London were after her and she knew just how to play them off against each other. After she had her tonsils and adenoids out she wrote a letter to one of her admirers saying she was only able to write one letter and of course her thoughts had turned to him. It turned out that she had written verbatim letters to six other men. Lord Louis recognised that she was 'deceitful' but he could not help admiring the 'clever little minx'. He added: 'How any girl can be so pretty and alive at the same time beats me.'[11] He confessed that he would give anything to be married to her. However, his friends were wary and warned him not to rush into anything.

Full page photographs of Audrey in *The Sketch* and on the cover of *The Tatler* show a girl with attitude; she looks very young but there is a moodiness and defiance in her eyes. Audrey was typical of the post-war single girl. Frances Donaldson, who was growing up at this time, set out how social conventions had changed. For the first time, girls were starting to have more freedom and go out without chaperones. High-spirited girls like Audrey deliberately set out to scandalise the older generation and find a new morality. Most did not give up their virginity as easily as they would have encouraged people to believe, but they gave the impression that they might because they liked to shock.[12]

When Lord Louis returned to England after the Australian tour, Audrey refused to make up her mind about whether she would marry him or not. He sent the Prince of Wales to act as a go-between and get a straight answer. After discussing her relationship with his cousin, Audrey decided that it could not work and broke it off.[13] In March 1922 she married Captain Muir Dudley Coats, heir to a cotton-manufacturing fortune at the Brompton Oratory. The joke in society was that Audrey had chosen the arms of Coats over a coat of arms.[14] Muir had served in the Scots Guards during the war and he had been awarded the Military Cross. However, he had been so seriously wounded in the chest that he never fully recovered his health. Freda was a guest at the wedding; her daughters were going to be bridesmaids but on the day they were ill.

After less than a year of marriage the Dudley Coats' relationship was failing. Audrey was spending time with the Prince of Wales. Audrey was a keen horsewoman and she met Edward again out fox-hunting with the Belvoir Hunt. Since the war the prince had become a dedicated rider. He worried his family by taking part in point-to-points and steeplechases. His assistant private secretary, Tommy Lascelles, described steeplechasing as the riskiest sport of the era. He estimated that of their contemporaries who had died violent deaths, apart from the war, two-thirds were as a result of racing falls.[15] Riding in a point-to-point in 1924, the prince had a bad fall that left him unconscious for half an hour and suffering from concussion. He had to remain in a dark room for a week and in bed for three more weeks. He spent this time crocheting – the skill Queen Mary had taught him as a child. He said it did for him what detective novels did for statesmen: it relaxed his mind.[16] After this incident the Labour prime minister, Ramsay MacDonald, wrote to the king complaining about the unacceptable risk the heir to the throne was taking. His father agreed, and he asked Edward to give up steeplechasing and take part in hunting and polo instead, but the prince refused to listen.

When he was not racing, Edward also enjoyed hunting regularly. He hunted first with the Pytchley Hunt, in Northamptonshire, then the Beaufort in Gloucestershire. When he moved to the Quorn, Cottesmore and the Belvoir in Leicestershire he rented a flat at Craven Lodge, a redbrick house which had been turned into a hunting club in Melton Mowbray. He enjoyed the social life during the hunting season, finding it lively and unpretentious. The prince discovered that riding helped him to switch off from his duties. It also fulfilled his need to excel and compete with other men on equal terms. He wanted to show that where physical courage and endurance mattered he could hold his own.[17] Always needing to prove himself, Edward was attracted by danger and enjoyed taking risks. Out hunting, he would always choose the most direct and riskiest route and inevitably he regularly fell off. His falls were no more frequent than any other keen rider, but because he was the heir to the throne they were widely publicised and his propensity to fall off became an international joke. Caricaturists and comedians across the world ridiculed his riding abilities. Tommy Lascelles complained that the prince's name was getting 'a sort of pantomime association'.[18]

When Freda visited her parents in Nottingham, she occasionally went hunting. There is a charming photograph of her outside Lamcote, holding a riding crop and looking very elegant in a riding habit. Beside her are her two little girls in matching hacking jackets, jodphurs and checked caps.[19] However, the hunting field was more Audrey's territory than Freda's. She shared the prince's risk-taking approach and was a courageous huntswoman. On one occasion, she had broken her arm in three places out hunting during the morning, but she just rode home, had a splint put on and hunted for the rest of the afternoon. She then had her arm re-set without an anaesthetic.[20] A few years later, while hunting with the Cottesmore, she broke a leg when her horse fell on her.[21] It was a serious break; she had to have several operations and she spent many weeks in Melton Cottage Hospital. However, she would not let her injury stop her from socialising for long. Her hairdresser came regularly to the hospital to shingle her hair so that she looked her best to receive the many friends who visited her.[22] Once back in London, while she was still unable to walk, she went out to dinner or the theatre in a carrying chair. She arrived draped in her Chinchilla cloak, which hid her splints and bandages. Although she was escorted by her two nurses there was always a fight among the young men in her circle over whom would be the chosen one to carry her to her table.[23]

Audrey was the prince's type of woman. Half-American, she was sexy and tough, with a harsh, rasping voice. She also had an irreverent streak and liked to shock. On one occasion, she made an entrance at a party by having herself announced as 'Mahatma Gandhi's mother'.[24] However, it was Edward's compassionate side that brought the couple together. In February 1923 Audrey gave birth to a son who only survived a few days. After she lost her baby the prince stepped in and comforted her. As Freda spent more time with Michael, Edward retaliated by visiting Audrey. The prince wrote to Freda that he had not forgiven her for enjoying herself at Wilton with Michael and he told her that he had spent two hours in the afternoon with Audrey as 'a slight reprisal'. He added: 'You want a d——d good shaking that's what you want and it maddens me that I can't give you one tonight. Bad, Bad Fredie.'[25] As he grew more distant from Freda, the prince behaved increasingly badly. He drank too much and was often seen at the Embassy Club with Audrey. He later admitted to Freda that he went 'quite mad and off my nut' in April 1923.[26]

It seems that finally Freda had had enough of his childish behaviour, and so she broke off their relationship. They had a discussion where she put her 'cards on the table' and made him feel such a 'worm'.[27] Characteristically, Edward admired her for being so strong and 'getting down to bed-rock'.[28] Her change of heart was not just about the prince's behaviour, it was also because her relationship with Michael had become more intense and he was demanding more commitment from her. In her frank discussion with the prince Freda set out new conditions for their relationship. She agreed that they would remain friends and still have talks, but he must not worry her all the time. She now wrote to him as his 'devoted little chum'.[29] However, although they were supposed to be just friends Edward still told her he loved her and made emotional demands. He also constantly confided in her about all his amorous adventures, perhaps in the hope of making her jealous. In August, he wrote to her:

> If ever there was the slightest chance of my drifting away from you it would be now Fredie – I know that for sure for I do fancy Audrey a lot and am fond of her but I'm not madly in love and never will be again and she'll never mean a fraction to me of what you do.[30]

He promised that he would still always tell her exactly how he felt. Keeping his pledge, he wrote openly to her about being with Audrey and her husband as the guests of the Ancasters at Drummond Castle in Perthshire: 'Never have I had such an exciting week as this and the air is electric and it's all too tricky for words. I'm quite exhausted and shall be lucky if I escape without a hell of a row.'[31] Wearing a Fair Isle jumper and plus fours, he played a lot of golf with Audrey at Gleneagles, sometimes staying on the course until 8 p.m.[32] Back at the castle, they played poker all evening. However, even when he was infatuated with another woman he still needed Freda. He explained: 'I'm in a queer state of mind just now Fredie and do so want you to vet me and tell me what it all is – I feel very lost and all muddled up.'[33]

His unstable state of mind may have been accentuated because the courtesan he had a fling with at the end of the war, Maggy Alibert, had come back to haunt him. In the summer of 1923 she shot her Egyptian playboy husband, Ali Fahmy, in the Savoy Hotel, London. It seems that the prince's staff were very worried about what might come out at the murder trial. A recent book argues that Maggy used the prince's letters to bargain with the authorities. According to Andrew Rose, evidence suggests that a contract was made between Maggy and the royal household in which she returned the letters and in exchange there was an undertaking that her full character would never be revealed to the jury. There would be no reference to her affair with Edward and his name would be kept out of court. As usual during this crisis the prince turned to Freda as if she were his mother confessor. She came up to London to spend time with him at York House and he wrote to her afterwards that he felt much better for getting it all off his chest. In September Maggy was tried at the Old Bailey. She was portrayed as the helpless European victim of her sexually abusive Eastern husband. The sexual element allied with crude racism worked. Instead of being hanged for murder Maggy was acquitted in a wave of popular sympathy.[34]

In the autumn, the prince went to Canada to stay at his ranch. Before he left Freda told him that she was in love with Michael. Edward had always been jealous of his rival, but this was the first time Freda had admitted the depth of her feelings for the other man in her life. The prince told her that it was a 'big blow' to him but that he was glad to see her happy. However, he wrote: 'It's a horrid thought for me that I really mean nothing whatever to you now though you mean the hell of a lot to me.' During their intense discussion, Freda had also told Edward 'home truths', chastising him for being so self-pitying and spoilt. He accepted what she said, thanking her for 'showing me myself the other night darling and it's the first time I had had a look at "the brute" for months'. He promised to try to 'harden' himself up while he was away.[35] The ranch represented the real world for him in contrast to the artificial one he usually inhabited. He had built up a herd of shorthorn cattle there and wanted to inspect them.[36] For a few weeks he played at farming: he harvested, helped store the winter feed and cleared out the cowshed.

However, as usual he got into a romantic scrape and wrote to Freda about it. In Quebec he met an attractive American journalist. He was 'all over her' and danced with her most of the evening. It was not until the next morning when she asked to see him that she told him what her job was. The prince admitted he had been 'had for a mug' but she was very nice about it and said she would not say too much although she 'got off with me'. The newspapers were full of the story, but the prince told Freda that he was past caring because nothing mattered now he was no longer in a full relationship with her.[37] When he returned from Canada it seems that Freda relented, and they became lovers again. In November, he wrote to her: 'I'm in a daze after our happy evening together and oh! So puzzled!!'[38] With the prince back in her life Freda asked Michael to draw back. He was not happy about it, but he had little choice.

In July 1924 Freda persuaded both the prince and Michael to go with her in the same car for a treasure hunt. These hunts had become the favourite society game of the year. Lady Diana Cooper described them as 'dangerous and scandalous, but there was no sport to touch them'.[39] Members of the smart set would rush around London in their open cars in the early hours of the morning, following carefully laid clues that required knowledge and concentration to follow. One clue might lead treasure hunters to a city courtyard where they would find a 'lady in distress', with a dead duellist at her feet. She would then hand them the next clue, which took them to a plague spot where a pockmarked ghost would whisper a riddle that took the hunters to their next destination. At Seven Dials, women in expensive dresses crawled on all fours searching for an elusive clue that was chalked on the pavement. On their travels competitors would collect an eclectic range of objects ranging from a police helmet to a horseshoe. The winners of the hunt were the ones who had collected the most items and they won a coveted prize.[40] The search would end with a splendid breakfast, where hunters were serenaded by a string orchestra, at Norfolk House, St James.

During the July treasure hunt, Lady Diana Cooper described Michael's face, flushed 'shocking pink' with the pride of success, as he had found the corset of a courtesan signed by her famous clients.[41]

However, her husband Duff noticed the tension between Freda's competing lovers. He wrote that Edward was charming, but Michael was 'terribly proprietary over Freda in front of him'.[42] Michael did not want to share Freda again, but he had to accept the situation or lose her.

For years Duddie, Michael, Freda and the prince were locked in a toxic cycle that made none of them happy. The prince continued to be away often. In 1924 and 1925 he toured America, South Africa and South America. Since 1915 less than a third of his life had been spent in England, and such long absences were difficult for Freda and Edward.[43] If she had relied on just the prince for company she would have been lonely. During a private visit to America in 1924 the prince visited New York to watch the international polo matches played on Long Island. While in New York, he was entertained by millionaires on a grand scale. He went out to all-night parties and enjoyed dancing to jazz. His father was furious about the newspaper headlines his playboy behaviour inspired.[44]

During his South African trip the following year, the prince became increasingly concerned because he did not receive any letters from Freda although he wrote to her almost every day. He thought it was Michael's fault. Edward's equerry, Joey Legh, agreed. He thought that Michael's influence over Freda was so great that he would not allow her to write. The prince had confided in Joey that just before he left on his tour he had had a 'desperate row' with Michael because he had forbidden Freda to go to a dinner at York House. Edward said that he would not be surprised to hear that Freda had run away with Michael.[45]

While one of the prince's mistresses was proving elusive, his other one was all too eager. Audrey Coats wrote to him by every mail with the greatest regularity. Audrey was too available to be a challenge to the prince. Joey wrote to his wife that he did not think Edward cared 'two straws' about her except for purely physical reasons. On their voyage from South Africa to South America, Joey gave his friend a long lecture. He told him that he ought to marry as soon as possible because he would never be happy until he found 'Miss Right'. The prince agreed.[46] In Argentina, there were complaints that he looked bored and was not bothering to acknowledge the crowds. He was depressed and there were rumours that he was having a breakdown.

During this period Freda also suffered from bouts of depression; she was trapped in her marriage and unsure of which of her lovers she would choose if she were free. Perhaps neither of her potential partners was exactly what she was looking for. From the earliest days of their relationship, the prince's letters were rarely even remotely erotic; they show a man who was really obsessed with himself rather than his mistress. They are all about him and his needs – not hers. His assistant private secretary, Tommy Lascelles, who knew the prince very well, wrote that Edward was so isolated in the world of his own desires that he never felt 'absolute, objective affection' for anyone, even his lovers or family.[47]

Michael's letters show slightly more concern for Freda's feelings. They focus a little more on her as a person, but he too comes across as self-centred. He constantly made emotional demands that Freda was unable to fulfill. By 1924 Freda and Michael were rowing frequently. Freda's large blue eyes would fill with tears and then they would say cruel things to each other. Michael was hurt to the core when she told him that she got nothing out of their relationship and no pleasure at all from being with him.[48]

Michael became worried about how depressed Freda was getting. He said that he would do whatever she wanted to make the situation better. He admitted that he had bullied her and been 'awful'. He now promised he would be a changed man and more reasonable. He would not worry her so much or be so jealous.[49] Although he still hoped one day that everything would turn out all right and they would be married, he realised that the only way to cope until then was to live day by day and not face the future. Freda was just living for the moment too. Many years later she told an interviewer that through all the years that she loved the prince she realised that no good would come of it. There was no future in it and when it ended it would be to her disadvantage.[50]

The photos of Freda during this period capture her mood; there is one of her in profile looking painfully thin and miserable and another portrait of her with her pet dogs in which her expressive eyes show her sadness. Rather than being a promiscuous femme fatale who enjoyed playing her lovers off against each other, she looks like a woman who was trapped in a difficult situation and did not know what to do for the best. It seems that she genuinely feared Duddie would take their children if they got divorced. She loved both Michael and Edward, but she could not marry either of them. Neither of her lovers would let her go. They both threatened that they would go mad or commit suicide if she finished with them. Each man believed that she was the only woman in the world for them and essential to their happiness. As Michael accurately wrote: 'Really everyone loves you so much, too much, that is the trouble.'[51]

Freda's family loved and needed her too. She always spent Christmas at Lamcote and as her parents became older and increasingly unwell she was required to be in Nottingham more often. Michael and Edward resented the demands made on her by her parents. Michael told her not to let her mother act as a tyrant and be selfish. He believed that she was such 'an angel on earth' and that she did too much for them.[52] The atmosphere was often strained when Freda was at Lamcote because her parents did not approve of her complicated love life. Rather than speaking to her about it directly, her father spoke to her sister Vera about it. Neither of her lovers was welcome at Lamcote. Once Michael sneaked in for a visit while her parents were away, but whenever her mother saw him elsewere she gave him black looks.

The prince was equally unpopular. In February 1925 Vera married Major James Seely, a member of another well-known Nottingham family. The prince turned up at the last minute to attend the wedding, which rather eclipsed the bride's arrival. At three minutes before 2 p.m. the crowded congregation heard a roar of cheers from outside the church. Instead of the bride, the Prince of Wales walked in to a perceptible rustle of excitement. Some of the wedding guests even stood up on their pews to get a good view of him and started clapping.[53] Unperturbed by all the attention, he walked up the aisle to sit in a front row seat next to Mrs Birkin. There was a hush again and then Vera walked in a few minutes later accompanied by her bridesmaids, Pempie and Angie. Unusually for a very conventional man, Colonel Birkin did not attend his daughter's wedding. Instead, Vera's young brother Charles, who was still at Eton, escorted the bride up the aisle and her mother gave her away. The colonel had been ill in the months preceding the wedding with heart trouble, but it is also possible that the prince's unexpected arrival caused such a row that the respectable colonel refused to attend if he was there.[54] It seems that Colonel Birkin resented the man who had played around with both his daughters. Freda and Vera's mother, Claire, was more tolerant and smoothed things over. After the vows had been said, the prince followed the wedding group into the vestry and signed the register too. The bride and groom then walked down the aisle followed by Edward and Mrs Birkin. There is a photograph of the bride's mother with the prince on the wedding day; while she appears rather strained he looks as nonchalant as ever. 'What a lovely wedding it is,' he exclaimed to one journalist.[55]

Even though he often strayed, the prince always returned to Freda and her involvement in his life continued until he met Wallis Simpson. He told her that anybody else in his life was 'a complete and utter side show compared to what you've been to me'.[56] As well as the brief flings, there were constant rumours about official alliances for the prince. In his memoir Edward wrote that although his parents never pushed him into marriage, he knew that they thought it was time for him to settle down. They wanted him to take his chance in what he called the 'grab bag' of the royal marriage market.[57] At various times throughout the 1920s his name was linked to at least nine continental princesses. There was the Queen of Italy's daughter, who was a Roman Catholic; the King of Spain's daughter Beatrice; and, most implausibly, Princess Eudoxia of Bulgaria, who was a bulky, 39-year-old musician.[58]

One of the most promising candidates was the elegant Princess Marina of Greece. She was the granddaughter of King George I of the Hellenes; her family had been expelled from Greece and were in exile. In many ways Marina was Edward's type of woman. She was beautiful, slim and sophisticated with dark hair and large eyes. Her conversation was also stimulating as she was witty and intelligent. Although Queen Mary had learnt that it was counterproductive to interfere in her son's love affairs, she arranged for the princess to meet the prince at Windsor.[59] Edward liked Marina very much and thought she was attractive. Their meeting was so promising that her brother-in-law, Prince Paul, was almost certain that she had won his heart.[60] However, while Freda was in Edward's life there was no real vacancy for another woman. Instead of marrying the heir to the throne, Marina was to become a close friend of Freda's, and in 1934 she married Edward's brother Prince George.

Many years later, in his memoir, Edward set out his attitude to matrimony. He explained that he had no quarrel with marriage as an institution. Indeed, it was very much his intention to marry one day, but the idea of an arranged marriage was repugnant to him. When asked why he was not married he always repeated that he would not be hurried. He would only marry for love and under no circumstances would he agree to a loveless marriage. His choice would be dictated by his own heart, not considerations of State. He had seen too many unhappy couples to risk it for himself. He was also particularly careful because he realised that his royal position would make a divorce almost impossible if he chose the wrong bride.[61]

His continuing devotion to Freda was plain for all to see. In a letter to his wife, Clementine, in 1927, Winston Churchill described the prince's love for his mistress as 'so obvious and undisguiseable' that it was 'quite pathetic'.[62] Churchill had gone to Nottingham to make an important speech and, as Freda's parents were very involved in the local Conservative party, he stayed with them at Lamcote. The prince was still not welcome by Colonel Birkin, so he stayed with Freda's sister Vera who lived half a mile away.

In 1927 Audrey Dudley Coats's husband died. For several years Audrey and Muir had been leading separate lives. Since 1925, she had been running a small shop called 'Audrey's' in Davies Street, just off Berkeley Square. She sold an eclectic mixture of merchandise; there were exclusive scents called 'Divan Noir' or 'Doux', silk stockings and feathered fans. She also offered a renovation and repair service for antique furniture.[63] She told one journalist she hoped to help people solve 'the wedding present problem'.[64] Her friends Lady Curzon, Lady Beatty and Lady Edward Grosvenor were among her customers.[65] During the season, she took her boutique to Cowes. She shared her shop with a well-known beautician, and it became a recognised meeting place for her friends who enjoyed popping in for a manicure or a massage.[66] After the war it had become fashionable for society women to play at shopkeeping; Angela St Clair-Erskine (sister of Millicent, Duchess of Sutherland) and the prince's other mistress, Lady Victor Paget, also ran dress shops for a while. However, their ventures did not last long; as Angela St Clair-Erskine explained, lack of business experience proved a problem and 'initial mistakes usually end in costly failures'.[67]

Audrey's husband was rarely in London. For several years he suffered from frequent bouts of pancreatitis; Michael Herbert had seen him in San Moritz looking very thin and ill. Muir was a keen shot and fisherman. While Audrey was socialising and shopkeeping, he spent much of his time in Scotland with his parents. The year before he died he bought the 19,000-acre Perthshire sporting estate the Barracks, Rannoch. However, he was only able to enjoy it for a few months before he became seriously ill.[68] In the spring his parents took him to their Cannes Villa, where his mother looked after him. On the Riviera, he seemed to rally and he managed to play a round of golf.[69] However, it was only a brief respite as when he returned to Scotland he went into an Edinburgh nursing home. He died in August following an operation on a pancreatic cyst, at the age of just 29. His parents, not his wife, were with him at the end. Just days before his death Audrey was at Goodwood races.

Now Audrey was available, and as she was a widow rather than a divorcee the prince could have married her. The younger generation of the royal family liked her; she was a friend of Edward's sister-in-law, the Duchess of York, and his sister, Princess Mary. However, Edward's relationship with Audrey had been primarily physical and he had no intention of committing to her. After her husband's death, Audrey gave up work and went on holiday to Antibes and then Le Touquet.[70] In November she was one of the few women at the opening meet of the Quorn Hunt. Wearing her distinctive silk top hat and a riding habit, she was photographed lighting a cigarette before the hunt began. She looked every inch a match for the prince who was there in his spotless buckskin breeches, pink coat and silk hat.[71] However, although Audrey was free Edward was not interested so she began to look elsewhere. In 1930, she married Marshall Field III of the wealthy Chicago department store family and moved to Long Island.[72]

The situation changed in Freda's life too. In 1927 she tried to break the stagnant circle created between Duddie, Michael and the prince by having an affair with the American polo player Rodman Wanamaker.

Rodman's father, Lewis Rodman Wanamaker, was the owner of famous department stores in New York and Philadelphia and of *Wanamaker's Magazine*. He was known as 'the richest shopkeeper in the world'. He had become friends with George V and presented the king with a gold, ruby and diamond communion plate set for Sandringham Church and a gold processional cross for Westminster Abbey.[73]

Freda went to Paris with Rodman and she also stayed at his exclusive estate in Palm Beach. Both the prince and Michael were jealous but willing to put up with the situation to keep Freda in their lives. For the first time in eight years Michael began to see other women, but none of his flirtations were serious. After exchanging bitter words with Freda, he wrote to her that they had both had a 'testing and exhilarating fling', but he begged her 'not to try and kill our love for each other which is the only really living thing in my life because of a temporary crossness and lapse on both our parts'.[74]

As Freda's affair with Rodman continued, Michael became unwell and unhappy. He described 1927 as the worst year of his life and he accused Freda of being cruel. His beloved brother, Sidney, was constantly ill following a serious operation on his leg, which eventually had to be amputated. Michael was also ailing; he suffered from recurring chest infections, which were becoming increasingly serious. The two brothers travelled abroad searching for cures that might improve their health. They visited Switzerland, Biarritz and Berlin with friends, but Michael missed being able to rely on Freda's support when he was frightened about the future. In September 1928 Michael was diagnosed with bronchial pneumonia. He was distraught without Freda and became very depressed. He told her that he was in tears much of the time and looked like a ghost. He added: 'everyone must notice your future in my poor longing eyes.'[75] Michael's doctor advised him to winter abroad, which meant he was separated from Freda for four months. As he travelled around America on business he wrote letters home most days. He told her that he had never loved her more and that he would give years of his life for them to be together now. He explained that it was not good for his health to be so miserable and if she did not write to him to show that she loved him 'it will just be murder for it will kill me'.[76]

While Michael was in Nassau with his brother and their mutual friend, Lady Diana Cooper, Freda was in Palm Springs with Rodman. Known as 'the American Riviera', Florida was a millionaires' paradise as wealthy American stockbrokers and businessmen socialised with celebrities from around the world. As evening fell, the actor and writer Noël Coward could be found sipping cocktails with the Vanderbilts. One newspaper described it as 'a sun-baked garden with spacious lawns, surrounding lovely homes, framed with palms and bordered with flaming pointsettas, hibiscus and bougainvillea; and everywhere glimpses of turquoise blue and jade green sea'.[77] Freda was having fun, swimming, golfing and then dancing the night away. The smartest place to dine was the palm-framed terrace of the Colony Club. While Freda was staying, Mr and Mrs Cornelius Vanderbilt Whitney of New York gave a dinner at the club for Rodman and his house party.[78] Michael found it torture to think that Freda was so near and yet so far away from him. They met up for a tantalising few hours, but Michael got the impression that she did not really want to see him. He felt insane with jealousy.[79]

It was also a very unhappy time for the prince. Edward was drinking heavily and one night he turned up in the casino at Le Touquet so drunk that he was incapable of standing.[80] His behaviour was worrying his staff. In 1927, during a tour of Canada, his assistant private secretary, Tommy Lascelles, was so concerned that he arranged a private meeting with the prime minister, Stanley Baldwin. He told Baldwin that in the pursuit of 'wine and women' and whatever selfish whim obsessed him at the time, the prince was rapidly going 'to the devil'. Unless he changed his behaviour, he would be an unfit king. Lascelles admitted that sometimes when he was waiting to get the result from a point-to-point the prince was riding in he could not help thinking that the best thing that could happen for the country was for Edward to break his neck. To Lascelles's surprise, Stanley Baldwin agreed with him.[81]

Without Freda permanently in his life, the prince was going off the rails. While she was absorbed in her affair with Rodman, her good influence on Edward was absent, leaving his bad behaviour uncontrolled. Like Michael, Edward tried to be understanding, comparing Freda's affair to the purely sexual flings he had had in the past. He wrote to her:

I know you like me better than anybody else deep down yet you have a crazy physical attraction an affair on just now – And you like still another very much in another way to me. I know our two lives aren't absolutely satisfactory and I'm afraid they won't ever be now. But I do know my angel – That I love you too much to ever be able to love anybody else again ever.[82]

In autumn 1928, the prince went on a tour of East Africa. He told his staff that he had begun to find England 'a little cramped'.[83] Tommy Lascelles, who was now his principal private secretary, believed that only two things kept Edward in England: riding in point-to-point races and Freda – but either of these might end at any moment. Apparently, the prince admitted to him that his relationship with Freda would not last forever.[84] With Freda often abroad with Rodman the prince did not wish to be in England. He was seeking distraction. His trip to East Africa was hastily arranged and he told his staff that it should be a strictly informal tour with no uniform more elaborate than khaki.[85]

Once in Africa, he wrote to Freda that he wished that she was with him and it was 'so d—d silly' that they were not married as she would be happier with him than 'with any bloody Pappapacker'. He added that his 'kind' were all right for an affair but not for anything more serious.[86] Freda asked if he was keen on anyone in Kenya and he denied it. However, as usual there had been some flirtations and flings, which infuriated his staff. After 'princing' during the day he partied all night at the Muthaiga Club with the so-called 'Happy Valley' set. They were a group of aristocratic fugitives who were notoriously decadent; there were rumours of orgies, wife-swapping and stripping.[87] The prince spent a great deal of time with one of the most outrageous women of them all, Gwladys (pronounced Gladys), Lady Delamere. Known for her scandalous behaviour, she was very thin, with pale skin, bright lipstick and jet-black hair.[88] Edward told Freda that she was very keen on him, but it was not reciprocated. During one dinner, Gwladys literally threw herself at him. First, she chucked pieces of bread at him. It hit Karen Blixen, the author of *Out of Africa*, who was sitting beside him and gave her a black eye. Next, Gwladys rushed at him, overturning his chair and rolling him around on the floor.[89] Gwladys was not the only woman infatuated with Edward. Even Karen Blixen, who was sceptical about the royal family before the prince's arrival, was won over by his slightly childish shy charm. She wrote, half-joking, that she was so much in love with him that it hurt.[90]

The Muthaiga Club was the prince's sort of place. It had a golf course, squash courts, croquet lawn and a ballroom. Inside the pink pebble-dash building with its small doric columns there were comfortable armchairs, chintz and parquet floors. Drinks were available at any time of day. Pink gins were served before lunch, then gin fizzes at teatime followed by cocktails, then whisky and champagne until bedtime. For the more adventurous, cocaine and morphine were also available.[91] However, when the resident drug dealer, Frank Greswolde Williams, offered cocaine to the heir to the throne in between courses at dinner, it was considered too much, even by Happy Valley standards. Williams was manhandled out of the room by a white hunter.[92]

In the evenings there was bridge, backgammon and dancing. Syd Zeigler and his band played on Saturdays while on other nights the prince and his party danced to gramophone records. One night, Edward got frustrated and complained that they were the wrong kind of music, he then picked up all the records and threw them out of the window of the old ballroom. During his stay, he would go to bed at 4 a.m. and be up at 6.30 to go riding.[93]

After Nairobi, the prince went on safari. His main aim was to observe and photograph big game rather than shoot animals. However, the safari turned out to be more eventful than planned. A one-tusked elephant charged the party and had to be shot. The next crisis was when the prince's stalwart supporter and assistant comptroller, Brigadier-General 'G' Trotter, had a serious heart attack. During the trip, the king also became dangerously ill with pleuropneumonia and a severe case of toxaemia caused by an untreated abscess behind the diaphragm.[94] The prime minister, Stanley Baldwin, sent urgent cables begging the prince to come home at once. At first Edward did not take it seriously; he spent the evening completing his successful seduction of Mrs Barnes, the wife of the local commissioner.[95] Eventually, it became clear that he would have to travel home as it seemed at one point as though the king might die, and Edward would ascend the throne.[96]

Tommy Lascelles was appalled at his boss's callous attitude. He resigned shortly after their return to England. Lascelles had become increasingly disenchanted with the prince, saying it was like working for the son of an American millionaire rather than the next King of England. After working for him for eight years and observing him closely, he feared that the prince was too self-absorbed and lacking in any sense of duty ever to be fit to become king.[97] When Lascelles told him his reasons for resigning, Edward did not argue back, he just thanked him for the talk and said that he supposed the problem was he was the wrong sort of person to be Prince of Wales.[98]

Back in England, while the king was ill the prince took on many of the monarch's duties. As he took on more responsibilities he got on much better with his father and mother, and they wrote some warm letters praising his behaviour. Edward even stopped steeplechasing, which had been a constant concern for them. He gave up his rooms at Craven Lodge, Melton Mowbray and sold his string of horses. He turned to the safer pursuit of golf for relaxation instead.

The king and queen were also pleased with the way Edward had looked after his younger brother Prince George. The two siblings had become close friends; they shared a sense of humour, love of jazz and passion for keeping fit.[99] After leaving the navy, Prince George moved into York House. The brothers were often seen at Quaglino's and the Embassy nightclub together. Artistic and hedonistic, George was attracted to men and women. He loved the theatre and enjoyed dressing up. He counted among his girlfriends the African-American singer, dancer and comedienne Florence Mills who was appearing in one of Charles B. Cochran's revues, *Blackbirds*. His name was also linked with the film stars Lois Sturt, Tallulah Bankhead and Gloria Swanson as well as the playwright, composer and actor Noël Coward.[100]

Inevitably, Prince George's parents did not approve of his choice of partners, but they became increasingly worried when he started seeing a glamorous American called Kiki Whitney Preston. Known as 'the girl with the silver syringe', she introduced the young prince to drugs.[101] Edward was as concerned as his parents. He intervened by breaking up the destructive relationship. After persuading Kiki to leave England, he took George off to the country and took charge of his drugs rehabilitation.[102] While he was helping his brother recover he turned, as always, to Freda for advice. He knew that he could rely on her discretion. She recommended qualified nursing staff who were a great support to Edward while he looked after his brother. Edward's care of George showed his compassionate nature; he dedicated himself to being there for his younger sibling and when the cure was at a critical stage he would not leave him, even to see Freda. It was a stressful and draining time. Edward would sit for hours in the sickroom with his brother, embroidering a stool cover for him. He told Freda: 'It would make you laugh and maybe cry a little too.'[103]

It seems that as Edward took on more responsibilities and seriously faced the prospect of becoming king he reassessed his hopes of a future with Freda. Her fling with Rodman Wanamaker had changed the dynamics of all her relationships. The prince now saw Michael as a fellow victim, not a rival, and wrote: 'Poor Herbert, I'm sorry for him and we might conceivably become friends. But Wanamaker – NO.'[104] Michael also felt a degree of sympathy for Edward during the king's illness. He wrote to Freda: 'I am glad to see the king is better, the poor Prince of Wales must have had a hard time but now you needn't go on comforting him much need you?'[105]

Although there was a powerful physical attraction between Freda and Rodman, after two years the affair burnt itself out and she returned to her long-term lovers. Michael loved her more than ever and told her that every moment away from her felt like time stolen from his short life. He was still hoping she would get divorced and marry him. The prince reacted differently. After the Wanamaker fling, he became more realistic. He wrote to her:

> I do now at last realise that you can't feel quite the same as you used to and that you have other interests and friends which prevent you being as much in my life as I want you to be – I guess I'm a fool and have been living on the idea of a situation that just can't be.[106]

THELMA

9

SECOND BEST

While Freda was increasingly preoccupied with her other commitments, the prince started seeing a twice-married American, Thelma Furness. Once Freda had chosen to distance herself from him, Lady Furness became increasingly important to the heir to the throne. However, although his affair with Thelma was Edward's most serious relationship since he had met Freda, she was no real replacement for the exceptional woman who had shared his life for more than a decade. Thelma was kind and very beautiful, but she could only provide the physical, not the emotional, support the prince needed. She lacked the maturity and confidence of Rosemary and Freda, so she proved to be only a temporary substitute until their true replacement, Wallis Simpson, filled the vacuum.

Whatever the reality of their relationship, in her memoirs Thelma Furness told the story of her romance with the prince as though it was a fairy tale. She recorded in breathless detail their first meeting in 1926. She could hardly contain her excitement as she got ready for a ball at the home of society hostess Lady Londonderry. An American who was just entering London society as the young bride of Viscount Furness, she was particularly impressed by the thought that royalty would be at the event. She tried to imagine whether Princess Mary, the Duke of York, or most thrillingly of all, the Prince of Wales would be among the guests.

Londonderry House was at its most spectacular that night. It was filled with banks of flowers, and there were footmen in powdered wigs, knee breeches and white stockings to wait on the glamorous guests. Thelma had just begun to dance with her husband when a murmur, then a hush spread through the room. Lord and Lady Londonderry had entered the ballroom with the Prince of Wales at their side. Thelma whispered to her husband: 'Look, darling, the Prince of Wales!' The heir to the throne looked boyish and slightly shy as he stood in the doorway. Thelma noticed that in a nervous gesture, his hand frequently touched his white tie and as he spoke he held his head to one side, but he seemed younger and more handsome than she had expected.

As the music came to an end and Lord and Lady Furness walked towards the supper room Thelma heard her name called close behind her. When she looked around Lady Londonderry and the Prince of Wales were beside her. As her hostess presented Lady Furness, beneath her long dress, Thelma's knees would not stop shaking. As the prince put out his hand, she put her gloved one on his. Unable to say anything, she just made a deep curtsy. 'Welcome to England,' he said politely. 'I hope you will be happy here. May I have the next dance? I believe it's a Viennese waltz. I do hope you like them.' After they danced together, the prince thanked her, and Thelma curtsied again.[1] She would never forget that Viennese waltz. Although according to her account she did not see the prince again for nearly three years, the heir to the throne had made an indelible impression.

It was as if Thelma had been preparing for this romantic moment all her life. Her ambitious mother had brought her up to use her good looks to rise up the social ladder and in two and a half decades she had reached the top. Born in 1904 in the Hotel Nationale overlooking the Lake Lucerne, Switzerland, Thelma was one of twin daughters born to an American diplomat, Harry Hays Morgan Senior, and his dominating wife Laura. Mrs Morgan was half Irish-American and half Chilean. Proud of her ancestry, she was the daughter of General Hugh Judson Kilpatrick, who had fought ruthlessly in the American Civil War and was then appointed as American minister to Chile. Her Chilean mother was a descendant of the grandees of Spain.[2] However, Thelma claimed that her mother often dramatised her background and she never allowed facts to get in the way of the fantasies she created. Reading Lady Furness's memoir, it seems that these tendencies were passed on to her daughter.

The Morgans already had a son, Harry, and daughter, Consuelo, but their twin daughters Thelma and Gloria became the focus of Laura's attention. The two girls were identical; even their parents and later their lovers found it hard to tell them apart. As they grew older, the only difference which distinguished them was that Thelma had a scar from roller-skating.[3] The twins were so close that they almost seemed to be telepathic and throughout their turbulent lives they stood together against the world. Due to their father's career, the family lived a nomadic life moving from Switzerland to Holland then to Barcelona. No single country felt like home, which led to the children lacking a firm sense of identity. They spoke English but with a French/Spanish accent and a slight stammer.[4] Their education was haphazard; they had a disconnected knowledge of some things but remained ignorant about many others.[5]

It was a rootless upbringing that made the girls insecure. Their mother was the centre of their world, but she was a volatile character who smothered her daughters with love one moment but then flew into terrible tempers the next. Laura instilled into her girls that they should never trust anyone. She advised them never to make intimate friends, as there was no such thing as real friendship because people always wanted something. She also warned them never to give anyone anything without a return.[6] She believed that women had to use their feminine wiles to manipulate men to get what they wanted.[7] However, it appears that she did not always take her own advice as she was difficult to live with and it seems that her husband had affairs. When Mr Morgan was appointed consul general at Hamburg in 1913, his wife refused to accompany him. Instead, she stayed with the children in Barcelona.[8]

At the start of the First World War, the family left Spain. Their mother finally joined their father in Hamburg while Thelma and Gloria were sent to a French boarding school in England. It was the twins' first experience of being away from their mother and they missed her and were homesick. As they spoke very little English, they felt like 'misfits' at the school. They found it hard to make friends and as usual had to rely on each other. They disliked everything about England from the cold weather to the boiled food.[9] After the twins had spent their summer holiday in Germany with their parents, Laura decided to move them to a school in Switzerland. However, they had only been there a short time when their parents decided to go to America. Gloria and Thelma had never been to the United States and they were determined to go too. Although at first their parents thought it would be too dangerous to risk taking their daughters across the Atlantic in wartime, the girls outmanoeuvred them. Working as a team, they falsified a telegram, pretending it was from their father, to get accommodation on the ship. Faced with a fait accompli, their parents relented and took them to America.[10]

From the moment they arrived in New York, in September 1916, the striking 'Morgan Twins' attracted publicity. Both girls were very happy to talk to the press. Newspapers ran the story of how they got themselves to America. While their parents continued to travel due to Mr Morgan's career, the twins were sent to the Convent of the Sacred Heart in New York. Over the next three years they only saw their mother four times as she joined their father in his postings to Cuba and then Brussels. With their real mother absent, they formed a close bond with the head of the convent, Reverend Mother Dammen, who became a trusted confidante. After the girls left school, when they were just 17, they moved into an apartment together in a brownstone house in the centre of New York. Characteristically, Thelma and Gloria's first action on moving in was to fill the flat with flowers and name it 'Chez Nous'.[11] For two teenage girls to live alone together at such an early age was very unusual. Their parents were living in Brussels, so their landlady agreed to keep a motherly eye on them.[12]

It was an exciting time to be in New York and the twins perfectly suited this era. In 1920 prohibition of alcohol had been introduced but within weeks 2,000 speakeasies sprang up in New York, flouting the law. The affluent were able to continue to drink alcohol with no problem because, although it was against the law to manufacture, transport, sell or possess alcohol, it was not illegal to purchase or consume it.[13] As well as speakeasies, nightclubs flourished. El Fey, Club Richman, the Embassy and the Regent's Club were the trendsetters. They were noisy, crowded and glamorous, featuring live entertainment including comedians, dance troupes and jazz bands. Jazz music reflected the atmosphere of rebellion that pervaded the period. The modern Manhattan nightclubs were a product of the new prosperity as well as Prohibition. There was a building boom in the city and the new money of traders and speculators was competing with the traditional wealth of established families like the Vanderbilts, Whitneys and Astors. There was a democratic feeling in the nightclubs where Broadway stars, dukes and society women danced side by side with ex-convicts, film extras and bootleggers. The clubs were cosmopolitan as people from all walks of life were drawn together by the intoxicating beat of the music and the liberating experience of defying the rules.[14]

This more egalitarian atmosphere made Gloria and Thelma's entrée into New York society easy. Although they were on a limited budget, the girls lived a sophisticated life. They were soon seen at nightclubs, debutante parties and tea dances. Cocktails were a novelty for the twins, but cigarettes were not, as they had been smoking since they were 13 years old.[15] Cocktails were the height of fashion because it was a way to disguise the unpalatable ingredients in bootleg liquour. F. Scott Fitzgerald popularised Orange Blossoms, a mixture of gin, orange juice and sugar syrup, while another favourite was the Pink Lady, a combination of applejack, grenadine, gin and egg white served in an elegant long-stemmed glass.[16] The twins' penchant for cigarettes was not unusual. Like drinking cocktails, it was a way of showing they were thoroughly modern girls. In the early 1900s women could be arrested for smoking in public. Two decades later promoters of Lucky Strike cigarettes linked smoking with female emancipation, and attractive young women were photographed lighting up what they described as 'Torches of Liberty' at New York Suffragist parades. Perhaps more importantly for the twins, smoking was also promoted as a way to keep fashionably svelte.[17]

Thelma and Gloria were both skilful needlewomen and as there was little spare money available they made themselves chic clothes. When they were invited to a fancy dress ball they wore identical medieval pageboy costumes they had designed themselves.[18] Together Thelma and Gloria made a striking impact. The 1920s was the 'Age of Personalities' where the most popular newspapers relied on sex, sensationalism and pictures of pretty New York girls to attract their readers.[19] The gossip columnist Maury Paul, who was known as 'Cholly Knickerbocker', became a good friend of the twins and he helped to turn them into celebrities, calling them 'the Magical Morgans'.[20] The photographer Cecil Beaton wrote of them in *The Book of Beauty*:

> The Morgan sisters [...] are alike as two magnolias and with their marble complexions, raven tresses and flowing dresses, with their slight lisps and foreign accents, they diffuse [...] an Ouida atmosphere of hothouse elegance and lacy femininity. They are of infinite delicacy and refinement, and with slender necks and wrists, and long coiled, silky hair, they are gracefully statuesque. Their noses are like begonias, with full-blown nostrils, their lips richly carved, and they should have been painted by Sargent, with arrogant heads and affected hands, in white satin with a bowl of white peonies near by.[21]

With their exotic good looks, the girls received a great deal of male attention. However, Thelma claimed in her memoir that they had 'a strong sense of propriety' which made affairs unthinkable. They were naïve and romantic and what they were looking for was romance, love, marriage and children.[22] While she was still a teenager, Thelma met James Vail Converse Junior at a dinner party. After falling in love, they eloped to Maryland to get married. James came from a wealthy family but had lost most of his fortune on an oil deal. When Thelma and James moved to Palm Beach the twins were separated for the first time. Away from Gloria, Thelma experienced an overwhelming sense of loneliness.[23] Her marriage was short-lived as James was an abusive alcoholic. After a few months Thelma knew she had made a mistake but she only made up her mind to leave him after she suffered a miscarriage following a fall. While she was seriously ill in hospital it was Gloria, not James, who stayed by her bedside.[24]

While in California getting a divorce, Thelma decided she would like an acting career. Hollywood was a modern Babylon, where new wealth, luxury and ambition burgeoned.[25] Thelma was one among many eager starlets who hoped to find fame on the silver screen. Film was one of the first industries in which women were able to compete on roughly equal terms with men, writing, producing and directing as well as acting.[26] However, fame proved elusive for Thelma. While she lived in Hollywood she played small parts in a few movies. In one film, she appeared as a Spanish señorita who just had to wink.[27] Although her acting career never really took off, her social life did, and she was soon mixing with 'Hollywood royalty'. She went swimming at Pickfair, the home of Mary Pickford and Douglas Fairbanks. Through the new medium of film the couple had experienced an unprecedented degree of fame. Mary Pickford was the first great film celebrity. Known as 'little Mary' and 'America's Sweetheart', she was the first actress to earn more than a million dollars a year.[28] When she married her fellow actor Douglas Fairbanks in 1920, she was probably the best-known woman in the world. The Fairbanks' Hollywood home was known as 'the Buckingham Palace' or 'the second White House' of the film world. On their rambling estate in the Los Angeles Hills they gathered together an eclectic range of guests, including Albert Einstein, Lord Louis Mountbatten and the writer F. Scott Fitzgerald. Mary admitted that Douglas was always bringing 'funny people' home to dinner and celebrities might find themselves sitting next to a tramp, a wrestler and two homeless cats.[29]

At Pickfair Mary created a cultured, civilised atmosphere. There was vintage wine, caviar in iced boats and sumptuous dinners created by French chefs. However, the atmosphere was relatively staid, with very little alcohol on offer.[30] On rare occasions dinner was followed by dancing, but only the waltz or two-step were allowed as the hostess did not approve of jazz music. More frequently guests played a round of bridge or they watched the latest film in the Fairbanks' screening room drinking a cup of Ovaltine. Evenings ended early as Mary and Douglas liked to be in bed by 10.30 p.m.[31]

The Fairbanks were great friends with the British-born actor Charlie Chaplin. The trio had set up United Artists together in 1919, which allowed artists for the first time to produce and distribute their own work and to be properly credited for their role in creating it.[32]

Chaplin and the Fairbanks lived close to each other in Beverly Hills. Thelma went out with Chaplin; they saw a great deal of each other and there were even rumours in the newspapers that they were to be married, but in fact they were just good friends.[33] Chaplin was known to be a womaniser; he had countless flings with women who were keen to be seduced by one of the most famous men in the world.[34] To avoid more gossip, Thelma stopped seeing Chaplin so often and within months he was married to Lita Grey.[35] Attracted to older men, Thelma began a relationship with the actor Richard Bennett, who was in his 50s. However, she soon discovered that acting was not her gift and that she did not want to marry Bennett. Looking for fresh adventures, she left the movie world to travel to Europe to see her parents and sister Consuelo.

Unlike Rosemary and Freda, Thelma lacked a strong sense of identity. She was a social chameleon who adapted to suit her surroundings. Once she was in Europe, it did not take her long to reinvent herself again. At a dinner in Paris she met Marmaduke Furness, the owner of Furness and Withy shipbuilders. Viscount Furness was one of Britain's wealthiest men. His father Christopher was a self-made man who had started life as a docker in Hartlepool but became a multimillionaire, member of parliament and the first Baron Furness of Grantley.[36] His son Marmaduke was considered one of the most brilliant businessmen in the City. Rumour had it that the sale of the Furness–Withy line for £9 million was concluded by him on the back of a menu.[37] However, he was far from urbane speaking, with a slight Yorkshire accent, and he swore frequently.

Dapper, with sandy, brilliantined hair, 'Duke', as he was known to his friends, was more than twenty years older than Thelma. He had been married before and gossip surrounded the death of his first wife, Daisy Hogg. In December 1920 she had a serious operation. After making a good recovery, she travelled with her husband on board his yacht the *Sapphire* to visit his mother in Cannes, but during the voyage she had 'a sudden relapse and passed away peacefully'.[38] Her death was never fully explained. Although there was a fully equipped hospital and a doctor on board she could not be saved. Despite the availability of refrigeration on the ship, she was hastily buried at sea.[39] From his first marriage,

Lord Furness had two grown-up children, Averill and Christopher (known as Dick), who were only a few years younger than Thelma.

In her memoir, Thelma described the first evening she met Lord Furness. After dinner Duke took her dancing in the Paris nightclubs. They ended the evening at Casanova, a fashionable Russian club where champagne and caviar were served while violins and balalaikas played and a Cossack choir sang. As dawn broke over Montmatre, they bought flowers in the flower market near the Madeleine. Duke was returning to London the next morning but after breakfast a huge box of roses arrived at the Ritz for Thelma from him. He sent a card that said he hoped the flowers would keep fresh until they met again. True to his word, he was back to see his new girlfriend two days later.[40]

During their courtship, Duke came to Paris most weekends. As Lord Furness was a racehorse owner, the couple often went racing at Longchamp in the afternoon and then spent the evening at nightclubs. Thelma was attracted by Duke's power; she felt that there was 'nothing he could not do'. When they went to restaurants they were always given the best tables. His vast fortune meant he could indulge her every whim. Thelma could not recall when he proposed; instead she explained that they both just took it for granted that they would marry.[41] However, one night at the Embassy Club in London, Duke asked her when her 'bloody divorce' would be finalised. Thelma explained that her first husband still hoped for a reconciliation, but this did not stand in Lord Furness's way as he had made up his mind to marry her. He arranged for detectives to follow James Converse Junior and within the month Converse had agreed to a divorce.[42] When Thelma's old lover, Richard Bennett, heard she had divorced he announced that when she returned to America he intended to marry her. Thelma denied the report and her mother went a step further by holding a press conference to announce her daughter's engagement to Lord Furness.[43]

Thelma married Duke in June 1926 at St George's Register Office, Hanover Square, London. She wore a Patou wedding dress, in bois-de-rose crepe de Chine with a matching long coat trimmed with lynx and a matching turban.[44] After the ceremony a reception was held for a few close friends at Duke's Arlington Street house. It was an austere setting for a celebration; the house was more like a museum than a home with statues lining the hallway and glass cases filled with Lord Furness's collection of rare glass and silver placed around the reception rooms.[45] Full of memories of Duke's life with his first wife, Daisy, the house never felt like home to Thelma.

Before she married him, Thelma knew that Duke was a difficult man. When he was in a bad temper he would shout and swear at anyone who got in his way. However, in the first months of their marriage she saw little of this side of her new husband's personality. She later wrote that she had never been happier in her life. She believed that Duke was a perfect husband; he was clever, worldly-wise and amusing company.[46] As one of the richest men in the country, Lord Furness provided Thelma with the lifestyle she craved. They travelled in his yacht, plane or private train carriages. His customised Rolls-Royce had solid silver handles, the Furness crest on the door and room for two chauffeurs.[47] In August, the Furnesses went to stay at Duke's Scottish estate, Glen Affric, near Inverness, for stalking and fishing. There were also visits to Ireland to see Lord Furness's stud in Gilltown, where he bred racehorses. Thelma found herself thrown into a world of endless parties, sociable weekends and days at the races. For most of the year, the newly married couple divided their time between Duke's London house and Burrough Court, near Melton Mowbray in Leicestershire.

At Burrough Court the Furnesses entertained in style. It was a large hunting lodge that could sleep up to thirty guests. The house was built around two courtyards, and its exterior was covered in ivy creeper. On Friday nights, when friends arrived for the weekend, cars would fill the courtyard. Once guests had driven down the mile-long avenue leading up to the house they would be greeted at the front door to the house by a butler and two footmen, who had been notified of their arrival by staff in the gatehouse. Their hosts would meet them inside before they were ushered up to their bedrooms to change. It was a comfortable place to stay; each bedroom had its own bath and central heating. At Burrough Court guests always dressed for dinner and the women would waft down the stairs in their long evening dresses to meet the gentlemen gathered in the great hall for cocktails. After drinks they would have dinner in the dining room. Reflecting Duke's passion for horses, the room was lined with paintings by George Stubbs. It looked out over a formal garden with box hedges cut into the shape of peacocks and pyramids. At dinner, footmen in the Furness livery of plum knee breeches with yellow stockings would stand behind each chair, before a butler and two footmen would bring in each course.[48]

During the hunting season Burrough Court was always full of guests who hunted with the Quorn. The house took on the atmosphere of a club. The guests had their own private jokes that no one else could understand and all the conversation was about horseflesh. After breakfast on a Sunday morning, Duke took all his guests down to the mock-Tudor stables to watch his grooms parade his thoroughbreds. Guests entered the stableyard through an archway with a clock tower to find dozens of loose boxes and a tack room displaying silver cups and trophies. There was a special boot room next to the butler's pantry where shoes and riding boots were kept. Lord Furness was obsessed with tidiness and always had to look immaculate. A boot boy spent all day polishing and cleaning his shoes, and the laces had to be ironed before Duke would wear them.[49] His horses also had to look as smart as their owner; each one had four blankets and sheets in the Furness colours of plum and gold, which were washed and ironed after every use. Not a strand of straw from the horses' bedding was permitted to ruin the pristine appearance of the freshly painted white chalk in front of the stable doors.[50]

Thelma found this preoccupation with everything equestrian dull because she did not enjoy riding. More to her taste was organising the hunt ball at Burrough. Everything had to be perfect for the Furnesses' special night. The ballroom was decorated in the Furness racing colours and every few feet bales of straw dyed black, white and red were held together with exotic flowers from Burrough's greenhouses. All the men came dressed in their pink coats while the women wore full evening dress and jewels. To add to the sophistication of the evening, Thelma hired Harris's band from the Embassy Club to play for her guests.[51] The ball went brilliantly. The new Lady Furness passed her first test with flying colours, proving herself to be the perfect hostess.

In March 1929 Thelma's happiness seemed complete when she gave birth to a boy named William Anthony (known as 'Tony'). Although she was now a mother, Thelma's routine changed little. She was part of a generation of society women whose children were taken care of by nannies. Excessive preoccupation with your children was thought to be a bourgeois characteristic.[52] Later, when Thelma was on the defensive about her lack of a maternal instinct, she blamed English nannies for totally taking over the care of a baby as soon as a mother handed her child over to them. She claimed that she spent as much time with her son as his nanny would allow.[53] Her niece, Gloria, partly corroborated her story. She recalled that Tony's nurse was 'awful'; she insisted on wearing a hat all the time and hated it when Thelma came into the nursery. Gloria nicknamed her 'Old Witch Nurse'. [54] Freda Dudley Ward was unusual in being such an involved mother; Thelma was more typical with her arm's-length approach to childrearing.

Lady Furness and most of her circle of women lacked meaningful occupation. No longer were hours taken up with letter writing as the telephone by the bedside was the new means of communication with friends. Yet, instead of spending their spare time with their children, their days were spent in a round of social engagements. They usually dined out most evenings, lunched out every day and went to the country for house parties at weekends.[55] Their purpose was primarily decorative rather than practical. However, Thelma soon found herself redundant even in this limited role. According to her memoirs, only a few months after she gave birth Duke's eye began to stray. One evening, they were at the Embassy Club when a glamorous American called Peggy Hopkins Joyce walked in. Thelma had known Peggy in her past. Mrs Hopkins Joyce was known as 'the queen of alimony'; she had been married to five millionaires and it is said that the term 'gold-digger' was invented to describe her. It was claimed that she refused to let one of her husbands into the bedroom until he had signed her a cheque for $500,000. She later hit him over the head with a champagne bottle but excused herself by saying that he seemed to like it. Like Thelma, she had dated Charlie Chaplin.[56] For some inexplicable reason, Thelma bet Duke £10 that he could not get Mrs Hopkins Joyce to dance with him. Duke won the bet, and after his dance with Peggy they started having an affair. Shortly after they met, Duke went to stay at his new mistress's villa in Monte Carlo. Apparently, Peggy was not his only lover; there were also rumours that Lord Furness was having an affair with a young widow.[57]

Thelma claimed that if Duke had remained a faithful husband she would have been a faithful wife. She was deeply hurt by his infidelity and she felt very alone in a strange country.[58] According to her memoir, it was in the summer of 1929, shortly after she discovered Lord Furness was having an affair, that she met the Prince of Wales again at an agricultural show in Leicestershire. As she saw a young man pinning a blue ribbon on one of the prize cows, she realised it was the prince, with whom she had so enjoyed dancing three years before. When he saw her he immediately came over and congratulated her on the birth of her son. He then asked if she planned to come up to London during the summer. When she said that she came to London regularly, he asked her to meet him for dinner the following week. Disillusioned with her husband and attracted to the prince, she accepted eagerly.[59]

A woman friend of the prince claimed that she was told a different story by Thelma about how the affair began. Lady Furness had been at a house party one weekend and met Edward. By chance, they were both on the same train coming back to London. To her surprise, the prince's equerry knocked on the door of her train compartment and asked her to join the heir to the throne because it was such a long journey and he was bored.[60] Newspaper and magazine accounts also suggest that Thelma's story in her memoir may not be totally accurate. They show that although she claimed not to have seen the prince for several years after their first meeting, they were at some of the same events and even danced together before the summer of 1929. In December 1926 *The Tatler* described a party at Craven Lodge where the Prince of Wales and the Duke of York were guests. It had been given by Mrs Jackie de Pret, who arranged for the Café de Paris band to be brought down from London to play. The prince danced the Charleston 'strenuously without ceasing'. The gossip columnist recorded that his partners included Lady Furness, Joey Legh's wife Sarah and Freda's youger sister Vera.[61] The prince and Thelma were also both at the Melton Hunt Ball in January 1928 but the prince in 'hunting pink' had plenty of other distractions that evening as Freda, Rosemary Ednam and Audrey Dudley Coats were also at the dance.[62]

It seems strange that Thelma did not mention these earlier meetings in her memoir. It is highly unlikely that Thelma would have forgotten dancing the Charleston with Edward. It was a momentous event for any young woman to dance with the Prince of Wales, particularly for one as starstruck by the heir to the throne as Thelma clearly was. Perhaps she omitted it because it did not fit the fairy tale she was trying to create. Any subterfuge also had more pragmatic reasons. It was important for Lady Furness to establish with precision the date when her relationship with the prince began because her son Tony was born in 1929. According to Duke's stepdaughter, Lord Furness doubted whether Tony was his child. He always referred to him as 'the bastard' and rarely saw him.[63] There is no conclusive evidence either way about who fathered Thelma's only child. It seems unlikely that he was the prince's son. As an adult, Tony always denied it and it was said that he bore a striking resemblance to his paternal grandfather.[64] However, by the time Thelma wrote her memoir, two decades later, it was essential to establish her son's legitimacy as he had inherited the Furness title and much of the fortune. To allay any suspicions about Tony's paternity, she had to minimise any reference to contact she had with the prince before her son's birth. Ironically, by covering up meetings Thelma drew attention to the timing and cast doubt on her story: it makes it look as though she had something to hide.

Thelma showed no similar amnesia about her first date with the prince. In her memoir, Thelma recorded in detail the dinner that was to prove such a turning point in her life. They sat by the fire and drank cocktails at the prince's home, York House, before going out to dine at the Hotel Splendide. Thelma found that Edward was easy to talk to. They discussed her elder sister, Consuelo, who was married to a diplomat, Benjamin Thaw. When the prince visited Buenos Aires, the American ambassador was away so the Thaws entertained the heir to the throne. Edward had got on very well with them and they became friends.[65]

The Hotel Splendide was famous for its food and its Viennese orchestra. During the evening, Thelma and the prince waltzed again. Thelma described the admiring looks the prince gave her as they danced. When they talked, it seemed as if they had always known each other. It felt natural and right for her to be with him. At the end of the evening, when the prince asked if he could call her again soon, she readily agreed.[66] Lady Furness and Edward began to see each other regularly. Thelma said that he was just what she needed at this time. He was the opposite of Duke, and his gentleness and shyness appealed to her.[67] They were seen at the newly redecorated Café de Paris which, when it reopened in 1929, had been painted red, green and gold. In keeping with the new fashion, short dresses were replaced with svelte long evening gowns. Thelma led the trend by wearing glamorous, figure-skimming dresses with her distinctive necklace of large black pearls.[68]

As the months went by, Thelma was seen more often than Freda in nightclubs dancing with the prince. However, Lady Furness's relationship with Edward was always less deep than his bond with his established mistress. Attractive though Thelma was, she could never replace Freda, as she lacked the intelligence and integrity of her rival. Elsa Schiaparelli explained that although Thelma was very beautiful she was 'heavy' to talk to. She was friendly and always chattering, but she had no repartee.[69] Edward's attraction to Thelma was superficial and throughout their affair Freda was always there in the background. Thelma was light relief; their conversations were never profound, they just discussed trivialities and gossiped about people they knew.[70] Unlike with Freda, he did not bare his soul to her or discuss his deepest beliefs. Thelma recognised that he was a complex personality, but she never came near to understanding him. He did not need her to, as Freda was still there, playing the role of mother confessor in his life. She no longer wanted to party all the time and according to her family it is unlikely that Freda was still in a sexual relationship with the prince, so Thelma conveniently acted as an attractive substitute.

In 1929 Edward found his first real home of his own. He persuaded his father to allow him to use Fort Belvedere, a castellated folly in Windsor Great Park above Virginia Water. Although when he took it on it was a run-down ruin, the prince could see the Fort's potential. The Fort had been built in the eighteenth century but eighty years later the architect Sir Jeffry Wyatville enlarged the folly for George IV to include a tall tower and create the effect of a castle in a forest. Reflecting her superior position, it was Freda, not Thelma, who advised Edward on the redesign and decoration of his home. While he was away, she visited the Fort to oversee the work. New central heating and bathrooms were put in, built-in wardrobes were added, and a swimming pool and tennis court were created in the grounds. Freda's understated good taste predominated throughout. Thelma's influence on the design was more minimal; this was fortunate judging by the changes that she did make. She had one guest room decorated in shocking pink and she added Prince of Wales feathers to the top of the four-poster bed. Apparently, the prince was very amused by this display of vulgarity.[71]

In the early stages of their relationship Thelma had a dilemma. She wanted to spend as much time as possible with the prince, but she also had to keep up appearances and not flout their affair or she would antagonise her powerful husband. In public Thelma continued to play the loyal wife, attending balls, charity galas and garden parties with Duke. In private she shared her life with the heir to the throne. As always, her twin Gloria helped her. She came to England and rented a house called 'Three Gables' at Sunningdale, which was very close to the Fort. Gloria provided a safe place where Thelma and Edward could meet away from public view. Thelma's older sister, Consuelo, also supported her sibling. Her husband, Benjamin Thaw, had been made diplomatic attaché to the Court of St James. The Thaws moved into a town house in Farm Street, thus providing another private place for the prince and his new girlfriend to meet.[72]

Inevitably, Thelma soon became the prince's mistress. In 1930 Edward continued the East African safari he had cut short due to his father's illness. The following month, Lord and Lady Furness were also in Kenya. As Thelma explained, her sophisticated husband took her relationship with the heir to the throne in his stride. Duke had sometimes joined the prince and Thelma at the Embassy Club and he even invited his rival to stay at Burrough Court. Sharing his wife with Edward while they were in Africa did not seem to bother him either. When the prince invited the Furnesses to join his safari, Duke turned down the invitation and allowed Thelma to go on her own.[73]

Safaris were full of adventure and the risk of danger, but the camps were as luxurious as money could make them. When they returned in the evenings hunters would drink sundowner cocktails or chilled champagne, then have a relaxing hot bath in a canvas tub. They would then sit down to dinner, often in their pyjamas and dressing gowns, on tables in the open air. As the night grew cooler a large campfire would be lit.[74] Guests slept under mosquito nets in green canvas the size of a ship's cabin. In her memoir, Thelma described in ecstatic terms her idyllic holiday with the prince. There were forty guests on the safari, but Thelma was only interested in Edward. Each morning he woke her up in her tent before he left for the bush in search of wild animals. As he filmed wildlife with his camera, she followed him with her Bell-Howell camera, recording his every move. The prince's tent was next to hers and once all the other guests had gone to bed, the lovers would meet up and sit by the embers of the dying fire beneath the vast, star-studded African sky. She described East Africa as their 'Eden', and wrote in purple prose about their lovemaking.[75] Like Freda before her, she lived for the moment, not sure when her affair with the Prince of Wales would end. She claimed that she never wanted or expected to become queen.[76]

When the 'enchanted' safari was over, Thelma was due to rejoin her husband.[77] Edward decided that he would drive her in an open-top car the 40 miles across trackless country to meet their train. However, his romantic gesture went disastrously wrong. Halfway through the journey Edward suddenly became seriously ill; he slumped over the steering wheel and was breathing shallowly. Thelma was terrified that he might die. Somehow, he managed to continue driving, and they reached the train but by the time they arrived his temperature was 105 degrees. Doctors diagnosed him as suffering from malaria. Distraught though she was, Thelma had to leave him in Kenya while she returned to England with her husband.[78]

Unknown to Lady Furness, while she was waxing lyrical about her romance the prince was still writing love letters to Freda. At the start of the safari, he wrote to his long-term mistress calling her 'My darling angel', and sending 'all my love darling from David'.[79] There was none of the sense of the euphoria he had felt in the early days of his relationship with Freda at the start of his new affair. Evidently, he was doing some soul searching while he was away. He told Freda that he dreaded returning to his duties in England. He felt that he was getting too old for 'stunting' which he complained was 'artificial nonsense' and made him look a 'fool'. He added: 'How sad it is to get as old and cynical as I've gotten and as discontented.' It seems that Thelma was unable to bolster his confidence and shake him out of his moods in the way Freda could. He told his trusted confidante that he felt 'sunk' and his 'inferiority complex' was worse than usual. He wanted to cry to her because he knew that she would understand.[80] In another letter, he told Freda he wished that she was with him. He was excited about returning to her. He added: 'I do love you so but you know that. All my love and blessings are yours, David.'[81]

Throughout his affair with Lady Furness, he continued to telephone Freda every morning and visit her most afternoons. There was no doubt that she still came first in his affections. When their old friend Sheila Milbanke (formerly Loughborough) invited the prince to the Derby Ball in 1930 he would only accept the invitation if Freda also attended.[82] Like so many of his other flings, Freda knew about Edward's relationship with Thelma and, to his disappointment, she was unconcerned. She even teased him about his American girlfriend's romantic illusions.[83] She could tell that Lady Furness was no permanent threat to her position. The prince also remained as involved as ever in Freda's domestic life with her daughters. Angie would visit him on her own at St James's Palace for tea or play golf with the prince.[84]

Although there was no prospect of exclusivitiy, back in England Thelma's affair with the prince intensified. They saw each other all the time and Duke no longer joined them. It seems that Lord Furness minded more than his wife was willing to admit. In his diary, the gossip columnist and diplomat Sir Robert Bruce Lockhart wrote that Duke had been seen at Le Touquet, while Thelma was 'going great guns' with the prince at Bayonne. Mutual friends thought that he was miserable about his wife's affair.[85]

The prince and Thelma spent weekends together and were seen at nightclubs and private parties as a couple.[86] However, she remained second best, not his first choice. It was Freda's decision, not the prince's, that they saw less of each other. Friends believed that she could get Edward back if she wanted but, apparently, she did not want to.[87] While Edward was involved with Thelma, Freda had many distractions in her life meaning there was less time available for his demands. Her daughters had grown into beautiful young women and they were beginning to have love affairs of their own. When they were sent to Munich to learn German Pempie fell in love with a much older man who was head of the opera. Freda often visited the girls in Germany. On her return to England, Pempie came out as a debutante. She was featured among 'the bevy of beautiful buds' photographed for *The Queen Magazine*.[88] It was said that Freda looked too young to be chaperoning Pempie, and they seemed more like sisters than mother and daughter.[89]

With her daughters increasingly living their own lives, in June 1930 Freda finally divorced her husband on the grounds of adultery. The correspondent was a woman called Lilian Gallifent of 15 Matheson Road, West Kensington. The adultery was alleged to have taken place at the Hotel Metropole, Brighton.[90] Until the Matrimonial Causes Act of 1937, to get a divorce it was not only necessary to prove a husband's adultery, it was also important to demonstrate that the divorcing couple were not colluding by putting up an agreed story. If there was any doubt, a government official known as the king's proctor would investigate the truth of the case. In practice many rich couples, like the Dudley Wards, divorced by mutual consent if the husband was willing to provide evidence for his wife by a procedure known as 'a hotel bill case'. This often involved a young woman being hired to stay in a hotel room with the divorcing husband. She would then be found in bed with him next morning when breakfast was brought up to them by a member of staff.[91]

Freda's case in court was that about five years previously she and Duddie had ceased to live in the same house. There was a disagreement and she discovered that her husband had a house elsewhere. There was no actual separation and they remained friendly. The year before, while she was in Paris, her husband called and saw her. When he said that he did not want her to go to his hotel her suspicions were aroused. Shortly afterwards she discovered he was being unfaithful. On hearing the evidence, the judge granted a divorce to Freda and custody of her two daughters.[92]

The divorce came too late for Michael. He was increasingly unwell, but as his health deteriorated he still hoped that Freda would marry him. Too ill to work, Michael sat in his garden all day just staring into space, waiting for a phone call, letter or visit from Freda. He wrote to her: 'I didn't know it was possible to long for anything like I long for you, I can't think of anything else.'[93] The prince was sympathetic, telling Freda he knew how much anxiety she was suffering from. If she could not get away from the nursing home where Michael was being looked after to visit him, he understood and she need not worry about him.[94] In September 1932 Michael died from an abscess on his lung, bronchio-pneumonia and cerebral toxaemia, at his home in Hill Street, Mayfair. He was only 39 years old. Freda was devastated. Her family believes that he, rather than the Prince of Wales or either of her husbands, was the love of her life. After Michael's death, she wrote to their mutual friend Duff Cooper about her feelings of guilt and regret:

> Darling Duff,
> Thank you for your sweet sympathy. I am so sorrowful and desolate and haunted by so many memories – sad and gay – but all so poignant. I know how much you and Michael loved one another and that you will miss him so often in times to come and at so many places. But you need have no regrets. While mine are intolerable and take all consolation from my sorrow. I am very touched that you should have thought of writing to me darling – Thank you so much.
> Freda.[95]

The seriousness of their relationship was reflected in Michael's will, which he made just before he underwent an operation in August. He left £80,000 of his £500,000 fortune to Freda. Half of his wealth was left to his brother Sidney. A clause in his will directed that all his locked boxes and attaché cases with their contents should be destroyed unopened.[96] It is likely that they contained love letters from Freda because, although she kept his letters to her, none of her letters to him survive. Michael was buried in the Temple Copse at Wilton. In 1939, when Sidney also died prematurely, he was buried beside his brother.[97]

As well as losing her lover, Freda also lost both of her parents within a short space of time. Her father had never fully recovered from the head injuries he sustained during the war, and had also developed heart disease; he died in 1932 aged 67. Her mother became unwell shortly afterwards. She had a gall-bladder operation while visiting France and died from complications two years later. Freda was with her when she died.

Freda was now without her husband, her lover and her disapproving parents. For the first time, the prince could have been the only man in her life and he could have had her to himself. Yet, unlike a few years later when Wallis divorced Ernest Simpson, Freda's divorce was not a prelude to marrying the heir to the throne. As with Michael, her freedom had come too late, and her relationship with the prince was past its peak. She never pushed to marry him. Instead, she continued to accept her role in his life without asking for more. However, the question of who would be the future king's bride had become an increasingly important issue. Various European royals were still rumoured as potential partners. At Edward's suggestion, Lord Mountbatten came up with a list of seventeen princesses, including Princess Ingrid of Sweden and the 15-year-old Thyra of Mecklenburg-Schwerin.[98]

Even Hitler tried to intervene in the matchmaking. The prince had expressed sympathy for the views of the Nazi party. He admired their policies to deal with unemployment and housing, and argued that Germany's internal affairs were their own business.[99] The German government appreciated his attitude and Hitler believed an alliance with a German princess could bring the two countries closer. He asked the Duke of Brunswick to arrange a marriage between the Prince of Wales and his 17-year-old daughter Princess Friederike. Her royal pedigree was excellent: like Edward, she was a descendant of King George III and her father was head of the House of Hanover. From Hitler's point of view, she was a model candidate. Her father regularly donated funds to the Nazi party and the princess was a member of the League of German Girls, the female branch of the Hitler Youth movement.[100] However, the Brunswicks were not keen on the idea as Friederike's mother, now the Duchess of Brunswick, was the Kaiser's daughter who had been matchmade with the prince in 1913. The Brunswicks believed the age gap was too great and that their daughter should be free to choose her own husband.[101] Nor was Edward enthusiastic about a child bride.

In March 1932 the king had a rare personal discussion with his son. George V began the conversation by telling Edward that he had no intention of having a row with him, he just wished to put certain ideas before him. He added that until now he had talked to him as a father, but now he wanted to speak to him as a reigning monarch to his successor. He told Edward that the public 'worshipped him and that he was at the zenith of his popularity – but would this last when the Public began to realize at last the more or less double life that the prince was leading?' The king believed that 'the great non-conformist conscience of England' would not accept Edward's private life if it was revealed. The prince disagreed, saying that people were more tolerant nowadays, but the king would not accept this and told his son that the days when royal princes had well-known mistresses and families by them was over and the the British public now expected their royal family to have a decent home life. He added: 'All young men sowed their wild oats; but wasn't the prince at 38 rather beyond that age?' The king was particularly critical of Edward's affair with Thelma Furness. He asked his son if Lord Furness could be entirely trusted not to make trouble. The prince assured him that he had no anxieties about that.

George V then asked his son if he was genuinely happy; he added, did Edward 'not sometimes long to have someone he could turn to for sympathy and true affection as apart from mere physical satisfaction'. The prince admitted that he was not particularly happy. The king replied that he never looked very happy. They then discussed the future of the throne and the empire. The king pointed out that England had never had an unmarried king and that it would be an 'invidious' position. Edward would feel lost living on his own in Buckingham Palace. The prince told his father that one of the reasons he had not married was his distaste for marrying a foreign princess and he understood that the king would not wish him to marry a commoner. The king replied that times had changed and that he would be willing to consider 'a suitable well-born English girl'. The prince claimed that this was the first time that this had ever been suggested to him. He admitted that there was only one woman he had ever wished to marry and that was Freda Dudley Ward, and he still wanted to marry her. However, the king said he did not think that would do. The interview then came to an end. It had been a highly charged encounter for both men. During their conversation the prince had smoked countless cigarettes and frowned most of the time, but on the whole it had been 'amicable'.[102]

Afterwards the prince told Sir Lionel Halsey and Sir Godfrey Thomas that it had been 'a very satisfactory interview' and it had 'cleared the air'. He said that the king had been 'very nice, though he had spoken with complete frankness'. Sir Lionel Halsey thought that for the first time the prince had taken notice of what his father had said. Edward felt that the king was 'a bit old-fashioned' and he rather resented what he had said about his friends but other than that he admitted that his father's criticism of his behaviour was 'fair comment'.[103] Edward added that he hoped to have another talk with the king, but this seems to have been the last conversation the prince ever had with his father about marriage.[104] It was telling that in his interview with his father he told him that it was Freda, not Thelma, he wanted to marry. Both Freda and Edward knew they were trapped in an untenable situation, they had spent more than ten years trying to find a solution and failed. Neither could make a complete break or the commitment that would have allowed them to move on, but soon a catalyst from outside would change the situation forever.

Unlike Freda, Thelma was not seen as a good influence on the prince. One of the criticisms of Lady Furness was that she separated him from his old friends and surrounded him with her own dissolute circle. The economic crisis, which left over a million men unemployed, made observers more critical of the prince's lifestyle than they had been in the previous decade. It was felt that he was socialising in a 'fast' set who danced until dawn and then lay in bed until 2 p.m. the following day. At least part of the negative reaction to Thelma's circle was because they were predominantly Americans and thus considered alien.[105] Rosemary's mother, Millicent, Duchess of Sutherland, complained that Edward was more irresponsible than in the past. She blamed Lady Furness, who failed to restrain him in the way Freda had done.[106] The prince's behaviour in public and private deteriorated. He was seen looking bored at visits to hospitals and was often unpunctual for events.[107]

A joke circulating in society at the time was: 'If the Lord saved Daniel from the Lions' den, who will save David [the prince] from the fiery Furness?'[108] The diarist Chips Channon claimed that Thelma was the first woman who 'modernised' and 'Americanised' him. He blamed her for making him 'over-democratic, casual and a little common'.[109] Channon's judgement seems a little unfair; all those tendencies were already there in the prince – Thelma just reinforced them. However, some of the royal servants agreed that Lady Furness was Americanising their employer and bringing a touch of vulgarity to his household. Edward's butler-valet, Finch, a plain-speaking Yorkshireman who had cared for the prince since he was a child, thoroughly disapproved when Thelma introduced cocktails at York House. When Finch refused to mix these American innovations, his boss came to a compromise with him. Finch would make the drinks but only on the condition that he would not have to take part in the un-English fashion of adding ice to the concoction. Once the rebellious butler had brought the shaker into the drawing room, the prince was left to put the ice in himself.[110]

One summer, Lady Furness rented a house with her friend, the American socialite Betty Lawson Johnston, near the Chiberta golf course in Biarritz. The prince and his brother Geroge came to stay. In the interwar years, the resort on the Basque Coast of Spain attracted many British and American socialites. As one gossip columnist explained, Biarritz had 'a youthful, reckless, last week of the holidays feeling'.[111] Life and gossip revolved around the various villas. There was always plenty to do. For the energetic there were tennis tournaments, polo or golf. On the beach, Thelma was seen in her scarlet beach pyjama suit combing her long black hair, then she stripped off to her yellow swimsuit to bathe in the bracing Atlantic Ocean.[112] The prince attended an unorthodox dog show in which prizes were given for the worst dog and the dirtiest dog.

For visitors who wanted to go further afield, there were excursions along the coast to St-Jean-de-Luz. At St Jean visitors could dine at the Auberge or visit the yacht club in the tower overlooking the harbour. St-Jean was the centre of the sardine industry so on certain days the smell could be quite pungent. On the way back there was the choice of bathing at Guethary or going to a tea dance at the Grand Hotel at Ilbarritz. The Grand was known for its modernist garden. The hotel was perched on a cliff top above concrete terraces punctuated with statues. In the evenings the Bar Basque was a favourite meeting place for cocktails. After dinner everyone decamped to the Château D'Espagne, the nightclub in the casino.[113]

As a Catholic, Thelma decided that she would like to visit the shrine at Lourdes. She encouraged Edward to come with her. Lourdes attracted thousands of sick and disabled people who hoped to be cured. During Lady Furness and the prince's visit, halfway through the ceremony, the priest passed by carrying the Blessed Sacrament. Everyone, including the prince, knelt. Edward and his party were then shown around the shrine and taken to a house full of pictures of people who had been cured at Lourdes. Inside the house the prince was surrounded by hundreds of people who had heard that he was there.

The visit to Lourdes caused outrage back in Britain. The prince received dozens of letters complaining about Lady Furness taking the Protestant heir to the throne to a Catholic shrine. There was a protest by the Scottish Reformation Society who believed it could be interpreted as 'indicating some favour for an alien system of religion'. They feared that it could be used to compromise the constitutional position of the country. The prince's private secretary replied that the incident was 'devoid of any religious significance'.[114] Naïvely, Thelma could not understand why people were so outraged and she was angry about the attack on her. However, she received many letters from Catholics telling her to keep up the good work.[115] The visit to Lourdes, and Thelma's reaction, demonstrated her lack of understanding of the British constitution and history. When the prince became king, he would be defender of the Protestant faith. Thelma's faux pas was the type of misjudgement Freda would never have made.

To portray Lady Furness as a malign figure would be over-emphasising her influence and misjudging her character. She was kind and easy to get on with. The Duke and Duchess of York liked her very much. During Thelma's five-year affair with the prince the two couples socialised often.[116] At the time the Yorks were living at Royal Lodge, Windsor, which was near the Fort. Years later, Thelma remembered skating with the Duchess of York on the frozen pond in Windsor Great Park. They held on to kitchen chairs to get their balance and were soon laughing together.[117] Thelma just lacked the strength of character or inclination to discourage the prince's worst side. During his relationship with her he became more spoilt and petulant. Lacking depth herself, she encouraged his more superficial side.

However, to see their relationship as primarily about partying would be wrong. As in the prince's relationship with Freda, his affair with

Thelma was also about domesticity. Thelma hosted house parties and dinners at Fort Belvedere for their closest friends. It was an unusual move for a bachelor household and it emphasised Lady Furness's status in her lover's life. To explain Thelma's frequent visits to his home the prince announced that no unmarried woman would be entertained at Fort Belvedere. The press fell for his ruse and he was congratulated for the discretion he showed in not inviting his unmarried girlfriends for weekends.[118]

At the Fort, Edward would greet his guests at the door and lead them into an octagonal hall with white plaster walls and a black and white marble floor. In each of the eight corners was placed a bright yellow leather chair. The yellow colour scheme was continued in velvet curtains in the drawing room which, like the hallway, was octagonal. There was Chippendale furniture, Canaletto paintings on the wall and a baby grand piano.[119] Meals and clothes were informal during the day, but guests dressed for dinner and the prince put on a grey and red tartan kilt at night. After cocktails, dinner was served in the panelled dining room with equestrian paintings by George Stubbs on the walls. Up to ten guests would sit down at the walnut table to eat a simply cooked healthy meal. Food often came from the Duchy of Cornwall; there would sometimes be oysters from the prince's own oyster beds followed by roast beef. After dinner, guests played cards, did jigsaws or danced to the latest records played on a gramophone. To the strains of 'Tea for Two' Edward would take Thelma in his arms and sweep her into the octagonal hallway.

The prince told his guests that there were no rules at the Fort. Although he went to bed before midnight and was up early, they could stay up as late as they liked and get up when they wanted.[120] Yet even at the Fort informality only went so far; at one dinner a woman who had become part of the prince's intimate circle called him by his first name. Edward allowed it to pass, but when she did it again he turned to her and told her that he would rather she did not call him by his Christian name. The prince was not quite as democratic as he liked to seem and, when he chose, he expected to be treated with the respect due to his rank.[121]

As well as entertaining friends, Thelma and Edward also enjoyed quiet, intimate weekends together shut away from the world. At Fort

Belvedere the prince could relax and escape from the formality and artificiality of his public life. Gardening had become one of his passions and he enjoyed pottering in the grounds, pruning his trees, moving shrubs and planting herbaceous borders.[122] His favourite flowers were old-fashioned ones and he planted delphiniums, Sweet Williams, nasturtiums and phlox.[123] After gardening, before dinner, the prince would have a steam bath in the basement. Recreating the happiest times in Edward's childhood, when he had sat in Queen Mary's sitting room embroidering, during the evening Thelma and the heir to the throne would sit for hours stitching their latest tapestries together. Thelma wrote about how happy she was, content with the simplicity and lack of drama in their life together.[124]

Whenever the couple were separated they had a special ritual of exchanging two pairs of pink and green teddy bears which Thelma had bought at Harrods. If they went on a trip away from each other they swapped bears, so that they would always have something of each other with them. When the prince wrote to Thelma from abroad he never failed to send love from his teddies to her's.[125] Edward's pet name for Thelma was 'Toodles'.[126] He was fond of her, even though she did not inspire the grand passion he had felt for Freda. Mary, Duchess of Buccleuch, recalled how Edward used to fuss over Lady Furness. Before taking her out in his motorboat on Virginia Water, he would meticulously check that her life jacket was safely fastened, even though there was little risk on such shallow water.[127]

10

THE ACCIDENTAL
MATCHMAKER

Rather than being remembered for her great love affair with the prince, Thelma Furness is most well known for her role in introducing Wallis Simpson to the heir to the throne. A fellow American, at that time Wallis was married to her second husband, Ernest Simpson, who was an Anglo-American shipping broker, when she met the Prince of Wales. During her first years in London Wallis had been lonely; she felt that she did not fit into British society. She searched for like-minded friends among the American colony in the city. Ernest and Wallis began to socialise with young diplomats and managers of American banks and businesses.[1] It was an important moment for Wallis when she first met Thelma's sister Consuelo, who was married to Benjamin Thaw, first secretary of the American embassy in London. Consuelo and Wallis became close friends and then Consuelo introduced Wallis to Thelma. The two women immediately got on well as Thelma found Wallis 'fun'.[2]

In their memoirs, Thelma, Wallis and the Prince of Wales all recorded slightly different versions of how and when Edward first met

Mrs Simpson. According to Thelma, it was in late 1930 or January 1931, when Consuelo first brought Wallis over to cocktails at Thelma's house. Gloria and her friends also dropped in, making an impromptu party. The prince arrived to see Thelma and she introduced him to her new friend, Mrs Simpson. Thelma later wrote that it was an uneventful meeting; there was no electric tension between Wallis and Edward that night.[3]

Edward remembered it differently. He recalled in his memoir that he first met the woman he would marry when he went to Lady Furness's country house, Burrough Court, for a weekend's hunting with his brother George during the winter of 1931. Wallis was there with her husband. She did not ride, and she was suffering from a bad cold. The prince made conversation with her, saying that she must miss central heating. Always prepared to say what she thought, Wallis told him that, on the contrary, she liked cold houses. A mocking look came into her eyes when she said that every American woman who came to England was asked that question and she had hoped for something more original from him. Her willingness to challenge him immediately attracted Edward's attention and made her more interesting to him.[4]

In her memoir, Wallis corrected both Thelma's and the prince's accounts. She agreed with Thelma that their first meeting was in the winter of 1930–31, but it was at Burrough Court, not in London. Biographers confirm that the fateful date was 10 January 1931.[5] Thelma had planned a hunting weekend with the heir to the throne. Lord Furness was away on safari so, to keep up appearances, a married woman was required to act as chaperone. Wallis and Ernest Simpson were invited because Consuelo could not be there. At this point, Wallis hardly knew Thelma as they had only met at a couple of parties. At first, she was reluctant to go because she did not know what would be expected of her. However, she agreed to help her friend and because she was 'dying' to meet the heir to the throne.[6] As she admitted to her Aunt Bessie in a letter, she had made up her mind to meet the prince ever since she first arrived in London, but she never expected to do it in such an informal way.[7]

Ernest had no qualms about going; he was delighted to be asked and saw it as an honour. On the way to Melton Mowbray by train, Benjamin Thaw taught Wallis how to curtsy. Her nerves about the weekend were made worse by the fact that she had a stinking cold. Once at Burrough Court, when she first met the prince, Wallis was surprised to discover how small he was. At 5ft 7in he was only 2 inches taller than her, but she was immediately attracted by his *joie de vivre* and his naturalness.

Wallis also recorded her version of her first conversation with her future husband. She admitted that she was very nervous and had to censor what she would normally say because she had been told that with royalty you should not discuss politics or controversial topics.[8] Lady Kimberley, who was at the dinner, recalled that Wallis was sitting opposite the prince. She leant forward and asked him if he thought she was like Rita Kruger, a woman he had courted in New York. Edward replied abruptly, 'Good God! No!' and turned back to his neighbour.[9]

On her way back to London at the end of the weekend Wallis decided that the prince was one of the most attractive characters she had ever met. She was also fascinated by the air of melancholy that she had detected in him. Wallis asked Benjamin Thaw if he thought Edward would ever marry. He told her that the prince had been in love with several women, but nothing ever came of the relationships. Thaw doubted that, having waited so long, he would marry.[10]

After this first meeting, Wallis thought it unlikely that she would ever meet the prince again, but thanks to Thelma she did. The prince was sent to South America in a bid to boost the British export trade, which had dropped drastically due to German and American goods taking much of the market during the Depression. To prepare him for his trip, Thelma frequently spoke to Edward in Spanish. She helped him practise his speech for the opening of the British Empire Trade Exposition in Buenos Aires in March 1931.[11] From South America Edward wrote to Thelma to tell her how much he was missing her. In terms that echoed his earlier letters to Freda, he explained: 'I love you and that it is wonderful to think that every day is bringing us nearer together. That is a wonderful thought, my darling, and about the only thought that keeps me alive and doing what I have to on this trip.'[12]

On the prince's return from South America, Thelma held a reception for him at her house. When Edward saw Wallis, he recognised her and asked Thelma who she was. He then came over to Ernest and Wallis and said how nice it was to see them again.[13] In the following months,

Wallis became part of the Morgan sisters' circle. When she was presented at court in June, Consuelo Thaw lent her the dress she had worn for her own presentation while Thelma lent her the train, feathers and fan. At the presentation, the prince walked past Wallis with his great-uncle, the Duke of Connaught. She heard him say that something ought to be done about the lighting because it made all the women look so awful. When Wallis saw Edward afterwards, at a party at Thelma's, she teased the prince about this remark. Her challenging attitude evidently appealed to Edward, because he gave the Simpsons a lift home in his car. When Wallis asked him if he would like to come in for a drink, he said he could not that night, but he would like to see her flat another time.[14]

Wallis did not hear from the prince for the rest of the year, but in January 1932 the Simpsons received an unexpected invitation to Fort Belvedere for the weekend; from then on, the Simpsons became regular guests. It was largely due to Thelma that Mrs Simpson saw the prince so often. At first, when Thelma had suggested Wallis and Ernest should be invited to the Fort the prince had resisted the idea. He did not find Ernest Simpson stimulating company as he was a reserved, bookish man. However, Edward eventually gave in thanks to Thelma's persuasive powers.[15] Thelma considered Wallis to be one of her best friends. Mrs Simpson later played down the friendship, saying that although they often lunched together at the Ritz or Claridge's it was usually with other women. They were not intimate and did not exchange confidences.[16] However, they were close enough to spend Christmas together and Thelma gave her an expensive present of three rings: one sapphire, one ruby and one of diamonds. Sometimes, Wallis would come to the Fort without Ernest, to act as chaperone to Thelma for the weekend. Thelma collected her friend in her car and then they would drive down to the Fort together. After dinner Thelma, Wallis and the prince would have coffee together in the sitting room in front of a roaring fire. While Thelma and Edward embroidered, Wallis would read to them.[17] In her letters to her confidante, Aunt Bessie, Wallis painted a less harmonious picture; she complained about the experience when Thelma read aloud, saying that she could not stand 'the Morgan voice'. To escape from it, she made an excuse to write a letter in the dining room.[18]

It seems that initially Thelma encouraged Edward to invite Wallis because she feared that she was losing her power over the prince. She tried to find witty guests outside of his usual circles to keep him amused. Perhaps at first Thelma did not see Wallis as any threat. Although the two American women had a similar style, wearing their dark hair in the same sleek chignon and dressing immaculately, Thelma noted that Mrs Simpson was not beautiful or even pretty; she had large hands which she used too much to emphasise points. Nor was she as thin and chic as she was later to become.[19] Perhaps Thelma also felt secure because Wallis was supposed to be one of her best friends. At this stage, Wallis wrote that if the prince was at all attracted to her she was not aware of it.[20]

However, Wallis's sharp wit and repartee piqued the prince's interest more than his mistress had intended.[21] Perhaps the first sign that Edward was attracted to Wallis came in June 1933, when he gave a dinner party for her at Quaglino's for her birthday. The restaurant had been started by the two Quaglino brothers, one short and plump, the other tall, slim and intellectual. Situated just off Jermyn Street, it had become one of the most fashionable places to eat. The Prince of Wales frequently dined in the grill where snipe, woodcock, grilled sole, roast chicken and caviar were on the menu. Every year the two Quaglino brothers would travel abroad looking for new ideas to keep their restaurant fresh and exciting. On one trip they bought exclusive eau de Cologne for the finger bowls; another tour led to white truffles being added to the menu. As special patrons entered the restaurant, Van Straten's dance orchestra would play their favourite tune. Lady Furness was known to particularly like the accordion and tango tunes.[22]

At Wallis's birthday party, the prince gave her an orchid, which he assured her would bloom again within a year. The following month, Wallis organised a dinner at her flat for the Fourth of July. She prepared a special American menu of black bean soup, grilled lobster, fried chicken and a raspberry soufflé for ten guests including the prince, Thelma and Consuelo. The prince was placed at the head of the table, Ernest at the foot.[23]

In 1933 Thelma divorced Duke on the grounds of adultery with a woman called Helene Griselain in a Paris hotel. The suit was undefended.[24] According to Lord Furness's stepdaughter, Duke did not divorce Thelma for her infidelity because he would not have wanted to cite a member of the royal family as correspondent. However, he was very angry about the situation and never forgave Thelma.[25] As with Freda's divorce, there was no suggestion that this was to make Lady Furness available to marry the prince. Thelma admitted to dreams of living permanently with the man she loved, but she knew deep down that it was just a fantasy.[26] There was still great stigma attached to divorce and nowhere more so than at court. In Edward VII's reign no divorced person, even if they were the innocent party, would be received at court. This rule was relaxed slightly as divorce became more common after the First World War. During George V's reign the innocent party could be invited to court, but except for a few rare exceptions the guilty party continued to be excluded.[27] As divorced women, Thelma and Wallis were only able to be presented at court because they were the innocent parties. The Prince of Wales did not approve of such old-fashioned conventions and he had decided that once he was king he would try to end this form of social ostracism.[28] However, while such rigid rules were still in place, the chances of a twice-divorced woman like Thelma marrying the heir to the throne seemed extremely remote.

When Edward heard Thelma was divorcing Duke, he held her close and said that he was sure she had made the right decision. He was very happy about it, but he did not make any commitment to her.[29] Like Freda before her, Thelma began to feel that she was trapped in an emotional dead end. She could be the prince's mistress but not his wife. She confided in her old friend, the journalist Maury Paul, that her life was at a standstill. She did not want to be queen, and even if she had, she knew that a twice-divorced commoner would be unacceptable.[30] It seems that only Thelma's mother, the indefatigable Mrs Morgan, held out any hope for their long-term future. When someone said to her: 'You surely don't expect her to become Queen?' Mrs Morgan immediately replied: 'Stranger things than that have happened!'[31]

Unlike Freda, Thelma began to trade on her royal connections. She had become a style icon whose every outfit was analysed by the newspapers. One journalist enthused that she could 'wear a backless dress better than anyone else I know'.[32] In January 1934 she appeared in an advert for Pond's Cold Cream. The cosmetic company paid many leading socialites in both England and America to appear in their adverts. Lady Diana Cooper and Sheila Loughborough had also promoted the face cream. Pond's used these aspirational models to change their image and appeal to middle-class women. Using cosmetics was becoming more fashionable as ordinary women wanted to bring a touch of Hollywood glamour into their own lives. During the 1920s the middle-class market had favoured more expensive European brands such as Helena Rubinstein and Chanel because they were perceived as more exclusive. Pond's rebranding strategy worked and there was a boom in sales.[33] In the advert, beneath an alluring photograph that emphasised Thelma's dark eyes and porcelain skin, Lady Furness was described as moving 'among the most exclusive set'. Thelma endorsed the product by telling potential buyers that she cleansed her face with Pond's Cold Cream several times during the day. She explained: 'It prevents the pores enlarging. I find it more effective than anything else for keeping powder on.'[34] Although many society women also took part in this promotion, it certainly was not the behaviour of a potential future Queen of England. Loathing as he did women wearing make-up and any form of vulgar self-advertisement, one can only imagine King George's reaction, if he heard about this latest venture of his son's American mistress.

Early in 1934, Thelma decided that she should travel to America to see her twin sister Gloria. They planned to meet in New York and then travel to California. When Thelma told the prince that she would be gone for five or six weeks, he did not try to stop her, but he said that he would miss her very much.[35] A few days before she sailed she invited Wallis Simpson for lunch at the Ritz. When Wallis said that the prince would be lonely without her, Thelma asked her to look after him while she was away and to make sure he did not get into any 'mischief'.[36]

Wallis took her friend at her word. While Thelma was in America her supposed friend spent a great deal of time with the Prince of Wales. Wallis wrote to Aunt Bessie that she had 'inherited' him from Thelma. At first, she felt that he was just calling on her because he missed Lady Furness.[37] However, although Edward was regularly in contact with Thelma by telephone or cable, gradually she was being supplanted. The prince asked Wallis to a dinner party he was giving at the Dorchester.

During the evening, Wallis impressed him by showing a genuine interest in his work. He began calling regularly at Wallis's daily cocktail parties at Bryanston Court. Although she did not have a great deal of money to spend, Wallis had exquisite taste and created an elegant home and gave her guests delicious food. She gathered around her an eclectic mixture of diplomats, politicians and intelligent women. They discussed new ideas about Hitler, Mussolini, Stalin, Roosevelt and Chiang Kai-shek.

Unlike Thelma, Wallis was very well informed about politics. Like Freda and Rosemary, she had strong views and was willing to express them. Wallis explained in her memoir that she thought it was important to be interesting and that she was prepared to argue her ideas 'spiritedly' against men.[38] The prince admired her feistiness and the fact that when she disagreed with him she stood up to him and argued with him.[39] Wallis was a challenge to the prince; Thelma was not. According to his memoir, Mrs Simpson was the most independent woman he had ever met.[40] Her wit stimulated him. She was one of the few people who could make him laugh out loud. Friends said that at dinner he would lean forward waiting for one of her witticisms and then he would roar with laughter.[41]

Once the parties were over the prince stayed on at the Simpsons' flat. At first it was just for supper, but as the weeks went by he used to stay up late with Wallis long after Ernest had gone to bed. As Freda had experienced in the first stage of their affair, he was soon telephoning Wallis two or three times a day and he seemed at a loose end.[42] Like Freda, Mrs Simpson built up his confidence and made him feel good about himself. She mothered him and bossed him around but, unlike Freda, with Wallis there was sometimes an edge of cruelty in her tone. She lacked Freda's genuine warmth, kindness and integrity. The prince's biographer Frances Dondaldson wrote that all his life Edward had been looking for a masculine woman who would dominate him. Wallis was that woman; she was made to dominate.[43]

As the prince was seen with Wallis, there began to be gossip that she was his latest conquest. Wallis told her aunt that she was not in the habit of stealing her girlfriends' boyfriends. She denied an affair had begun while Thelma was away, claiming that she just made him laugh and they liked to dance together. She added that they always had Ernest around, so it was safe.[44] However, emotionally her relationship with the prince had deepened.

While Edward and Wallis drew closer, Thelma was having a flirtation of her own in America with Prince Aly Khan. Thelma was almost 30, while Aly was only 23, but the sexual chemistry between them was instant when they met at a dinner party in New York. Aly's father, the Aga Khan, was seen by Muslim Ismailis as the direct descendant of the Prophet Muhammad. He was the world leader of the Nizari Ismailis, the second-largest branch of Shia Islam, a non-radical sect with 15 million followers in twenty-five countries.[45] The Aga Khan was one of the world's wealthiest men and an international celebrity. His son Aly lived a playboy lifestyle, racing cars and horses. However, he also took his role as heir apparent to his father seriously, and he spent three months of the year visiting followers in Asia, Africa and South America. He was worshipped by Ismailis as a living deity. Like the Prince of Wales, he was often mobbed on his tours and he found the experience both exhilarating and exhausting.[46]

In his private life, Aly was irresistible to women. The American author and songwriter Elsa Maxwell described him as 'un homme fatal' with 'animal vitality'.[47] Not only was he dark and very handsome, he also knew just how to make a woman feel good about herself. He loved women and took a delight in the way they walked, dressed, spoke and thought. Adding to his attraction, there was also a hint of danger about him because he was an exciting, risk-taking figure.[48] He knew that all women believed in the *coup de foudre* (love at first sight), and he made each woman he seduced feel that was what he felt when he first saw her.[49] As Elsa Maxwell explained, when he fell in love with a woman he fell madly and deeply. He would make her feel that no other person existed for him. He would be absorbed with her to the exclusion of all others. He would dance cheek to cheek with her 'slowly and rapturously', as though it was the last time he would ever hold her in his arms. It was intoxicating, but the only problem was his infatuation might last for only one night.[50]

When he focused his attention on Thelma she found it hard to resist. Although she claimed that she was flattered but not interested in a relationship, Thelma went to dinner with him the following night. The next morning Aly sent her a huge box of flowers. Before Thelma was due to return to England they dined and danced together again. When she reached her cabin on the *Bremen* it was full of red roses from her new admirer. She then discovered, to her surprise, that Aly had booked himself on board the ship. During the crossing, they dined together every night.[51] The fact that she was the mistress of the Prince of Wales made her more attractive to Aly. He was competitive and liked to prove his prowess. He often seduced women who were married or in a serious relationship. If he detected restlessness or frustration in a woman he would capitalise on it.[52] Knowing that there was no long-term future with the Prince of Wales, Thelma was receptive to Aly's seductive wiles. Gossip soon spread about Thelma and Aly, and it was said that she now had captured both the White Prince and the Black Prince.[53] Inevitably, some of the rumours reached the Prince of Wales's ears and he was not amused.

By the time Thelma returned to England in March 1934 everything had changed. When she was reunited with the prince at her Regent's Park house, he was polite but distant. He told her that he had heard Aly Khan had been paying her attention. Thelma asked him if he was jealous, but the prince did not answer. The following weekend they met again at the Fort. When her lover was still cold towards her Thelma met Wallis at her Bryanston Court flat to get her advice as a friend. Both Thelma and Wallis gave different accounts of this meeting. According to Lady Furness, when she asked Wallis if she knew why the prince's attitude had changed, Mrs Simpson assured her that Edward still loved her. She added that he had been lost without her. However, Thelma began to have her doubts when at the end of her visit Edward called to speak to Wallis, not her, on the phone.[54] Wallis recalled the afternoon differently. Apparently, Thelma said that the prince was avoiding her; she then asked her friend 'point-blank' if he was 'keen' on her. Wallis had been expecting the question and answered that she thought he liked her and might be fond of her but, if she meant was he in love with her, the answer was no.[55]

According to Thelma's memoir, the next weekend, she joined the prince and the Simpsons at Fort Belvedere. The first night Thelma went to bed early as she had a cold. The following evening, at dinner, Thelma noticed that Edward and Wallis had developed little private jokes. When she saw her supposed friend playfully slap the prince's hand as he picked up a salad leaf with his fingers, Thelma shook her head at Wallis, but she just looked back at her defiantly. Thelma was shocked that Wallis treated the heir to the throne in this way; she would never have dared to behave with such familiarity.[56] Perhaps that was why her hold on the future king was less than her successor's. Thelma was always slightly in awe of the prince, partly because she was so in love with him but also because of his status. She was far more subservient than Freda, Rosemary or Wallis ever were, even lighting Edward's cigars for him.[57] She failed to realise what the other important women in his life quickly understood: the prince liked to be treated strictly, sometimes even cruelly, by his women. Rather than a pampered prince, he wanted to be chastised like a naughty little boy. Wallis was already perfecting this technique. She admitted to one friend that she always kicked him hard under the table if he was going on too much in a conversation, then she would kick him again to continue.[58]

There has been much speculation about Wallis's sexual hold over the prince but it seems that, as in his relationship with Freda, her power over him was at least as much psychological as physical. When Edward and Mrs Simpson first consummated their relationship is a subject of debate. Contemporaries who wanted to discredit Wallis believed that she used sexual techniques she had learnt to ensnare the prince. However, the Windsors' biographer, Michael Bloch, points out that Edward always rejected suggestions that Wallis had been his lover before they married. A judicial inquiry in the winter of 1936–37 found no evidence that they had been guilty of an adulterous relationship. Bloch writes that his letters to Wallis reveal a 'mother–son relationship'; they were full of baby talk and were childish and adoring, pleading for her affection.[59] These letters have the same characteristics as his letters to Freda, although the ones to his earlier mistress are perhaps even more effusive and loving. As Freda drew back from the prince's life, Thelma had not been able to fill her elegant shoes. Edward had now found someone who was ready, willing and able to do so. He was Wallis's slave – a role he had long desired in Freda's life but one she had rejected.

After watching her friend and lover together, Thelma knew what had happened: she had been replaced. When the prince came up to see her in her bedroom, Thelma asked him directly: 'Darling, is it Wallis?' The prince's features froze, he told her not to be silly and walked out of the room.[60] Thelma left Fort Belvedere the next morning, never to return. Someone else at the Fort that evening told a different story. The prince was having a dinner party and Thelma was not there. She then arrived, banging on the door so loudly that it sounded as though someone was trying to break in. She stormed into the party and then the prince went into the library with her. The guests could hear her voice coming from the room but not his. She then stormed out, leaving the Fort forever. Edward returned to the dinner party without saying anything about what had happened.[61]

Whatever the precise denouement, the outcome was the same; as Wallis wrote to Aunt Bessie, Thelma's rule was over.[62] In May 1934 Thelma's old friend Maury Paul reported: 'Over in London, the Prince of Wales, who once was noted as the frequent dancing partner of Lady Furness, now is tripping the light fantastic with a Mrs Simpson. And the air becomes frigid whenever Lady Furness and Mrs Simpson happen to meet – which, fortunately, is not often.'[63]

Thelma was not the prince's only mistress to be banished. The callousness with which Edward treated Freda, his lover, confidante and best friend, shocked their mutual friends. In the early days of Wallis being on the scene Freda and her daughters were still part of his life. When in 1933 Angie was presented at court, the prince was there to give her moral support. The girl chosen by journalists as the deb of the year was Primrose Salt. The prince teased Angie, warning her that she had better go to the hairdresser, stand up straight and lower her voice, or she would never measure up to Miss Salt. The king was unable to attend the presentation as he had an attack of rheumatism, so the prince was going to lead his mother to the throne. The night before Angie's presentation Edward boosted her confidence by saying that when the ceremony was over and he came down among all the debutantes she would outshine Miss Salt because it would be Angie he talked to. True to his word, on the day, the prince, dressed in his Welsh Guards uniform, singled out his favourite.[64]

Wallis knew about Edward's continued attachment to Freda and seemed to believe that his long-term mistress would remain. She told her aunt that although the prince was attentive to her he saw equally as much of Mrs Dudley Ward.[65] He was open with her, saying that he would visit Freda in St John's Wood before stopping off to see her at Bryanston Court.[66] As late as February 1934 the prince was seen at Ciro's dancing with Freda.[67] Members of the king and queen's household also thought that his affair with Mrs Simpson would not last and he would return to Freda.[68] The diarist Chips Channon wrote that Wallis was determined to 'storm society' while she was the prince's favourite, because she was aware that he would eventually leave her because he left everyone in time.[69]

However, as Edward fell more under Wallis's spell, Freda's days were numbered. At first she had not noticed that the prince was visiting her less. She had heard gossip about Wallis, but Edward had never mentioned her, and she was not concerned. Freda had been distracted because Pempie had been dangerously ill with appendicitis. For several days Freda had thought her daughter might die and she anxiously kept a vigil by her bedside. For many weeks the invalid was not well enough to do more than lie quietly in Freda's garden. When Pempie was on the mend Freda had time to realise that she had not heard from Edward. The end of their sixteen-year relationship was brutal and abrupt. When Freda called St James's Palace she was told by the operator: 'I have orders not to put you through.' Freda and the prince never spoke again, and she was deeply hurt by his neglect.[70] Many years later, Freda told an interviewer that she had always known their affair would end sometime, but she wished that he had had the courage to tell her face to face.[71]

It was thought by many people that Wallis had insisted that the prince cut off all communication with his former mistresses. Chips Channon wrote that Mrs Simspon had banned Thelma and all her circle from York House.[72] However, in an interview many years later Wallis denied she had been responsible. In the case of Thelma, she said something had happened between Lady Furness and the prince that had destroyed the warmth and easiness of their relationship. As for Freda, Wallis always admitted that she was the prince's first true love. She said that she had known that Edward was very attached to his long-term mistress. At first

Wallis had encouraged hostesses to invite Freda to parties where the prince would be present, but it seems that she had turned down the invitations.[73] There is a ring of truth to Wallis's story. When the prince was first with Freda he had behaved unchivalrously to old girlfriends like Lady Coke, not because Freda requested it, but because that is what he thought she wanted. Perhaps he was just repeating the same pattern in his new relationship with Wallis.

The prince's behaviour towards Freda and Thelma was the talk of society. Friends divided into three camps, each supporting their chosen mistress. The diarist Chips Channon wrote that it was 'war to the knife between the past and the present'.[74] As an act of solidarity some of the prince's old friends refused to socialise with Wallis. However, Chips Channon and the society hostesses Sibyl Colefax and Emerald Cunard rallied round Mrs Simpson. Lady Colefax claimed that the criticism of Wallis was very unfair and due to the jealousy of the women he had liked in the past. She told the novelist Maire Belloc Lowndes that they had all made him 'dreadfully unhappy'. None of them had been faithful to him and that had made him feel 'wretched'.[75]

Supporting the new regime was controversial. Lady Cunard was attacked by the prince's old flame Portia Stanley for befriending Wallis.[76] At a weekend house party at Portia's country estate, the first woman member of parliament, Nancy Astor, wrote in her diary that the Duke and Duchess of Kent and Sheila Milbanke (previously Loughborough) were there. They were all friends of Freda and they hated the way the Prince of Wales was 'pushing' Mrs Simpson. He had refused point blank to attend a court ball unless Wallis was invited. Lady Astor complained that everyone seemed to be suffering from a new disease, which she dubbed 'Simpsonitis', which involved sucking up to Wallis. Apparently Emerald Cunard was the biggest sychophant around 'Queenie Simpson'.[77]

Other members of the prince's circle remained loyal to Thelma. The prince's household comptroller, 'G' Trotter, wrote to Edward criticising his transfer of affection from Thelma to Wallis. The heir to the throne did not want to hear what his old friend had to say and when 'G' mentioned it again he was dismissed after years of loyal service. However, not everyone in the prince's set was sorry to see Thelma or Freda go. Edward's equerry John Aird thought there was little to choose between

Mrs Simspon and Lady Furness; in his opinion, they were both 'tough girls' who deserved to be treated with the callousness the prince had shown.[78] Chips Channon was critical of Freda's circle, writing that while they were 'amusing and witty' the set was 'small and suffocating with their high-pitched voices and pettiness and criticism and anti-everything'. He claimed that Wallis was a better woman than them all.[79]

Many people commented that Edward's behaviour had improved under Wallis's strict rule. The diplomat, writer and politician Harold Nicolson was impressed by the way she had changed the prince. He thought Edward was more relaxed and seemed less nervous and shy. While he was with the couple at the theatre, Wallis stopped Edward smoking during the interval. However, Nicolson thought that for all her good intentions, she was separating the prince from the type of people he should be mixing with.[80] Duff Cooper, who spent many weekends with the couple at Fort Belvedere, also thought she was a sensible woman. However, he believed she was as 'hard as nails' and did not genuinely love the prince.[81] His wife, Lady Diana, went further: she thought Mrs Simpson was bored by her lover, and was cold towards him not as a strategy to lure him in, but because he irritated her. Although Diana found Wallis amusing, she described her as common and like Becky Sharp, Thackeray's aspiring heroine in *Vanity Fair*.[82]

Wallis's political influence on the prince was even more controversial and has been the subject of decades of debate.[83] Many of Edward's friends noticed that the prince was becoming more pro-German; both in public and private he argued for a strong friendship with Germany.[84] There was a great deal of gossip about the Prince of Wales's Nazi leanings. According to Chips Channon, he had been influenced by Emerald Cunard, who admired the German special envoy to Britain, Joachim von Ribbentrop.[85] More recent research suggests that the link was more direct. Hitler had told Ribbentrop to flirt with Wallis and become intimate with her in order to influence Edward. The German diplomat began to send her seventeen red roses or carnations each day. According to some observers, this gesture was to remind her of the number of nights they had spent together.[86] However, Wallis's recent biographer believes that although she enjoyed a flirtation with Ribbentrop there is no evidence of an affair.[87]

Whatever other people thought of his new mistress, the prince had made up his mind that he wanted to be with her. It seems that he had learnt from his experience with Freda that exclusivity was essential for a fulfilling relationship. He was not willing to get caught in another toxic circle where no one felt secure. His feelings for Wallis had much in common with his bond with Freda. His old friend Walter Monckton wrote that it would be a great mistake to believe Edward was in love with Wallis purely in the physical sense of the word. He had found a spiritual affinity with her. He believed that they were made for each other and that she was an inspiration to him to be at his best and to do his best.[88] Anyone who has read his letters to Freda would recognise these sentiments. However, this time he was not willing to listen to reason and take no for an answer; he was determined to make a lasting commitment no matter how great the cost.

PART TWO

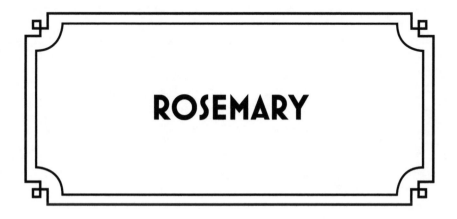

ROSEMARY

11

ROSEMARY IN LOVE

n the spring of 1918, once Rosemary knew that her relationship with
the prince would not end in marriage, she did not waste time on self-
pity. Like Edward, within months she was more deeply in love than
she had ever been before. However, as with Edward's affair with Freda,
Rosemary's relationship with her new lover was to prove complicated
and at times painful.

A year after Rosemary's romance with the prince came to an end,
she walked down the aisle with a handsome war hero. In March 1919
Rosemary married William Ward, Viscount Ednam, at St Margaret's
Westminster. Dressed simply in a long tunic of white chiffon edged
with point de Venise lace, Rosemary was the perfect post-war bride.
Her twelve bridesmaids were dressed in yellow chiffon with touches of
green to represent spring while the daffodils they carried symbolised
hope for the future. It was a celebration of a new era; during the war
ceremonies had been scaled back and even the numbers of bridesmaids
were rationed. Recognising the past, while looking forward to the
future, Rosemary promised that 'every friend she has ever had is to be
invited to the wedding'.[1]

Although Rosemary had not been considered suitable to marry into the royal family, many of its members attended her wedding. Queen Alexandra, her daughter Princess Victoria and Princess Alice, Countess of Athlone, were among the guests. However, all eyes were drawn to the man who had so recently wanted to walk down the aisle by Rosemary's side. When Pathé News filmed the occasion, as well as the doll-like bride and the groom in his army uniform, the film-makers could not resist showing the Prince of Wales, walking alone along the pavement with his cane. Eve, the gossip columnist at *The Tatler*, spotted him there and described him as 'one of the boys who won't grow up isn't he?' and added that he had decided that he wanted to see the world as a bachelor before he settled down 'into even the silken chains of Royal matrimony'.[2] In fact it was not quite that simple. As what the prince described as 'an engagement epidemic' swept through his contemporaries, he felt left out.[3] He found it particularly hard seeing the woman he had wanted to marry wed another man. He confessed to his new love, Freda, that the engagement had been a great surprise to him and he couldn't 'help feeling a little sad'.[4]

Inevitably, Rosemary also thought about what might have been. After she was greeted at one of her new husband's family estates by his tenants carrying hundreds of torchlights to welcome her, in her first letter to her mother following the wedding Rosemary wrote that it was a good thing that she had never seriously considered marrying the prince purely for the sake of glamour because she had now got that and the man she loved too.[5]

Like the prince, who had dived headlong into his love affair with Freda Dudley Ward immediately after the end of their relationship, Rosemary had not waited long to find new love; she was soon involved with William, Viscount Ednam, heir to the Earl of Dudley. Twenty-five years old, dark haired and very good looking, William, known to his friends as Eric, was considered a catch. He worked hard and played hard and, as one gossip columnist euphemistically explained, he had already been 'a good deal about in the world'.[6] Another added that he 'is something of a "lad"'.[7] At Oxford University he ended up in court for playing polo riding a bicycle in Merton Street with Lord Cranborne and Prince Paul of Serbia. The over-exuberant undergraduates were each fined 2s 6d and costs.[8] Eric loved sport, particularly if it had an element of danger. He was a keen horseman who relished the thrill of steeplechasing. His family owned land in Staffordshire and Worcestershire and some of the most valuable collieries and iron- and steel works in the country. During the war, he had served as a lieutenant in the 10th Hussars; he had been wounded once and awarded the Military Cross.

By May 1918 Eric was showing an interest in Rosemary. They had known each other since they were children but after meeting again in the heightened wartime atmosphere they began writing to each other. He had seen three photographs of her in *The Tatler* and wanted her to send him a picture of her to keep. As well as being attracted to her, like the prince, he was impressed with her war work. In one of his first letters to her he wrote with admiration about what she was doing. He told her that he thought it was 'wonderful' of her. As the battles intensified in the spring of 1918 Millicent's hospital moved to a château near St-Omer. Once all the huts and equipment had been transported it become a casualty clearing station. Eric wrote to Rosemary: 'Although you say you live in the lap of luxury at your chateau and have plenty to eat yet I expect you are having a pretty rough time really and everything must be very uncertain and then very noisy what with guns and bombing!!'[9] He was right: Rosemary had underplayed the danger she faced; a neighbouring hospital in the town had been hit and patients suffered fractured skulls and limbs. When Rosemary, Millicent and their team arrived at St-Omer there were no dugouts or trenches. While they were being constructed the nurses were given orders that if there was an attack those on duty were to remain in the wards, while those off duty should scatter into the surrounding woods and get under the trees where they were less likely to be hit by shrapnel.

While Rosemary assisted in the operating theatre at her mother's hospital, Eric was at the British General Headquarters in Italy. He promised to visit her when he returned to France. By the end of the war in November 1918 their feelings for each other had intensified. Unlike in her previous relationships, this time Rosemary was deeply in love. When Rosemary went to France with her mother and aunt, Tommy Rosslyn, to see the British troops' official entry into Lille, Tommy wrote to Eric telling him how Rosemary was counting the days until she would see him again. She added that her niece would go home tomorrow if Millie would let her, but the duchess wanted her by her side to share in the victory as she had been her second-in-command throughout the war. As they stood with Winston Churchill and Lieutenant Colonel Bernard Montgomery to watch the soldiers march past, it seems that Rosemary's thoughts were elsewhere. Tommy wrote to Eric: 'She could not be more in love, it's quite painful. The only happy moment in the day is the early morning when your letter arrives – after that complete gloom.'[10] In this relationship it seems Eric had the upper hand and Rosemary feared that he was not missing her as much as she missed him. She visualised him having the time of his life in London and not giving her a second thought. Tommy added: 'My dear!! You have no idea how the child loves you – Perhaps it's not good for you to know all this!'[11]

Unlike in her previous relationships with John Manners and the prince, this time it was the real thing for Rosemary. She admitted her feelings in a letter to Eric written from Inver Lodge, Galway, where she was on a fishing trip. She complained that she had not received a letter from him and asked whether this was due to 'laziness, stinginess […] or what!!' She rebuked him: 'You may be sure I could not be more annoyed.' She told him that she had been fishing on the lakes and caught mackerel, but although it was 'very peaceful and delicious' she was finding it hard to be apart from him. She wrote that she was 'getting through the day fairly well but it is very lonely without you my angel. And I want you to come back to your Rose so much and quick too please for I believe I must be in love.'[12]

In the post-war era, after so many young men had been killed in the conflict, the younger generation realised that life could be short. The moment had to be seized. When Duff Cooper, Rosemary's former admirer, met Eric and Rosemary at Lady Desborough's house party in January 1919 he suspected they were about to get engaged. They married just two months later; Duff and Diana followed them by marrying later that same year. Rosemary and Eric's alliance pleased the Sutherlands and the Dudleys: the *Illustrated London News* noted that it 'gives great satisfaction to the families on each side'.[13] Like Millicent, Eric's mother, the Countess of Dudley, had run a hospital in France during the war. Reflecting the interwoven circles in which the prince and his friends socialised, Rosemary's new husband was the cousin of Freda's husband William Dudley Ward. The prince had known Lord Ednam at Oxford but had not been impressed with him, describing him as 'coshy', meaning 'stuck up'.[14] At first, Edward was concerned about whether Eric was good enough for Rosemary. He wrote to Freda: 'I really only know Eric by sight though I'm sure he's nice and they'll be very happy; I only hope so for her sake as she's such a darling and I guess he's a very lucky man!!'[15] However, over the next few years Edward got to know Eric better and they became good friends.

In the first years of their marriage Rosemary and Eric were very happy. When their first son, Billy, was born in January 1920 Eric wrote with pride to his wife: 'All my admiring love to you my queen – I think of you the whole time and miss you so much that it just isn't worth a damn thing without you.'[16] When he had to leave his wife and his baby son to return to his cavalry barracks in Canterbury he wrote that 'it gave me a proper pang to leave you last night – looking so sweet and lovely with the little teardrops in your eyes – it gave me the sobs hot and strong. Quite a "movie scene"!'[17]

Unlike with many of his other ex-girlfriends, the prince remained close to Rosemary. He stood as sponsor to her eldest son and, shortly after the birth, he wrote to her sending a present for his godson. He explained that he would like to see her again before he sailed for Australia on his seven-month tour. Showing how their relationship had adapted to the new circumstances, he also sent his 'best love to you and Eric'.[18]

With their growing family, the Ednams needed a London home where they could settle permanently. In 1921 they bought a house in Cheyne Walk overlooking the river for £14,000. It was a fine Queen Anne building; most of the reception rooms were panelled and the drawing room led out into a delightful garden.[19] It had been the home of the artist James Abbott McNeill Whistler. Eric wrote to Rosemary: 'If you feel you'd never live anywhere else we'd better buy,' then he added a comment that was to prove all too prescient: 'tho' I feel we shall regret it!'[20] Like Freda, Rosemary was a talented amateur interior designer, and she enjoyed doing the house up. In the dining room, Rosemary had the walls painted with scenes of the River Thames and Chelsea Bridge in the era when picturesque sailing boats plied up and down.[21]

In the early 1920s, the first major sadness which was to marr the Ednams' life together happened; Rosemary lost a baby daughter late in her pregnancy. Naming her after her mother as Mary Rose, Eric poignantly described their sense of loss:

> Poor darling little Mary Rose – it makes me so terribly sad to think of her lying stiff and stark in her little piece of paper awaiting the doctor's inspection instead of warm and snug inside my Rosie! And she too so lovely and sad and weak in her bed – would to feel I was in it with you to comfort her.

Rosemary was very ill after the stillbirth, but Eric had to leave her to go with the army to Italy. He wrote an anguished letter to her explaining how he felt:

> My angel – I am in a terrible stew today – firstly worried about you – I hated leaving you in that state yesterday when I wanted to be with you more than at any time before – secondly because I am so terribly bored and depressed and have such an overwhelming fit of the blues. I feel I can't possibly live through the day [...] Was ever a man more highly tried? My life away from you is impossible and worse than death.

Describing his 'volcanic state of mind', he explained that it was because 'I love you so much, you divine sweet and my love grows daily so much stronger that I simply can't concentrate on anything else, or bear to be parted from you'. He ended the letter by writing: 'I love you to death always, and I'll never be away from you again as long as we live.'[22]

The couple went on to have two more sons, John Jeremy in 1922 and Peter four years later, but they never had another daughter. Rosemary reconciled herself to the situation and was very proud of her boys. Writing to Duff Cooper to congratulate him on the birth of his son, John Julius, she confessed: 'I like boys much better.'[23] Like Freda with her daughters, Rosemary was a devoted mother who was adored by her three little boys. Her love was reciprocated; in her papers, there is a letter written in French to her by her eldest son Billy when she was away sending 'mes meilleurs baisers' (lots of kisses).[24]

Although to begin with they were deeply in love, as the years went by Rosemary and Eric's marriage came under strain. They began to spend increasingly long periods of time away from each other. Both had parents to visit abroad; Rosemary often stayed with her mother in France while Eric's father also settled across the Channel. Partly vindicating the royal qualms about Rosemary marrying the prince, Millicent's love life had turned out to be messy. By 1919 her marriage to Major Fitzgerald was over. He had remained a womaniser and allegedly had fathered several illegitimate children. As he was a Roman Catholic Millicent obtained an annulment.[25]

A few months later, Millicent married for a third time. Showing her individuality, she wore a black wedding dress and sables.[26] Her latest husband was another professional soldier called George Hawes. He was a small man with a moustache who bore a striking resemblance to Charlie Chaplin. George had an eye for art and beauty and, at first, he appeared to worship Millicent, admiring her clothes and appearance. However, this relationship turned out to be another disaster because her new husband was homosexual. He often unleashed his cruel tongue and bad temper on her. Unwilling to be undermined further, she divorced him.[27] Acknowledging her matrimonial mistakes, Millicent charted her unhappy love life in an aptly named novel she wrote called *That Fool of a Woman*, published in 1925. With no wish to return to the censorious circles of England, Millicent made her permanent home in France. She bought a former monastery in Juigne, a village near Angers. The house had been derelict for years but Millicent brought it back to life, creating a charming home which her friends and family loved to visit. Rosemary came often, and the Prince of Wales visited once.[28]

In the early 1920s, Eric's father Lord Dudley was also behaving like a lovestruck teenager. After being widowed, he married the musical comedy star Gertie Millar. They moved abroad, and Eric often stayed with them in their villa in the Pas-de-Calais, France.

Separation was not good for the Ednams' marriage. At first, Rosemary and Eric just playfully complained to each other when they were apart. Each moaned that the other did not write often enough. When Rosemary was visiting her mother in France, Eric wrote: 'I really want you back more than I care to admit – tho' I could not loathe you more tonight for not writing to me. I am making this letter completely illegible out of spite.'[29] Rosemary wrote in a similar vein to him when he was away, telling him: 'You don't deserve a long letter as you never write to me or post the letters with any sense if you do. I love you all the same.'[30]

Although these comments were just light-hearted banter, there was a more serious side to their separations; too much time apart left them open to temptation. The Ednams' love life became as complicated as Freda and the prince's tangled affairs. Just a few years into their marriage, Eric had an affair with Venetia Montagu, who as Venetia Stanley had been the great love of the wartime prime minister, Herbert Henry Asquith. She had married the politician Edwin Montagu during the war but by 1918 she was mixing regularly with Eric as they were both part of the Diana and Duff Cooper set. Once Rosemary and Eric were married the three couples often socialised together. Evidence suggests that Venetia's only daughter Judith, born in 1923, was fathered by Eric. It seems likely that Venetia's husband Edwin knew the truth, but it was kept a secret from most of their family and friends.[31]

Although Eric was unfaithful to Rosemary he still loved her, writing to her while he was staying with her family in Dunrobin in March 1923: 'Sweetheart [...] I miss you like hell and am terribly lonely and lost without you with all these stiffs [...] I enjoy it all 100% less when you are not here.'[32] The Ednams moved in overlapping circles with the prince and Freda. In the hedonistic atmosphere of the post-war era infidelity was acceptable provided that everyone behaved with discretion and did not create too many embarrassing scenes. Reflecting this tolerant attitude, when Edwin Montagu died in November 1924 both Eric and Rosemary attended his funeral. After his death Rosemary and Eric continued to attend Venetia's house parties at Breccles Hall, Norfolk.

Breccles was a Tudor manor house which had kept many of its original features. It had an oak-panelled great hall, doors which were fitted with latches and stained-glass windows. In the bedrooms there was no wallpaper, beams in the wall and ceiling being exposed instead.[33] However, charming though these features were, the lack of modern

Rosemary and her mother Millicent in a car. (Sutherland Collection/Staffordshire Archive)

The Bystander, January 15, 1913   125

Wanted: A Speedy Recovery
AND THE CONFIRMATION OF AN INTERESTING RUMOUR

[Photograph]   **LADY ROSEMARY LEVESON-GOWER**   *[Lallie Charles]*

Daughter of the Duke and Duchess of Sutherland, an unconfirmed rumour of whose engagement to a prominent member of the nobility has recently been circulated. Lady Rosemary is the latest victim of a fashionable malady, from which we wish her a speedy and complete recovery

Rosemary, 'the girl of girls' in 1913. (© Illustrated London News Ltd/Mary Evans)

Rosemary in a nurse's uniform (staring straight ahead) with the Prince of Wales at her mother's hospital in France, 1917. (Sutherland Collection/Staffordshire Archive)

Eric, Lord Ednam, in uniform; by Bassano. (© National Portrait Gallery, London)

Eric Ednam (looking down) with the Prince of Wales and Prince George in Jamaica, 1931. (© Illustrated London News Ltd/Mary Evans)

Freda's wedding to William Dudley Ward, 1913. (© Illustrated London News Ltd/Mary Evans)

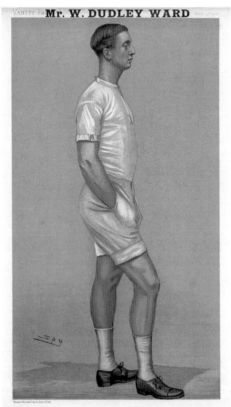

VANITY FAIR **Mr. W. DUDLEY WARD**

William Dudley Ward caricatured by Spy in *Vanity Fair*. (Mary Evans Picture Library)

Freda posing in a floaty
dress in 1916. (© Illustrated
London News Ltd/
Mary Evans)

Freda at the time she first
met the Prince of Wales.
(© Illustrated London
News Ltd/Mary Evans)

The Prince of
Wales in his cabin
on HMS *Renown*,
1920. (© Illustrated
London News Ltd/
Mary Evans)

Freda at the height of her affair with the
Prince of Wales. (© Illustrated London
News Ltd/Mary Evans)

The Prince of Wales in golfing clothes.
(© Illustrated London News Ltd/
Mary Evans)

Elegance at the Embassy Club by Mundo. (© Illustrated London News Ltd/Mary Evans)

"Charleston, Hey! Hey!" the "Darktown Strut" at the Embassy

Sketch by Fish of the Charleston dance at the Embassy Club.
(Mary Evans/Jazz Age Club Collection)

Freda with her two daughters Penelope (Pempie) and Angela (Angie).
(© Illustrated London News Ltd/Mary Evans)

Freda, the devoted mother
with her two girls.
(© Illustrated London News
Ltd/Mary Evans)

reda with Brendan Bracken and her sister Vera in
936. (© Illustrated London News Ltd/Mary Evans)

Bobby, the Marquis de Casa Maury; by Bassano.
(© National Portrait Gallery, London)

Freda on a ship with Lord Mountbatten and Bobby de Casa Maury (on the
right-hand side). (Ben Laycock Collection)

Freda looking chic in her 50s.
(Ben Laycock Collection)

Freda sunbathing in Malta.
(Ben Laycock Collection)

The Prince of Wales out hunting. (© Illustrated London News Ltd/Mary Evans)

Audrey Dudley Coats on the cover of *The Tatler*, 1925. (© Illustrated London News Ltd/ Mary Evans)

THE VISCOUNTESS FURNESS

The beautiful wife of Lord Furness, who was formerly Mrs. Converse, and is the daughter of Mr. Harry Hays Morgan, U.S.A. Consul-General at Buenos Aires. The first Lady Furness died in 1921. Lord Furness, who has large shipping and iron and steel interests, is also a famous breeder of blood-stock, and a former Master of the York and Ainsty hounds (1912-19), for the first two years jointly with Mr. J. Stapylton, and it was during his mastership that a very famous hound, Vandyke (1916), was bred. Vandyke was the sire of Critic, dam of the Quorn champion, Cruiser. Both Lord and Lady Furness are very popular personalities in Leicestershire. His seat is Burrough Court, Melton

Thelma with her baby son Tony. (© Illustrated London News Ltd/Mary Evans)

Thelma, Lady Furness, on the front cover of *The Tatler*, 1930. (© Illustrated London News Ltd/Mary Evans)

The Prince of Wales shortly before
he began his affair with Thelma.
(© Illustrated London News Ltd/
Mary Evans)

The Prince of Wales meeting coal
miners in 1929. (© Illustrated
London News Ltd/Mary Evans)

The Prince of Wales on safari in Kenya, 1930. (© Illustrated London News Ltd/Mary Evans)

. stylised image of Thelma by Autori in   .
© Illustrated London News Ltd/Mary Evans)

A caricature of Prince Aly Khan by Mel
in 1932. (© Illustrated London News Ltd/
Mary Evans)

Identical twins Gloria Vanderbilt and Thelma Furness. (© William Hustler and Georgina Hustler/National Portrait Gallery, London)

VISCOUNTESS FURNESS'S SISTERS : MRS. GLORIA VANDERBILT
AND MRS. BENJAMIN THAW.

Thelma's sisters Consuelo Thaw and Gloria Vanderbilt on the French Riviera. (© Illustrated London News Ltd/Mary Evans)

Prince Aly Khan with his
father the Aga Khan at the
races in 1932. (© Illustrated
London News Ltd/
Mary Evans)

Thelma socialising with friends.
(© Illustrated London News
Ltd/Mary Evans)

The Prince of Wales and Wallis Simpson during the royal cruise down the Dalmatian Coast in 1936. (© Illustrated London News Ltd/Mary Evans)

Edward and Wallis at Ascot in June 1936. (© Illustrated London News Ltd/Mary Evans)

Wallis Simpson at Quaglino's in April 1936. (© Illustrated London News Ltd/Mary Evans)

soundproofing was to prove a problem at Venetia's house parties as sometimes private conversations became public. The underlying tensions broke through the polished veneer one weekend at the end of July 1926. Duff Cooper recorded the denouement in a letter to his wife, Diana. The Ednams had both been invited to stay at Breccles but on the first evening it was just Rosemary, Venetia and Duff as Diana was away and Eric was arriving the next day. It was a low-key gathering; the trio played bezique and then went to bed early. The next morning Duff played golf with Rosemary before more guests arrived including Eric, Violet, Duchess of Westminster, and Sir Matthew 'Scatters' Wilson. Although on the surface Rosemary and Eric put on a united front, behind the scenes there were arguments. Duff wrote to Diana that he heard them having 'a royal row' in their bedroom. Rosemary had lent money to a dressmaker, but she had not told Eric about it, and Violet Westminster had given her secret away. Violet had been married to Bendor, Duke of Westminster, for only a few years, but the marriage was now over and by the time of the house party she was looking for a new love. Violet had arrived at Breccles with Eric, which made Rosemary suspicious that something was going on between them.

In her jealousy, Rosemary turned to her old admirer Duff, and spent much of the weekend with him. They played golf, tennis and bezique together. The simmering passions between the guests began to erupt as the weekend went on. The hostess, Venetia, made several scenes. It seems her affair with Eric was now over and she was sleeping with her long-term on/off married lover Scatters Wilson, but his attitude to her was far from gallant. Late on the Monday night the other guests tried to persuade Scatters to play cards for longer, but Venetia was not amused and hovered by the door. Eventually, Scatters said he would not play, saying instead that he thought 'he'd go to bed with old Venetia'. After this rude comment, she left the room, slamming the door in fury. The next morning, Rosemary told Duff that she had heard a row going on in Venetia's room far into the night. There was another scene when Violet Westminster said that she needed to motor back to London late on the Tuesday night with Eric. It seems that this idea made Venetia as jealous as Rosemary. Venetia said that she was sorry, but it would be quite impossible for her staff to pack their clothes that quickly. Determined to escape, her guests said they could pack their own cases, so Venetia had to let them go. No doubt to the relief of both Venetia and Rosemary, Duff decided to go back to London with Eric and Violet in her Rolls-Royce. Despite Eric's attempts to prolong the evening the duchess was dropped off first and he was left with Duff.[34]

As the Breccles encounter suggests, Venetia was not Eric's only lover. In the Dudley papers, there is a letter to Eric from Berlin in March 1926 from a woman called Enid which suggests another affair. Complaining that once Eric had left there was 'no more joy or party spirit', Enid asked if he was happy and whether he ever gave her 'an occasional thought'. She added: 'if you can persuade yourself to put anything in writing – I'd love to hear from you! In the mean-time you may know I don't forget you.' It seems Enid may have been an actress, as she mentions being in a show in first Paris and then London. She asked Eric: 'Will you be there? I hope so. After five months in Berlin – I think I deserve a little attention – don't you think so?'[35]

Rosemary also had flirtations, but they seem to have been more retaliatory reactions to Eric's behaviour rather than meaningful relationships. In her papers, there is 'Eulogic or Romantic Notes on "Rose"' written to her from White's Club in November 1926. The handwriting is neither Eric's nor the prince's. Her secret admirer wrote:

Dearest and most lovely and adorable and fascinating, charming and alluring <u>Rose</u>.
You are one in a million.
I love you.
<u>YOU</u> (nobody else).[36]

There were also rumours that Rosemary had resumed her relationship with the Prince of Wales. In the mid 1920s Cecil Beaton was told that the prince dined with her frequently and she was believed to be his mistress.[37] As Edward's relationship with Freda became less all-consuming and she turned her attentions to Michael Herbert, there are photographs of Rosemary at social events with her former royal boyfriend. In March 1924 newspapers noted that the prince danced with her at Sir Philip Sassoon's house.[38] A few months later in July, Rosemary was again one of his dance partners at a charity ball at the Ritz.[39] In November 1925 they attended the Armistice Ball at the Albert Hall together; Eric was not there but Rosemary's sister-in-law Eileen, Duchess of Sutherland, was with them. Since their time together in France in the First World War, Edward had been attracted to both Eileen and Rosemary and at the ball he danced a great deal with both attractive married women. Edward and Rosemary were spending time together when they were both having problems in their respective relationships with Freda and Eric. It is possible that they rekindled their affair, although Audrey Dudley Coats was the prince's main substitute for Freda at this time. We cannot know the extent of Rosemary and Edward's continuing relationship. Certainly, in the free and easy attitude to adultery in the prince's circle it is possible that they had an affair. However, as Lord Ednam's second wife Laura wrote, Eric could be a very jealous, possessive man and as the prince remained a lifelong friend perhaps it is unlikely that he was sleeping with his wife. Rosemary was also considered by her contemporaries to be more virtuous than many of her friends so an affair with the prince seems unlikely. Whether their relationship was sexual or not, it was important to them both. Rosemary was one of the few of his ex-girlfriends he never denigrated, and she remained a trusted, discreet confidante throughout his turbulent love life in the 1920s.

Whatever the nature of their relationship, the prince was a regular visitor to the Ednams' country house, Himley Hall in the Midlands. Rosemary and Eric inherited the house when his father Lord Dudley decided to spend more time abroad with his second wife. Himley is an E-shaped house without the centre bar which dates mainly from the eighteenth century. It had not been occupied for years when Lord Dudley gave it to his son and daughter-in-law. They intended to spend most of the year there as Eric wanted to live among his tenants and the workers at his family colliery.[40]

A natural homemaker, Rosemary used her interior design skills to turn Himley into the perfect country house, mixing modern innovations with traditional charm. She was an excellent needlewoman and good at carpentry and painting. As a girl, she had painted much of the furniture for her bedroom at Dunrobin. She had never lost her love of using her hands, and so she now used her skills in upholstery to give her country home a personal stamp.[41] She found rolled up in the attic some period chintzes left by Eric's grandmother, which she used for the curtains and loose covers. Each bedroom had a large bathroom in a different colour scheme to complement the shades in the chintzes. Walls were painted oyster colour or in pastel tones of peach, green and parchment, while large bunches of flowers, placed in white bowls or big vases, finished the rooms. One gossip columnist described it as 'one of the jolliest houses I have ever been in', adding that Rosemary was 'all that is English and lovely – like birch trees and apple blossom'.[42] As well as expressing her understated good taste, Rosemary also had fun with the interior design at Himley. When the servants' wing was demolished, an indoor swimming pool was built in its place. Rosemary employed the interior designer Guy Elwes to decorate the room. He painted a Venetian loggia scene on one wall and a Regency bathing party on the other.[43] Special lighting was put in which gave bathers a phosphorescent appearance. In the gallery of the swimming pool wing a fashionable cocktail bar was built.

The Prince of Wales, his brother and sister-in-law the Duke and Duchess of York and Rosemary's old friend the Queen of Spain were among the guests who enjoyed the Ednams' relaxed hospitality. The prince wrote to Freda Dudley Ward about one visit after he had spent the afternoon 'princing' in Dudley. Hinting at his continuing affection for Rosemary he wrote: 'I've loved our visit here but not as much as I love you.' He added: 'Rosie is very sweet and Eric has been nice and not too pompous and he certainly is very efficient.'[44] The prince told Freda that he hoped they might one day stay at Himley together.

In the first years of their relationship, Freda had been a little jealous when the prince visited Rosemary, but the two woman soon became firm friends. At first they met frequently at the homes of Rosemary's brother and sister-in-law Eileen and Geordie, the Duke and Duchess of Sutherland. In the early 1920s the two women and the prince socialised together at Dunrobin Castle, Scotland, and Sutton Place, the Sutherland's Tudor mansion in Surrey. In 1921, when the Duke of Sutherland was Colonial Office spokesman for the government, the Imperial Conference met in London to consider the foreign policy of the empire and the idea of establishing the League of Nations. Geordie and Eileen invited some of the international delegates to lunch at Sutton Place and among the guests were Freda and Rosemary, their husbands and the prince. In one photograph Edward is sitting cross-legged in the front row, looking tanned and boyish, between his former and present love.

Edward found the Sutherlands were relaxed hosts and he often invited himself to stay. Writing to Geordie that he hoped he would not regard him as 'cadging', he asked his friend not to make it too formal as he loathed that sort of thing. At Sutton Place there would usu-ally be dancing or a film show to entertain the guests. When the duke and duchess were in Los Angeles with some of their friends, including William Dudley Ward, they all appeared in a short comedy film with Douglas Fairbanks and Mary Pickford. They screened their celebrity home movie at one of their house parties.[45]

The Sutherlands also hosted some memorable parties at their London home, Hampden House. On these occasions the tennis court was con-verted into a ballroom, a special floor was put down and the room was lined with tapestries. The Sutherlands, like many of their contem-poraries, loved fancy dress. The Prince of Wales enjoyed it so much that he suggested to Eileen Sutherland that guests should change their costumes several times during the evening to keep their companions guessing their true identity. As he was so often the centre of attention, he relished even a brief interlude which allowed him to mingle with his fellow guests unrecognised. At one ball he arrived as Bonnie Prince Charlie then transformed himself into a Chinese coolie.[46]

The most memorable Hampden House fancy dress ball was in 1926 when the King and Queen of Spain were visiting England. It epito-mised the close-knit and incestuous circle which had formed around the prince. That night the Prince of Wales and his brother Prince Henry came dressed as Arab sheiks, unrecognisable in their black beards. There was much laughter and fun during the evening. In honour of the Spanish guests, there was a mock bull-fight in which Prince Obolensky impersonated the bull and Freda's lover Michael Herbert was the mat-ador. As another 'diversion', Duff Cooper 'coxed' the Eton eight – a crew of eight society women including Rosemary, Freda and Bridget Paget – across the ballroom in an imaginary boat race. Wearing a blue blazer that was far too tight for him and a straw boater, Duff directed his harem, who were skimpily dressed in white shorts with blue ribbons, tiny blue caps and vests with sweaters draped around their shoulders. As they 'rowed' vigorously across the room the rest of the guests started singing the Eton Boating Song.[47]

As the 'Eton' crew indicated, Freda and Rosemary formed a type of exclusive club of the prince's girlfriends who had been deemed unsuitable to be royal brides. Their camaraderie extended to girlfriends of Edward's brothers too. When in 1927 Prince George told his parents that he wanted to marry Poppy Baring, a friend of Freda and Rosemary, Freda said that if he stuck to his guns firmly they would not be able to stop him. Poppy was the daughter of the wealthy banker and MP Sir Godfrey Baring. Exotic, with huge dark eyes and a wide mouth, she was one of society's 'Bright Young Things'.[48] Rosemary joked that should Poppy lengthen her skirts and stop wearing lipstick, then she would win over the king but lose Prince George. Inevitably, Poppy, like her two friends, was soon rejected as an unsuitable bride by Queen Mary and King George. Rosemary and Freda were rather amused.[49]

12

THE TRAGIC HEROINE

Although Rosemary was at the centre of the set which surrounded the Prince of Wales, she was never just a decadent socialite. She had an integrity which many of the other women in her circle lacked. She was great fun, but she also had a serious side. Like Freda, she was interested in politics; when Eric decided that he wanted a political career and ran for parliament in the Hornsey by-election in 1921, Rosemary was one of his greatest assets. Although he stood as a Conservative many coalition Liberals, including his mother-in-law, Millicent, spoke for him. Eric and Rosemary recognised the importance of winning the support of recently enfranchised women. In the constituency women voters made up 21,000 of the 46,000 electors on the register. Eric's team arranged women-only meetings each afternoon which proved to be a great success. About a dozen women decided to parade the streets as 'sandwich-men' supporting Lord Ednam.[1]

During the election Rosemary was constantly by Eric's side, canvassing in his Hornsey constituency and providing moral support. She won him many votes with her persuasive arguments.[2] Her early training at her mother's charity events had made her ready with a quick retort and she was skilful at talking to all sorts of people.[3] Once Eric was in parliament she used her charm to woo senior politicians who could help advance her husband's career. In one letter to Eric she mentioned dining with Winston Churchill, who at this time was secretary of state for the colonies. She promised to 'get all I can out of him perhaps another job'.[4] Eric was praised by journalists for having ideas and the eloquence to express them.[5] Rosemary's charm offensive and his obvious ability were a powerful combination. In 1922 Eric was made parliamentary private secretary to Lord Winterton, the under-secretary of state for India.

However, Rosemary was not just a supportive political wife. Although for the three years her husband was MP for Hornsey she left all the politics to him, saying only a few words that she considered appropriate to the candidate's wife, during the 1924 general election she came out in her true colours. The 1924 election was held in October after the defeat of the first ever Labour government, led by Ramsay MacDonald. The Labour minority government had lasted only a few months. During the campaign, Rosemary gave a very carefully thought-out speech to Worcestershire Conservatives which set out her firmly held political beliefs. She described herself as 'an ardent, enthusiastic and lifelong conservative' who felt what she was saying 'intensely'. Appealing to women, she told her audience that this general election was the most important in the country's history as it was a fight between Labour and Conservative which would be decided by the women's vote: 'On us women lies a grave and great responsibility; in our hands are the welfare and the future of this small, but historic island and of all its great dominions overseas.'

Her speech showed what an asset Rosemary would have been if she had married the Prince of Wales. She was a stalwart supporter of the monarchy and everything it stood for in the modern era. In her speech Rosemary said that people needed to vote Conservative because otherwise a socialist government might threaten the king, the constitution and the empire. Speaking in terms that show that she shared many of the prince's beliefs and could have helped him modernise the monarchy for the post-war world, she explained:

I have the greatest respect for the genuine British labour man, I see no reason why he should not help to govern the country, he is out to help his own people, which is perfectly natural. I only wish he belonged to our party and not the Socialist party, for will he have the strength of character to predominate among the extremists and to get what he wants, for what he wants, we want, that is to say to get in a perfectly orthodox and sensible way better conditions for the working people of this country.

She added that the Conservatives' aim was that 'every man and woman in this country should be well-educated, well-housed and above all employed'.

Like the Prince of Wales, she made plain in her speech the effect the war had had on her. She explained:

In the Great War thousands of men, rich and poor, comrades together, side by side, died for their country. It is up to all of you to live for your country and vote for whatever government you think is going to keep these great principles of loyalty and patriotism and is going to do the best for the people of Great Britain as a whole.

Her speech demonstrates how different Rosemary was from the more controversial members of her mother's family. It shows how fundamentally she disagreed with her aunt, Daisy Warwick. The year before, in the December 1923 general election, the Countess of Warwick had stood as a Labour candidate for Warwick and Leamington. While Rosemary defended capitalism, arguing that only the Conservatives could deal effectively with unemployment by reviving trade rather than giving subsidies, Daisy had fought for more egalitarian principles. Her views were so radical that *The Times* correspondent had even wondered whether the red flag would be raised over Warwick Castle. With characteristic verve Lady Warwick, who was now in her 60s, drove a phaeton with a team of white ponies in red and gold Labour colours through the constituency. Supported by her 'comrades', the day before the poll she addressed nine meetings before her car was pulled by supporters through the streets of Warwick.

Despite her valiant effort, Daisy lost to the Tory high-flier and future prime minister Anthony Eden.[6]

In her speech, Rosemary made a vicious attack on Daisy's type of upper-class socialists. She ridiculed them as 'that fanatical intelligentsia, those so-called gentlemen who have been brought up in the lap of luxury, except when they step out of their limousines, pull on an old cap and go the last mile of their road into their constituency in the tram'. Rosemary's vitriol against these political opponents is shown by her initial use of the word 'lunatics' to describe them. She then crossed it out to add: 'I only hope these fanatical visionaries make their colleagues in their own party as sick as they make us.'[7] This uncharacteristic outburst makes a reader wonder whether Rosemary had ever forgiven her aunt for the embarrassment she had caused her and for perhaps being one of the reasons she was rejected as a royal bride.

Rosemary evidently enjoyed campaigning because during the 1924 election she went to Oldham to canvass for her old friend and admirer Duff Cooper. During the campaign, Rosemary and a group of friends including Duff's wife Lady Diana Cooper, Juliet Duff, Diana Westmorland and Maurice Baring moved into the Midland Hotel in Manchester. Early each morning they reported to the party's head-quarters in Oldham where they were given their canvassing orders for the day. At lunchtime they would meet up and exchange stories about their experiences that morning. At one of the mills the girls mobbed Diana and kissed her; in return, she promised them a clog dance if they voted for Duff. Their campaigning was successful, and Duff won.[8] As his friends, including Freda, heard the news at Mr Selfridge's election night party, Duff got the longest and loudest cheer of the night.[9]

Reading Rosemary's passionately argued speech and hearing about her love of campaigning makes one wonder if she had political aspirations of her own. It raises the question of whether she might have, like Lady Astor, followed her husband into parliament. It also makes us think about what a different political path the Prince of Wales might have followed if he had married Rosemary instead of Wallis. Although the prince had earlier admired Lloyd George, by the mid 1920s, like Rosemary, he was very supportive of the new Conservative prime minister, Stanley Baldwin. He disapproved of social injustice but was to the right politically and he was delighted with the Conservatives' victory in 1924. The Conservative leader Stanley Baldwin won 412 seats to Labour's 151. As always, the prince's political views were complicated and not clear cut. He was still concerned about the threat of communism, but he respected some Labour party leaders for understanding working people better than any Conservatives did.[10] With her carefully thought-out Conservative politics and firm moral compass, it seems far less likely that with Rosemary by his side Edward would have flirted with fascism in the 1930s.

Instead of pursuing a political career herself, Rosemary chose a less controversial path by continuing her mother's tradition of charity work. Her wartime experiences had affected her deeply. Determined to do her bit for those injured in the war, she replaced her mother Millicent as president of the North Staffordshire Cripples' Aid Society. She became a very popular figure as she worked tirelessly organising fundraising activities. Her aim was to modernise the Hartshill Hospital and make it better for people with disabilities. She was particularly concerned about improving conditions for disabled children. She told her fellow fundraisers that it 'left her cold' when she thought of the mothers with disabled children who were unable to secure treatment owing to lack of accommodation. She believed the need for more beds was urgent. She argued that they should not rest until every disabled child was given the medical help to be turned into a strong and healthy citizen.[11]

Rosemary was never just a cipher; she was a hands-on philanthropist who threw herself into her charity work with enthusiasm. To publicise the hospital's needs she invited prominent North Staffordshire residents to lunch and then she put forward her proposals for an extension of the building. In Dudley, she became particularly involved in the infant and maternity welfare movement. She laid the foundation stone of Rosemary Ednam House, an up-to-date maternity hospital. In October 1929 she opened a baby week and health week which ran concurrently at Wolverhampton. At the opening she told the audience that simple principles of hygiene ought to be taught to mothers, most of whom were only too eager to learn. She was very aware of the evils of overcrowding and she believed that something should be done to alleviate the problem.[12]

In all her charity work she was valued for her dedication and her wisdom. Both the hospital staff and the management committee learnt to love her for her 'beautiful disposition' and because her advice was so sound.[13] Her lifelong friend the writer J.M. Barrie wrote that she grew to be 'a very wise woman, so understanding that other wise ones took counsel of her, and there were few with a better sense of their duties which only lay lightly on her because of the gay courage with which she shouldered them'.[14] Like her mother, Rosemary was able to cut through class boundaries and establish a rapport with people from all walks of life and all ages. Her friend Lord Castlerosse wrote: 'She had something of the quality of St Francis of Assisi, who made everything he touched virtuous and attractive [...] She would break through the gloom of unhappiness like the sun dissipating the mist, and she was a stand-by to many.'[15]

When Rosemary was not doing her charity work she enjoyed country pursuits and travelling. Throughout the 1920s Rosemary frequently appeared in the society pages of newspapers and magazines at point-to-points, the races and out hunting. One newspaper feature focusing on the fashion for tweed raved about how well the country look suited her. The journalist wrote: 'Lady Ednam looks quite perfect in tweeds – it's sort of inborn, the tweed look – and her kind of fairness never goes blue with cold in a mist but takes on a sort of moonlight fairness and transparency which is accentuated by jerseyish clothes.'[16] A keen horsewoman, Rosemary often went hunting with the Quorn, Beaufort and Belvoir hunts. It was a passion she shared with both her husband and the Prince of Wales. The hunting world was at the centre of their social life and inevitably reflected its incestuous nature. By the end of the decade, when the prince attended hunt balls at Melton Mowbray, his past, present and future girlfriends, Rosemary, Freda and Thelma Furness, would all be there. There was safety in numbers and the presence of all three women threw gossip columnists off the scent; none of them could be openly with the prince, but each might get at least one dance with him.

The Ednams also spent part of the year abroad. They owned a house called the Villa Rosemary on the French Riviera where they entertained guests including Clementine Churchill.[17] At the end of January each year it had become fashionable for British aristocrats to leave behind the English winter and escape to the south of France. Cannes had become particularly fashionable; it was known as 'Deauville Deux'. One observer recorded how chic Cannes was, using some precise criteria, apparently 'hair is shingled much closer to the nape of the neck than anywhere else [...] In Cannes the pearls are worn much larger and much tighter around the neck than any other town in the Riviera.'[18] During their visits the Ednams and their friends would play tennis at the Carlton Club with the Duke and Duchess of Westminster and then dance or gamble at the casino.

They also often holidayed further afield with friends. In the summer of 1924 Lord and Lady Beatty invited Rosemary for a cruise on their yacht *Sheila*. After relaxing on the Lido at Venice, the party travelled all over Romania and parts of Transylvania. They visited the Dardanelles and Constantinople, where they were lavishly entertained in Turkish palaces. However, Rosemary and American-born Lady Beatty had grown bored with socialising and wanted an adventure. One afternoon while relaxing in a deckchair Lady Beatty read a translation of the legend of Hero and Leander. She was excited to discover that their yacht was anchored close to where the tragic love story took place. According to the legend, Leander swam through those same waters every night to visit Hero until one day the tide was too powerful for him and he was drowned. His body was washed up at the foot of his lover's tower. Hero, in despair, threw herself from the tower and died beside her love.

Talking about the story with their friends, Rosemary and Lady Beatty discovered that Lord Byron had swum the Hellespont a century before. As the two women had both been swimming a great deal that summer and were proud of their prowess they decided to try to emulate the poet. They chose a quiet, windless, moonlit night and persuaded a Turkish guide and boatman to take them out to the place where Leander swam from. The two women made it halfway across with little effort, but as they got close to the other shore the strength of the tide became too much for them. They were beginning to struggle and were swimming in circles to try to keep afloat when luckily the first mate, who had been watching them from the yacht, saw them. He called four other crew members and they set off in a launch to rescue Rosemary and the countess. Except for temporary exhaustion, they were fine and before they got back to the yacht they were laughing over their escapade.[19]

Wherever Rosemary went there was laughter. In January 1928 Rosemary and Eric went with Diana and Duff Cooper to Biskra. The foursome laughed a great deal, particularly after smoking a hubble-bubble pipe in Algiers. However, there was less laughter, except from Rosemary who could see the funny side in any situation, when a miscalculating doctor injected Eric with ten times the approved dose of streptococci needed for a vaccination. Luckily, Eric had no reaction at all. They laughed a lot too when they rode in the desert and ate on eiderdowns under the palms with some sheikhs.[20]

However, although Rosemary always tried to remain positive it was not always easy. During the decade after her marriage her family were to be struck by more than their fair share of misfortune. In June 1920 Eric's mother, the Countess of Dudley, drowned while swimming at Rosmuck, Connemara. She was an excellent swimmer, but she collapsed and drowned in sight of her maid, who was unable to save her. In 1921, while on a shooting trip in Rhodesia, Rosemary's younger brother Alastair was suddenly struck down with malarial fever and died aged only 30. The young man had everything to live for. He had fought bravely in the war and then married an American heiress; just a month before his death his wife had given birth to a baby daughter. Rosemary was very close to her brother and she was inconsolable after his death. At Alastair's funeral at Dunrobin his mother, Millicent, his wife and Rosemary dropped sprigs of lily-of-the-valley into his grave.[21] In 1929 another untimely loss hit the family. Rosemary's cousin, Lord Loughborough, the Earl of Rosslyn's son who had been married to Sheila, the friend of Freda and the prince, ended his life by committing suicide.

The tragedies continued at such a pace that Lord Ednam believed his family had been cursed. When Rosemary and Eric were in Egypt in the spring of 1929, Eric had a row at Luxor with the Rosicrucian Society, who were holding a celebration. They were angry with him and apparently cursed him. At first Rosemary joked about it, making a great after-dinner story out of it but as one disaster in the family followed another Eric began to take it seriously.[22] In December 1929 Rosemary and Eric's 7-year-old son, John Jeremy (known as Jeremy), was killed in a freak accident. Jeremy had been out with his younger brother Peter and their French governess, Mlle Paule Marie Sejuret. He had been riding his miniature bicycle along Chelsea Embankment to the park. When they left the park, Mlle Sejuret had forbidden Jeremy to get on his bicycle. They were returning home along the Albert Suspension Bridge when suddenly Jeremy disobeyed his governess and shot ahead on his bicycle. She did not see what was happening because she was pushing his brother in his pram with the hood up. When she realised, she ran after Jeremy but before she could catch up with him his bicycle collided with a lorry and trailer. The spot where the boy went off the pavement was hidden from the view of the driver by a lamp post, so he could do nothing to avoid the little boy. Jeremy was caught between the trailer's wheels. A man working on a cab rank close by said: 'I saw the boy and the bicycle wedged under the wheels of the trailer. We all rushed over and found that the boy was still conscious and was bleeding in many places, later he lost consciousness.'[23] A doctor, who was passing, had Jeremy rushed to the Victoria Hospital for Children but his injuries were fatal.

Rosemary and Eric were informed of the accident by telephone. By the time they reached the hospital their son was dead.[24] On hearing the news, Rosemary was prostrate with grief and would see no one, while Eric left for Oxford to bring their eldest son home from school.[25] In the following days and weeks their friends tried to comfort them. The Prince of Wales was one of the first people to call them and express his grief at the tragedy.[26] Messages of sympathy and flowers flooded in. Jeremy had been a very lively, charming little boy and was a great favourite with his mother's many friends.[27] In very shaky handwriting, Rosemary replied in pencil to Duff Cooper: 'Darling Duff, Your love and sympathy does help. Diana tells me you cried for us. Thank you dearest Duff.'[28] To another confidante, Elizabeth, Marchioness of Salisbury, she wrote: 'Darling Betty, I loved your sweet letter – I know you understand how we are suffering. Thank you for your love and sympathy darling – it helps. Rosie.'[29] At the inquest a verdict of accidental death was recorded; the jury concluded that no one was to blame.

After Jeremy's death the Ednams put their Cheyne Walk house up for sale. They could not bear to continue living in a house which constantly reminded them of his accident. In her grief, Rosemary dedicated her time to creating a garden of remembrance for her son at their country home. Jeremy was buried under the branches of an old apple tree beside a babbling brook in the grounds of Himley Hall. Using her artistry, she planned a garden with flag paths, a rockery, herbaceous bed and a small bridge across the brook. As she struggled to cope with her loss, day after day, she could be found planting forget-me-nots and rock plants or supervising the estate gardeners in laying the flagstones.[30]

Rosemary was not to outlive her son by long. In the early summer of 1930 she and Eric had decided to take a complete break and spend a few weeks in France at the Chalet du Bois, his stepmother's villa. Unfortunately, Eric developed typhoid fever while there, but Rosemary wanted to fly back to England for a meeting with the architect who was helping her to plan Jeremy's memorial garden. When Eric had recovered sufficiently to be left for a few days, Rosemary wrote to her mother that she was intending to pay a fleeting visit to Himley. She explained that if she did not see the flowers she would not know what to alter for next year. In a prophetic postscript, she added: 'It is just conceivable that I won't come back.'[31]

She already had a flight booked but one seat had become vacant on an earlier flight from Le Touquet to Croydon, which would give her more time to keep her appointment.[32] On 21 July 1930 Rosemary boarded the Junker plane with the society hostess Mrs Henrick Loeffler and her guests, the Marquis of Dufferin and Ava, and Sir Edward Ward. Mrs Loeffler's husband owned *The Albion*, the largest steam yacht in the world. She often entertained the Prince of Wales and his friends at her house parties at Le Touquet. During that last weekend, the American author and songwriter Elsa Maxwell and the prince's equerry Joey Legh and his wife Sarah had been staying with Mrs Loeffler. At the end of the weekend, Elsa had been planning to fly back to England but the writer Somerset Maugham, who was also in Le Touquet, said, 'Why go? Why not stay on here in my villa and play bridge?' Fortunately for Elsa, she accepted his offer.[33] Joey Legh had intended to take the one remaining seat on the plane, but on the morning of the flight Sarah woke up and heard a strong wind blowing. As she was particularly nervous about flying, she persuaded her husband to pull out and take her back to

England by sea. Joey warned her it would be a rough sea crossing, but he agreed to go with her, leaving a seat on the plane which was taken by Rosemary at the last minute.[34]

It should have been a quick and easy journey. Colonel George Henderson, who flew the plane, was very experienced. After learning to fly in 1915 he became a lieutenant colonel in the Royal Flying Corps. After the war, he became the principal of the Henderson Flying School at Brooklands. A famous flying ace, he was the first pilot to fly under Tower Bridge.[35] Before making the flight he had thought that there was 'something wrong'. It was found that an exhaust-pipe washer had worked loose but an adjustment was made, and Colonel Henderson was happy to fly.[36]

The plane took off in perfect weather, but as it reached England it flew into a gale. It then fell to pieces in the air over the village of Meopham in Kent. An eyewitness recalled:

> As the plane approached from the direction of the Channel, I saw at once that it was wobbling badly. It was pouring with rain at the time. The plane had passed over when there was an explosion, not a very loud one, immediately pieces of wreckage and what looked like little aeroplanes came floating down. We did not realise then that they were bodies.[37]

Parts of the plane were found as far as 2 miles away from where the accident occurred. As well as the wreckage, poignant personal items were found. It was estimated that £65,000 worth of jewellery was lost from the aeroplane. Rosemary had been wearing a valuable pearl necklace and a diamond clip brooch. When the bodies hurtled to the ground the necklaces worn by the two women broke and Rosemary's priceless pearls were scattered all over the orchard in which her remains were found.[38] One local man found what he thought was a piece of cut glass; in fact it was a diamond.[39] The bodies hit the ground with such great impact that they made deep impressions in the soft earth. As the shocked villagers became aware of what had happened, they recovered the remains of the victims and put them in a cart to be taken to a makeshift mortuary in a nearby barn. As the cart moved away from the orchard the heavy rain stopped for the first time during the day, the sun burst through and on the far horizon villagers saw a rainbow.[40]

When news reached London that evening about what happened, Chips Channon wrote that 'a gloom fell' on the city.[41] All parties were cancelled as a mark of respect.[42] As Eric was too ill to travel, Rosemary was identified by her brother, the Duke of Sutherland. On the Wednesday after the crash, an inquest on the victims was opened in a little timber tea room on the green at Meopham adjoining the barn where the bodies had lain since Monday. The inquest was adjourned until 13 August to give the Air Ministry time to make a full investigation. Eventually, a verdict of accidental death was returned.

Despite an intensive investigation into what had caused the crash, no single factor could be found to blame. The petrol tanks were intact, and all the vital parts of the engine were in order.[43] The cause of the disaster remains a mystery to this day. There were rumours of sabotage as important people used the air taxi; the Prince of Wales often flew back and forth from Le Touquet and one of the victims, the Marquis of Dufferin and Ava, was the speaker of the senate of Northern Ireland.

Rosemary was only 36 when she died. A few days after her death, her funeral was held at Himley. After the service, she was buried next to her son in the garden of memory she had created for him. The grief expressed that day was a testament to the lasting hold Rosemary exerted over the men who had loved her. Her husband, Lord Ednam, was too ill to attend the funeral but he sent a wreath of huge lilies to 'My beloved darling'.[44] Her ex-fiancé, John Manners, now the Duke of Rutland, was so devastated to hear of her death that according to his sister, Lady Diana Cooper, 'he took Belvoir's [his family estate] whole garden to her grave'.[45] Lilies, rosemary and ivy from him were used to line her grave.[46] Her old admirer and friend Duff Cooper wrote a poem to the woman he had been so attracted to. The last verse ran:

We shall remember you, Rosemary, always;
Life will be lonelier, sadder than before,
But not less lovely, because we shall remember,
Sadder and holier for evermore.

If years be given us which were denied you,
Age may dim eyes that today are blind with tears,
Yet we shall see that smile and hear that laughter
Echoing for ever through the empty years.[47]

Among the many floral tributes at her funeral there was a wreath of
pink and red roses from the Prince of Wales and a card that read simply:
'With love, from EP [Edward, Prince].'[48]

Reflecting the many lives Rosemary had touched, memorial services
were held for her at St Margaret's Westminster, Dornock Cathedral and
Golspie Church. The Duke of Sutherland and Viscount Ednam received
messages of sympathy from the king and queen and other members of
the royal family. Edward's own reaction was genuine and profound. He
wrote to Millicent shortly after Rosemary's death about how deeply
shocked he was by it. He explained: 'It's just one of the biggest tragedies
I've ever known and so big that it's hard to realise it has happened. It's
just one of those rare occasions when one wishes it had happened to
oneself instead.' He admitted to her mother the feelings that he still had
for the woman he had once wanted to marry, adding: 'I was so devoted
to her and like so many will miss her more than I can say.'[49]

After the Meopham disaster there was anxiety about the risks taken
by the Prince of Wales and Prince George when they flew. Edward had
bought a De Havilland Gipsy Moth and took lessons from a pilot at
Northolt aerodrome. The year after the Meopham tragedy the prince
flew, through dangerous conditions, to open the Rosemary Ednam
Memorial Extension at Hartshill. The idea for the new wing had been
launched by Rosemary on the very day that her son Jeremy was killed.
The extension had cost £20,000. About £6,000 had been raised by the
time of her death, but afterwards her friends and family turned it into a
fitting memorial for her and raised the rest of the money quickly.

The prince was met at the air base by Rosemary's widower, Eric,
then the two men travelled together to the hospital. As the prince and
Rosemary had first been brought together by their shared compassion
for a shell-shocked patient in a hospital ward, it was an appropriate place
for Edward to publicly acknowledge his admiration for his former love
and say a formal farewell. As the prince entered one of the children's

wards sixty voices called out from the beds: 'God bless the Prince of Wales.' The prince was touched by this unexpected welcome and said to the sister in charge: 'This is indeed a pretty sight.' Demonstrating his caring side, which had been such a bond with Rosemary, he expressed genuine interest in the work that was being done and insisted on being shown all around the hospital and talking to patients. He was particularly interested in the progress that had been made by one small girl called Mary Clewes. Thanks to the work of the hospital, in two years as an outpatient she had been completely cured of what had at first appeared to be an untreatable disability. 'It is absolutely marvellous. I would not have thought it possible,' he commented as he compared the child's legs with her original plaster casts. Rosemary's brother, Geordie, Duke of Sutherland, who was at the opening, noted that the prince did 'everything in just the way that would have pleased Rosemary herself'.[50] At the end of his visit, the heir to the throne paid tribute to the woman he had wanted to marry. He said:

> You all know, the wonderful work Rosemary Ednam did all the years she lived in these parts. It was she who inaugurated the idea of this hospital and started the fund [...] I now open this hospital, full of great thoughts and sacred remembrances.[51]

FREDA

13

THE SOCIALITE WITH A SOCIAL CONSCIENCE

Once Freda was permanently replaced by Wallis Simpson, instead of being bitter, she gracefully retreated from the scene. She demonstrated the discretion which had made her such an ideal royal mistress. As one of her friends said, she had 'pride, integrity and dignity'. She was determined to behave as well as she could in a difficult situation.[1]

However, Freda and Edward had not been the only ones affected by their sixteen-year-long relationship – her daughters Pempie and Angie had been involved too. They had provided the prince with the nearest thing he had ever had to a normal family life. When he cut off all contact with them Angie was very upset and angry. Fun-loving like her mother, Angie had developed a real rapport with the prince. Reflecting the closeness of their relationship, the only photograph of Edward that remains in Freda's albums is from him to her youngest daughter. Sent in 1932, it shows him looking his most handsome in a uniform and it is signed: 'Darling Angie from Little Prince'.[2] Pempie was less hurt because she had not been as close to the heir to the throne. More serious and censorious than her younger sister, she had begun to see through him and she disapproved of his affair with her mother.[3]

Some of the prince's family were also upset by the ending of the relationship. They had grown to respect Freda and saw her as a good influence on him. His brother Henry thought that she had been the best friend he had ever had.[4] Lord Louis Mountbatten was particularly disgusted by the prince's abrupt abandonment of Freda.[5] He knew how important she had been to his cousin, writing: 'There was something religious, almost holy, about his love for her. She was the only woman he ever loved that way. She deserved it. She was sweet and good, a good influence on him. None of the others were. Wallis' influence was fatal.'[6] Freda knew how weak and susceptible the prince was. She told one interviewer that his opinion on almost any subject frequently became that of the last person with whom he had discussed the issue.[7] If he had remained under Freda's influence it seems less likely that he would have made the links with Nazi Germany which were to tarnish his reputation. Her political views were moderate and tolerant.

Edward was to claim that one of the things that attracted him to Wallis in the early stages of their relationship was that she was the only woman to show an interest in his 'job'. She had listened attentively about his plans to improve the situation for the unemployed. Evidently, he had forgotten the long years in which Freda had served as a shrewd sounding board. During her ascendancy, Freda had supported his ideas for social reform, not his fascist tendencies. Both Edward and Freda had always cared about social injustice. During the Depression, as unemployment increased, the prince toured industrial areas. He visited the Midlands, Tyneside, Yorkshire, Lancashire, Wales and Scotland. He was shocked when he saw crowds of unemployed men with nowhere to go; they were milling about the streets or standing outside labour exchanges and pubs. At a soup kitchen, he saw men wearing coats without shirts under them, and spoke to a miner who had not worked for five years. Picking a house to visit at random, he held the hand of an underfed woman who was in childbirth. He was appalled by the levels of deprivation and he wrote to Prime Minister Stanley Baldwin about it. Although some of the men he met were apathetic, his sincerity impressed many of the unemployed; they believed he genuinely wanted to help them.

After one visit, a *New York Tribune* reporter found the prince pacing up and down asking: 'What can I do? What can be done?'[8] As he spoke out about what he had witnessed, his support for the unemployed infuriated some of the upper classes and he was accused of being too political.[9] In his memoir written many years later, he wrote that there was constant conflict within him between his desire to share in the social turmoil of the era and the constitutional restraints which prevented him saying anything too controversial or being overtly political.[10]

The slums he had visited were often so disgusting they left him feeling sick. Although as a member of the royal family his power was limited to suggestion, he was determined to do his best to improve housing.[11] He invited the Labour politician Ramsay MacDonald and the Conservative Neville Chamberlain to dinner at York House with a dozen experts to discuss solutions. In 1934, he told the American ambassador that there needed to be a change in social conditions in England to relieve poverty and that it would be achieved either constructively or, if not, violently, which would destroy the country.[12]

The prince had become patron of the National Council of Social Service, which organised voluntary organisations. He was keen to encourage job creation and see social centres set up in deprived areas. With him as a figurehead more than 700 schemes were put forward to the council in one year.[13] By the following year, 2,300 centres had been opened, helping up to a quarter of a million men and women.[14] One evening when Edward returned from a tour of a depressed area he told Freda that more ought to be done for the families of the unemployed. He explained that too often clubs and centres were run by the wrong sort of people. He added: 'People like you ought to run clubs.'[15] In 1934, at the prince's behest, Freda set up the Feathers Club Association, a society which helped the underprivileged in London who were suffering due to the Depression.

Edward allowed his crest of the three feathers to be used as the insignia of the charity and he became its patron. When the first club opened at Ladbroke Grove, the prince donated an electric refrigerator and carpentry and boot-mending tools. When the next club started at Notting Hill, Edward's own furniture designer made benches which were also lockers.[16] The clubs helped unemployed people in practical ways. They offered them nutritious meals at a minimal cost and, rather like a modern food bank, they distributed food. There were books and newspapers to read and classes which encouraged the unemployed to rebuild their self-confidence and get back to work. Most importantly, they were places where people could find companionship and compassion.

Under Freda's leadership, eight branches were set up. Each time a new club opened Edward gave her a tiny version of the Prince of Wales's feathers in diamonds, rubies and sapphires to add to a gold bracelet he had given to her.[17] Ironically 1934 was the year Mrs Simpson usurped Freda's position, but even when she was excluded from his life she continued with the charity work she had started in his name. Once the Prince of Wales withdrew, Freda's old friends the Duke and Duchess of Kent, who were newly married, supported her work. Princess Marina employed a member of one of the Feathers Clubs to decorate her bedroom in Belgrave Square. The Duke of Kent visited a club in Marylebone. Many of the women members were waiting with their babies to see the duke, who was introduced by Freda. When he entered the centre for children aged between 3 and 5 it was very noisy. He asked: 'Do they fight very much?' Freda assured him that they all got on very well.[18] Another lifelong friend of Freda's, Winston Churchill, also helped by doing a broadcast for the Feathers Clubs. Freda was a very dynamic leader of the charity. She not only drew on all her society contacts; she also thought of ways the association could reach more people. She wanted the clubs to be included in housing schemes and factories which would increase the subsidies given to the charity.

Freda did not just care for people through her charity work; she gathered around her anyone in need of help. When a young Italian film director, Giancarlo Capelli, was about to be deported for overstaying his permit under the Aliens Act, Freda supported him. She accompanied him to Bow Street Magistrates and stood surety for him when his counsel applied for bail.[19] Freda also had to step in when her sister Violet's marriage fell apart. Violet had met her husband Lieutenant Douglas Blew-Jones when he was convalescing at her mother's Nottingham hospital at the end of the First World War. The couple had married in December 1918 and then moved to the Blew-Jones's estate in North

Devon where they were very involved in the hunting set. During the 1920s and 1930s, the family exprienced financial problems; their daughter Bindy later recalled the embarrassment of being sent to answer the door to the bailiffs.[20] When Violet turned to alcohol, Freda took her niece Bindy Blew-Jones in and gave her a home. Younger than Pempie and Angie, Bindy idolised her aunt and cousins. As a teenager, she was a troubled girl who was expelled from several schools. On one occasion Freda took her to the station to go to school, and by the time she arrived home she found her niece sitting on her doorstep. Freda tried to give Bindy some stability. She became more important to her than her mother and was the young girl's emotional rock.[21]

Freda's relationship with her own daughters remained as close as ever as they grew up. She was a very relaxed and easy-going mother. Angie said that they were allowed to do whatever they wanted, but they would not have wanted to do anything to upset her. If they did do something wrong, she was understanding. One day, Angie came to her mother sobbing about some misdemeanour; Freda just comforted her and said: 'Don't worry, we all make mistakes.'[22]

By the 1930s Freda had established for herself and her daughters a firmly rooted place in society. Mother and daughters attracted an interesting circle of men around them. While staying with Freda's close friend Sir Philip Sassoon at Port Lympne in Kent, the artist Rex Whistler fell in love with Pempie. Freda commissioned Rex to paint a portrait of her two daughters. It was exhibited at the Royal Academy in 1934. It was set in a garden, with a broken fountain in the background and a black manservant in green livery unpacking a picnic basket. The girls were dressed in white, high-waisted dresses with narrow black ribbons edging the flounces. Whistler's aim had been to exemplify the spirit of youth. It was a great success, as one newspaper commented: 'It's done with more than a touch of nineteenth-century Romanticism and comes off triumphantly.'[23]

Brendan Bracken, the confidant of Winston Churchill and chairman of *The Financial Times*, was also fascinated by the trio. There were rumours of a relationship between Freda and Bracken, or Bracken and Pempie. He liked it to be thought that he was single because Pempie had turned him down. Whatever the nature of his relationship with the

Dudley Wards, he was devoted to all three women. When Angie left her cloth doll, 'Pinkie', which she had had since she was a child, on a train in France, she was in tears over its loss. She had slept with the toy every night of her life. Most of her friends thought she was being childish, but Brendan was sympathetic. He sent a detective, at his own expense, to investigate in France.[24]

Brendan greatly admired the work Freda did for the underprivileged. He became a member of the Feathers Club Association Council. In 1935, he suggested that Winston Churchill should recommend Freda to become a member of the central housing advisory committee. He explained that Freda knew more about housing than any woman in the country and through the Feathers Clubs she looked after about 3,000 unemployed people. Brendan emphasised that she never sought publicity and only wanted to join the committee because she thought that she could do some good work on it.[25] Churchill wrote to Kingsley Wood, minister of health, saying that he thought Mrs Dudley Ward would make a most suitable representative.[26]

Winston was already an admirer of Freda; they had known each other for many years and she was a great friend of his wife Clementine. Freda was often invited to Chartwell. Lady Diana Cooper recalled one visit when they all had fun splashing about in the swimming pool.[27] Brendan Bracken told the prime minister's doctor, Lord Moran, that Freda was among the few people who could shake Churchill out of his darker moods and make him talk. She would let Winston drink a glass or two of champagne and then get him chatting. He described her as 'a brilliant talker'.[28]

In the years after her relationship with the prince ended, Freda had many admirers. In 1932 Rosemary's widower, Eric Ednam, had become Earl of Dudley on his father's death. According to his second wife Laura, Eric was in love with Freda and would have liked to marry her.[29] In the years since his wife's death many women had chased him, but no one measured up to Rosemary for him. He had an affair with Rosemary and Freda's friend Lady Victor Paget (Bridget), who was also a former mistress of the prince.[30] Rosemary's mother Millicent, who was heartbroken after her daughter's death, was very critical of his choice. She wrote to her son-in-law harshly, telling him: 'All the time you associated with Bridget she was hardly the woman to succeed Rosemary, to whose purity and whose money, you owed so much.'[31]

When Eric's affair with Bridget came to an end, Freda was another of Rosemary's friends whom he hoped would fill the chasm left by her loss. Freda was often invited to Himley Hall for weekend house parties. In January 1935 Freda stayed there with Pempie, the other guests being Chips Channon, Emerald Cunard and her old friends Brendan Bracken and Sheila Milbanke. They arrived by train in bitterly cold weather. Chips Channon complained that although the house was modernised the bedrooms were cold. He described their host as being 'lovable and yet so moody and irritable', while Freda was 'tiny, squeaky and wise and chic'.[32]

Perhaps one deterrent for Freda from marrying Eric was that he was still great friends with the prince. The two men had drawn even closer since Rosemary's death; for years they telephoned each other at least once a day.[33] The prince knew that Eric was grief-stricken from the tragedy and in 1931 he decided to take his old friend with him as aide-de-camp on his tour of South America. He thought the change of scene would do Eric good, while his friend's industrial experience would be useful when he talked to South American financiers and industrialists. Eric was chairman of two colliery companies and of the family Round Oak Steelworks. He had also been president of the British Gas Industries. He had been examining the potential of America as a market for British steel products. During the trip Eric at times got depressed, finding it particularly difficult when they flew across the Panama Canal. It was the first time he had flown since Rosemary's death and, according to the prince, 'the poor boy was terribly upset'.[34]

Once Edward was with Wallis, Eric remained part of his circle. Lord Ednam was invited to weekends at Fort Belvedere and the new monarch knew that his old friend's house was a place where his new mistress would be welcomed. A few months after Edward had become king, in April 1936, he came to stay at Himley with Mrs Simpson. Wallis wrote about her stay in a letter to her Aunt Bessie, saying that it had taken her seven years to get to that sort of elite house party. There were eighteen guests staying in the house and they were 'the crème' of society.[35] Perhaps Freda decided not to get involved with Lord Dudley as she had had enough of moving in such incestuous circles.

The other main contender for Freda's affection was the sophisticated Pedro Jose Isidro Manuel Ricardo Mones, Marquis de Casa Maury. A Spanish–Cuban aristocrat and a racing driver, he was known as 'Bobby' to his friends but 'the Cuban Heel' to his enemies. He was an exotic figure, the opposite of many of the rather repressed Englishmen of the time. A profile of him in *The Bystander* described him as 'slim and sad-eyed, pale and gently gesticulating, he has smiled his half-smile (just the right-hand side of the mouth is raised) through misfortune after misfortune right into success'. It added that he smoked endless cigarettes and his eyelashes were 'probably the longest in London'. [36]

Bobby loved speed and danger. He drove Bugatti racing cars and owned the first Bermuda-rigged schooner in Europe. He took up flying and owned three planes, before he lost his money in the Wall Street Crash. [37] He was a risk-taker, but he was also deeply superstitious. He always carried a print of St Theresa with him wherever he went. His latest plane, *Toi et Moi*, had sacred pictures painted around the pilot's seat. When it was named by Edwina Mountbatten at Stag Lane Aerodrome, Edgware, London, Bobby insisted that it should also be blessed and sprinkled with holy water by a Catholic priest. [38]

The marquis had previously been married to Cecil Beaton's muse Paula Gellibrand, whose elegant, streamlined silhouette made her an art deco icon. She became one of Beaton's favourite models. He recorded her appearance in words and images in *The Glass of Fashion*. He described her 'perfect egg-shaped head' which gave her a look of a Modigliani portrait. [39] Paula knew just how to make a chic statement. For her wedding to Bobby in 1923, she dressed in the style of a nun, wearing a strikingly simple gown of white satin with a severe veil which perfectly showed off her 'calmly contemplative' face. [40]

The de Casa Maurys' London home became a byword in sophisticated, modern elegance. All the corridors were painted pure white, while the door fittings and curtain rails were chromium plated. In Bobby's study, a small cocktail bar was concealed behind a sliding panel in the mahogany wall. The bedroom was mirrored while the bathroom had greeny-silver walls and two black baths. The drawing room mixed many shades of blue: the walls and ceiling were painted a 'heaven blue', the chairs were covered with aquamarine velvet and the curtains were sapphire.[41] Adding to the exotic atmosphere, they kept a mongoose as well as a Siamese kitten and an Airedale dog.[42]

Bobby and Paula had been friends of Freda and Michael for many years. The two couples had often socialised together. However, the dynamics changed in 1932 after Michael died and the de Casa Maurys divorced. Shortly after the divorce, Paula married the former Unionist MP Bill Allen. As they were both now free, Freda and Bobby started seeing each other. Knowing her ex-husband's playboy tendencies, Paula wished Freda good luck. The two women were to remain great friends for the rest of their lives.

In March 1934, Bobby opened the Curzon Cinema in Mayfair, London's leading art-house cinema. It was a new type of cinema with 'no plush, no palms', no orchestra or organ.[43] With its simple, austere lines and stylish decoration it was described as a 'temple to movie art'.[44] The audience was encouraged to feel that they were the guests of the management and if they had paid for their ticket it was 'a mere formality which gentlemen will wish to hush up'.[45] Bobby took his new role very seriously and travelled all over Europe in search of the latest continental films to show at the Curzon. *The Bystander* wrote that the marquis was inspired by a 'realisation of the importance of intellectually satisfying films'. However, the journalist wondered if there was a large enough 'moneyed intelligentsia' to appreciate what he was trying to do. The article concluded: 'The Curzon is a "snob" cinema, and we want our "snob" public to show that they can understand and can lead public taste.'[46]

On the opening night, cars filled Curzon Street as the audience arrived. The men were in white tie and tails, the women in furs and long dresses.[47] Although Freda was at the premiere the marquis was photographed with Pempie, wearing a trademark red carnation in his buttonhole. At first it was hard to tell from the society pages whether he was courting Pempie or Freda as he appeared in photos with both mother and daughter at different events. The Dudley Wards' interests now overlapped with the marquis's, because Pempie had become an actress. After a successful screen test, she began appearing in films. In 1935, her first screen role was in *Escape Me Never*, which was filmed in Venice and London. One newspaper described her as having 'an ethereal look' and giving 'the impression of being ultra-sensitive and aloof'.[48] Another paper tipped her as the next Greta Garbo.[49]

The same year she appeared in Anthony Asquith's film *Moscow Nights*. She played the heroine, a war nurse, opposite Laurence Olivier, who played a Russian officer in the First World War. Critics wrote that she gave 'an excellent performance'.[50] At the premiere at the Leicester Square Theatre, her mother's old friend the Duke of Kent appeared in the audience as a surprise visitor.[51] It was evident that although the Prince of Wales had abandoned the Dudley Wards, his family had not.

Through her daughter and lover, Freda had a new circle of friends that included film stars. In 1935 Freda, Pempie and Bobby stayed at Carlyon Bay in Cornwall with Douglas Fairbanks Junior and Gertrude Lawrence. They all travelled down to St Austell together on the sleeper train from Paddington. Carlyon Bay was described as having a 'Riviera-ish atmosphere'. There was an elegant hotel with bungalows scattered around it. Pempie and Freda stayed in one bungalow while the actress Gertrude Lawrence and her daughter took another. The atmosphere was very relaxed; guests wore shorts or swimming costumes all day long, played tennis or squash or swam in the open-air seawater pool. Pempie wore brick-coloured pyjamas to lunch at the hotel and then put on an aquamarine swimsuit to bathe in the pool. On the occasional rainy day there were excursions to unspoilt fishing villages. The party went out in the lifeboat at Fowey and got soaked but thoroughly enjoyed it. The locals were fascinated; by the time the boat returned there were dozens of autograph hunters waving their books at the stars. According to *The Bystander*, the holiday was a great success and all the guests had 'a divine time altogether'.[52]

Freda's younger daughter Angie was also leading her own life. In 1935 she married Captain Robert Laycock, of the Royal Horse Guards at St Margaret's Westminster. Bob, as he was known, was also from a well-known Nottinghamshire family. The young couple had met during the hunting season. Angie did not ride but she was staying at the house of her late grandmother, Mrs Birkin, when she met the up-and-coming young officer. Angie had just had her first season. Although she was attracted to Bob, she did not immediately succumb to his charms. He was nine years older than her and on one occasion she accused him of being a 'cradle snatcher'. Shortly after they met, she went to America to visit some of Freda's relatives. Her aunt, Vera, told Bob that Angie was having such a good time she might not come back. When she did finally return, he proposed at Doncaster racecourse in November 1934.[53]

Angie was the first of her season's debutantes to marry. At only 18 she was such a young bride that one gossip columnist joked: 'We've always wondered how she's escaped matrimony so long.'[54] The wedding, at St Margaret's Westminster on 24 January 1935, reflected Freda's classless attitude. It was a stylish event with the bride dressed in a medieval-style brocade gown created by one of her sister's costume designers and a military guard of honour from the bridegroom's regiment awaiting her as she walked down the aisle. However, it was not all film-star glamour; Freda's social conscience was also emphasised as unemployed men and women who were members of the Feathers Clubs had seats reserved for them.[55] Angie's father William Dudley Ward had come from Canada to give her away; the only guest who was missing was the Prince of Wales.

As Angie had been so close to the prince, she begged her mother to send him an invitation to her wedding. She was very hurt when there was no reply. She received nothing from the man who had been in her life since she was a toddler, not even a card. According to Wallis Simpson, when she heard of the engagement she had said to Edward that she supposed he must be very pleased as it was an excellent match, but he had just brushed her remark aside, saying he no longer saw the family and would not be going to the wedding. When Wallis asked if he was sending a present he just said: 'No.' His new mistress was quite shocked; it was the first time she had seen the side of him which could permanently exclude people who had been important in his life.[56]

After Edward had abdicated at the end of 1936, he married Wallis Simpson in June 1937 at the Château de Cande in the Loire region of France. Their host was the controversial self-made millionaire, Charles Bedaux, who had extensive business and political connections in Nazi Germany. Until it actually happened, even Mrs Simpson did not know exactly what the outcome of her affair with the prince would be. In February 1936 she had written to her aunt that Edward was lonely as king without a consort. The English wanted him to marry a duke's daughter rather than a 'mangy' foreign princess but he would not marry without being in love.[57] Like Freda before her, at one point Wallis wrote to Edward breaking off their affair, explaining that they could only 'create disaster together'. However, like her predecessor, she also discovered that it was almost impossible to end her relationship with Edward.[58]

With Edward (now Duke of Windsor) married, Freda finally felt free to move on with her own life. A few months after Edward and Wallis's wedding, in October 1937, Freda married Bobby de Casa Maury at Marylebone Registry Office. Crowds encircled the bride's car and some people climbed on walls to see her arrive. Freda walked up the registry office steps with her brother Charles and sister Vera. Her outfit was understated; she wore a blue felt hat with a velvet bow and a 'smoke blue' suit with a stripe down the sleeves and a fur collar.[59] After the marriage, the bride and groom entertained a few friends and then left for honeymoon in Paris.[60] Freda's family believe that sex had a great deal to do with the suave marquis's attraction. He was known to take love-making very seriously. For him it was almost an art form; he collected erotic books and even had a Japanese model of a solid gold penis as a paperweight.[61]

As Freda began her new life, in the same month Edward and Wallis made their infamous trip to Germany. Knowing that it would provide the regime with a propaganda coup, the Duke and Duchess of Windsor's Nazi hosts welcomed them enthusiastically. Referred to as 'Her Royal Highness', Wallis was treated like a queen and shown the respect her besotted husband believed she deserved. When they arrived, Union Jacks alternating with Swastikas decorated the station as the crowd cheered 'Heil Edward'.[62] During the visit they met Hermann Göring, Heinrich Himmler, Rudolf Hess and Joseph Goebbels, but the highlight of their trip was tea with Hitler. Wallis grinned like an infatuated teenager as the Führer shook her hand. She later noted that he had 'great inner force'.[63]

Before the Second World War, Freda and Bobby led a stylish life in London. They were frequently seen at film premieres at the Curzon. However, there was always a more serious side to Freda and she was soon using her new husband's business to help her charity. Many of the premieres were in aid of the Feathers Clubs. Relishing everything modern, in 1937–38 Freda and her husband had a state-of-the-art house built in Hamilton Terrace, St John's Wood. It was commissioned from the fashionable Scottish architects Burnet, Tait and Lorne, who had already built the Curzon Cinema using the design of their architect Francis Lorne.

Built on the site of two Victorian houses, the new art deco house was featured in the *Ideal Home Magazine* of September 1938. Over six pages the magazine showed photographs of the house and analysed how the de Casa Maurys had created the simple, elegant style. Outside, blue-tinted bricks and white finish stonework and door and window frames complemented the clean lines of the house. Inside, light colours were used throughout. The hall was painted the palest yellow with a yellowish grey marble floor. In the sitting room the scheme was composed of pinkish-white walls and ceiling, the chair covers were blue and white with cushions and ruching of deep wine-coloured ottoman silk. One bedroom had blue satin covers and a buttoned bedhead; another used pink satin quilting. To make a bold statement, much of the furniture was designed by Doris Howard Robertson in satin-finished steel. The de Casa Maurys had all the latest technology; there was a television set in their second sitting room and they had the most modern heating and lighting. Mirrors were used throughout to reflect the light and make rooms look larger. The curved staircase was lit by portholes; during the day, natural light came through while at night artificial light from lamps in the thickness of the wall between the inner and outer glass lit the stairs.[64]

Freda had always enjoyed interior design and between the wars she was very successful at buying properties, doing them up, and then moving on. Her daughter Angie recalled that she had rarely lived anywhere more than two years. During the 1930s Freda built six houses in Wells Rise, Regent's Park which she then let out. She found the whole process very rewarding, describing the townhouses as 'so nice and my own creation'.[65]

As always in Freda's life, family was a priority and although they were now grown up, she remained close to both her daughters. When Angie gave birth to her first daughter Edwina Ottillie Jane (always called 'Tilly') in 1936, Freda became a youthful grandmother. Gossip columnists commented that she was 'the slimmest as well as the smartest grandmother in London'.[66] Two years later, in July 1938, the Laycocks had a son, Joseph William Peter.

In 1939 Bobby de Casa Maury opened a second cinema, the Paris, in Lower Regent Street. It could seat 500 people and like the Curzon it was decorated in the latest fashion. Its crinkled walls and ceilings were painted matt white, while the chairs and carpets were in pillar-box red and the dim lighting in the corridor was turquoise blue. The first film shown at the Paris was *La Bête Humaine*, a thriller based on Emile Zola's novel but directed by Jean Renoir, son of the famous painter. The gala premiere raised funds for Freda's Feathers Clubs. Noël Coward and Pempie were among the celebrity guests.[67]

By the late 1930s Pempie's acting career had taken off. She was in the pages of magazines more often than her mother and Freda was now referred to as 'the mother of Penelope Dudley Ward'. In 1938 Pempie made her debut on the American stage, appearing in Noël Coward's revue *Set to Music* in New York. While appearing in the show she fell in love with fellow actor Anthony Pelissier, son of the popular composer Harry Pelissier and the actress Fay Compton. Anthony composed music, painted, wrote and acted. After a short courtship, Pempie and Anthony married in December 1939. He was very well read, but he was a mercurial character and difficult to live with. A year after their wedding, the couple had a daughter, Tracy, but by that time their marriage was not working out.[68]

During the war Pempie appeared in some high-profile films, acting opposite Laurence Olivier and David Niven. While filming a short film, called *A Letter from Home*, made under the auspices of the British Ministry of Information, she met the film-maker Carol Reed. Carol was a tall, dark, restless man. The attraction between Pempie and Carol was very powerful. At the time Pempie was still married to Anthony Pelissier and Carol was about to marry another woman, Diana Wynyard. Carol married Diana, although he knew he was more in love with Pempie. Although she was deeply in love too, Pempie tried to do the honourable thing. She did not wish to break up someone else's marriage, so she left England to appear in *Lady Windermere's Fan* on Broadway. It was a great success and Pempie's career flourished in America.[69]

14

THE CHARITY WORKER

D uring the Second World War, Freda's connections kept her close to the centre of power; her friendships with Winston Churchill and Brendan Bracken deepened. In 1940 Winston nominated her charity, the Feathers Club Association, to receive the royalties on the records of his speeches which were being distributed by His Master's Voice Gramophone Company. He also sent her £500 from a fund sent to him by the Mutual Fire Underwriters Association of Ontario. Freda wrote to him saying how touched she was by his gesture. She explained: 'Any money that I get is so badly needed, and so inexpressibly welcome at the present time. We have much work to do and so little money available.'[1] The press baron Lord Beaverbrook also donated £200 to the clubs.[2]

Responding to wartime needs, the charity's role expanded. It was supplying food to thousands of homeless people and men and women doing war work. It got so busy that the Feathers Club Association called in a communal feeding expert to advise them. The clubs gained a reputation for giving a nourishing meal at low prices at lunchtime and in the evening. They also provided food to take home for people who had no cooking facilities. Feathers Clubs set up emergency nurseries to look after babies and children whose mothers had to go out to work to supplement the family income while their husbands were in the forces. In the evenings, the clubs were full of people of all ages from the overcrowded districts of London. They put on cookery demonstrations, first aid classes and knitting parties. To provide some light relief there were whist drives and dances. Many of the women who came were very lonely because their children had been evacuated and their husbands were abroad fighting.

Activities were still put on for boys and girls aged 14 to 18. It was felt that it was particularly important to care for teenagers. Without the clubs they would have had nowhere to go and nothing to do except hang around in the blacked-out streets. If they got bored it was feared they would turn to hooliganism. Instead, the clubs provided a warm cheerful place where, under the supervision of supportive adults, they could spend their evenings playing games or pursuing their hobbies. In an era when gender stereotyping was the norm, in one club the boys were making model aeroplanes to be judged by Bobby de Casa Maury, while the girls were making Christmas cards and redecorating dolls' houses.

The club activities continued until the night bombing became intense. Due to the Blitz, some of the clubs had to shut in the evenings but at the Kensal Road club an air-raid shelter was built adjoining the building so that the boys could come straight from work, have their supper and then continue with club activities. They slept in bunks in the shelter and then had breakfast before leaving for work the next morning.

Nightly attendance had been high, but it dropped when club members were called up or started war work. Some women and children members were evacuated to the country, and many said that they wished there was a Feathers Club near them. When soldiers returned on leave they would pop into the clubs. To provide a respite from the bombing in London, the Feathers Club opened a workers' rest camp at Chipperfield, Hertfordshire, where members and their families could go for a quiet weekend.[3]

Freda enjoyed her work for the charity. After staying with Vera in Nottingham she wrote humorously to Duff Cooper that her visit to her sister's house on top of 'a coal black bleak hill with all her children and their Nottingham accents [...] will gradually get me ready to go back to the slums without suffering too much hardship from a sudden change'.[4]

In January 1941 Freda was invited to Ditchley Park in Oxfordshire by Winston and Clementine Churchill for a weekend house party. Ditchley was the elegant eighteenth-century home of the Conservative MP Ronald Tree and his American wife Nancy; the couple were well known for their lavish hospitality. The niece of Nancy Astor, Mrs Tree was the owner of 'Sibyl Colefax and John Fowler', the well-known British decorating firm. She was credited with creating the 'English country-house look' which was based on understatement and comfort. She believed that a house should never look 'decorated' and that a designer should not stick slavishly to one period or a room would be turned into a lifeless museum. Her special touches were open fires, candlelight and masses of flowers.

When the Battle of Britain started in 1940, Churchill was advised not to go to Chequers, his official country residence, as when the moon was bright it was considered a target for bombing. Churchill invited himself and his War Cabinet to Ditchley for the weekend of 9 November 1940. He then returned for a further twelve weekends up to September 1942. As a junior minister in the Ministry of Information with the task of encouraging American relations, Ronald Tree invited many of President Roosevelt's inner circle to join them at Ditchley.[5] Freda was there at an important moment in the war. The American diplomat and foreign policy adviser Harry Hopkins was visiting the prime minister on behalf of President Roosevelt. The Churchills were trying to win him over and gain American support for Britain. It seems that Freda was part of the charm offensive; the guests had been carefully selected, and another of Winston's favourite women, Venetia Montagu, was also invited. Over a series of weekends, the strategy worked and the early stages of 'Lend-Lease' were agreed upon in the Trees' country house.

Dinner at Ditchley was in a dining room displaying Nancy Tree's impeccable taste. It was lit only by candles and a large chandelier. The table was simply decorated with four gilt candlesticks with tall yellow tapers and a single gilt cup. Despite wartime rationing, the food was excellent. After dinner, the party watched a film called *Brigham Young*, which emphasised the value of simple faith and the nobility of refusing to compromise your principles. Following the film, some German newsreels were played; the absurdity of the Nazi salutes and goose-stepping parades made everyone laugh. The prime minister's young assistant private secretary, Jock Coville, sat next to Freda. Afterwards, he wrote in his diary that he understood why the Prince of Wales had felt as he did about her.[6]

The next day there was a long lunch. The British physicist and scientific adviser Professor Lindemann, Churchill and Mr Justice Singleton discussed the strength of the German air force. While the conversation continued, other guests went for a walk in the grounds. At dinner, there was just the type of stimulating discussion Freda relished. They talked about how America coped with unemployment by providing work instead of a dole. The evening ended with another film show. While the guests were watching *Night Train to Munich*, the phone rang with the news that HMS *Southampton* had been destroyed by bombers in the Mediterranean. Churchill stayed up until the early hours of the morning, smoking a huge cigar and pacing up and down in front of the fire in the library. For Hopkins's benefit, he gave his assessment of the war so far.[7]

After her visit, Freda sent Churchill a 'health-giving lamp' or 'sunlight machine', which she had told him about during the weekend. She suggested he should use it for three minutes on his back and three on his front every other day. She told him that she used it and it made her 'feel like a million dollars'.[8] Winston warmly thanked her and said that he would try to fit it into his routine.[9] Freda was a regular guest of the Churchills because she was so good at entertaining the prime minister and so discreet. In May 1944 she was invited to lunch by Clementine, shortly before the D-Day landings. She wrote to Duff Cooper that 'the atmosphere seems charged with suspense and waiting'. She added: 'Our friend [Churchill] was in the most fascinating form, and seemed in the gayest of moods – I wish I could tell you about it because I think you would enjoy it – but I suppose I had better not.'[10]

Another long-term friendship which flourished in the war years was Freda's with Duff Cooper. As he travelled around the world in various diplomatic roles, he sent her gifts of nylon stockings and lipstick. Duff wrote to her from Singapore in 1941 that he would like to be lunching with her at the Bon Viveur or dining with her at the Coq D'Or. He wrote: 'I often think of you, always with love and passion – Darling – Duff.'[11] When Freda was ill two years later, Duff sent her a large bouquet of flowers. Freda thanked him, saying: 'It is lovely to be remembered and thought about – especially by people you love.'[12] Freda was ill for some time but characteristically, she made light of it, telling her friend that 'I shan't be able to keep up this dame of the camellias stuff much longer I'm afraid as it ill becomes me as I look and feel so well'.[13]

In the war, Freda's marriage to Bobby de Casa Maury was beginning to fail. He was a compulsive womaniser and they spent increasingly long periods of time apart. Throughout her life, Freda had been surrounded by admirers, but she admitted to Duff that she seemed to be 'bereft of gentlemen friends just now'. In her late 40s, she was feeling her age. She added that everyone she saw was 'either too young, or too old; either too grey or too grassy-green'.[14] Freda and Duff enjoyed flirting with each other and exchanging gossip but there was also a deeper bond because they both missed Michael Herbert; he had been one of Duff's closest friends.

The war was a worrying time for Freda and her family. Angie's children were sent across the Atlantic to join their grandfather Duddie in Canada. He had moved to Alberta after his divorce, but had remained on good terms with Freda. When he came to England, they continued to see each other for family occasions and they even holidayed together. It was thought that Angie's children would be safer in Canada than England during the war. Angie took them across the Atlantic but crossing the ocean in wartime was dangerous and both Freda and Bob Laycock were relieved to hear that they had arrived safely.[15]

During the Blitz, the houses Freda had built at Wells Rise, Regent's Park, were destroyed by bombing. In a letter to Duff Cooper, she described the bombs thundering over her head 'on their deadly destructive way'. Imaginative and entertaining even in adversity, she wrote that it had been like a fairy tale:

In each little house was one little maid dusting and polishing and burnishing on each little top floor – The wicked bomb came roaring and hurtling overhead and each little maid took her little heels and scurried downstairs at a terrified breakneck speed just in time to reach her little basement kitchen as the bomb tore through the six little houses, taking their tops off like the lids of biscuit tins; but the six little maids were safe and unhurt, without even a scratch! – I think that story has the Big Bad Wolf and the six little pigs licked to a frazzle.[16]

After the bombing, Freda went to the bombsite and picked through the rubble. There was little left of what she had created. She told Duff that she was 'defiant and challenging' the enemy. She wished that she had 'some sort of new metal-obliterating spray gun that I could take some pot-shots with, in a sort of roof-top guerrilla warfare, and see them disintegrate in the air as I obliterate them one by one with my deadly marksmanship!'[17]

Freda's former lover's attitude could not have been a greater contrast. In the Second World War, when Britain's future hung in the balance, Edward and Wallis's behaviour could at best be described as naïve, at worst, treasonous. While they were in Spain and Portugal in 1940, they were breathtakingly indiscrete and defeatist. According to Germany's ambassador to Portugal, the Duke said that if he had been king it would never have come to war. Apparently, Edward believed that continued severe bombing would make England ready for peace.[18] It was at this stage that the Germans hatched a plot to kidnap the Duke and set him up as a puppet king if Hitler invaded Britain.[19] Fortunately, this nightmare scenario never became a reality. Instead, an exasperated Winston Churchill sent Wallis and Edward as far away as possible to govern the Bahamas.[20]

Freda and Angie's husbands both played important roles in the war. Known as 'Lucky' Laycock, Angie's husband Robert was often in the right place at the right time. He had two powerful patrons, Lord Mountbatten and Winston Churchill, who rated his abilities highly.[21] His most important role was in the creation of the commandos. In 1940, when he was just 33 years old, Laycock became commanding officer of 8 Commando, a new 'crack' unit which was formed on Churchill's order.[22] Once they had been trained, a number of commando units were sent to the Middle East under Laycock's command and they were called

Layforce. However, all did not go to plan in the early years. When in May 1941 Crete fell, many of the commandos were killed or taken prisoner by the Germans. Later in the same year, against his better judgement, Laycock took part in Operation Flipper, 'the Rommel Raid' in North Africa. The abortive raid on Rommel's headquarters was carried out mainly by men from No. 11 (Scottish) Commando. The operation failed and all but two of the British commandos who got ashore were killed or captured.

Freda's husband was also involved in a controversial operation. At the beginning of the conflict, Bobby de Casa Maury had been working as an air intelligence officer in the West Country, then, to many people's surprise, Lord Louis Mountbatten gave him a high-powered job. The Mountbattens had been friends with both Bobby and Freda for many years. As the chief of combined operations, Mountbatten asked the marquis to head the Intelligence Section. It was a very controversial appointment; many military men opposed a racing-driver chum of Mountbatten's being given the crucial role, particularly as he was an unqualified amateur.[23]

Once at COHQ, Bobby was put in charge of military intelligence for a raid on Dieppe. Its aim was to find out whether a major port on the continent could be captured quickly in close to working order. It was doomed to failure from the start. There was imprecision about the objectives and too large a committee was involved in planning it. It went disastrously wrong with a massive loss of British and Canadian lives. In August 1942 Operation Jubilee, the seaborne assault on the beaches of Dieppe, met far greater resistance than expected. Many of the Canadians in the landing craft were killed before they even got on shore. The men and tanks that managed to land were pinned down and never reached the town. By the end of the day 20 per cent of the commandos and 68 per cent of the Canadians who had landed were dead or wounded. Almost 1,000 men died and 2,000 were taken prisoner. The raid proved how hard an invasion would be.[24]

Many leading figures in Britain were furious, particularly the Canadian press baron Lord Beaverbrook. The Dieppe raid had handed the Germans a major propaganda coup. The underestimation of German fortifications at Dieppe was considered a failure of British intelligence.

Although it was debatable who was most at fault, Bobby took the blame and resigned.[25] He returned to the film industry and was soon working for Rank on the production side. One of the first films he was involved in was *Caesar and Cleopatra*, starring Vivien Leigh and Claude Rains.

As Bobby de Casa Maury's military career came to an end, Bob Laycock's was taking off. After his escapes from Crete and North Africa, in the middle of 1943, Laycock had a very successful period commanding the Special Service Brigade in Sicily and Italy.[26] While her husband was busy with his new post Angie stayed in London at the Berkeley Hotel with her mother. She ran the canteen at COHQ in Richmond Terrace with the help of Freda. She also supported the Commando Benevolent Fund which provided assistance to the wives, widows and children of men who had served in the commandos. Following in her mother's fundraising footsteps, she organised dances, concerts and a premiere of Laurence Olivier's film of *Henry V* for the cause.[27]

In October 1943, Laycock was chosen to take over from Lord Mountbatten as the chief of combined operations. His youth made him a surprising choice; he became the youngest major general in the British army. In his new position he attended most of the important Allied conferences. He was head of an organisation which played a key part in making possible the Allied landings in Europe.[28] Recognising his role, in the New Year's Honours of 1945 he was made a Companion of the Order of the Bath.[29]

Freda was very proud of her son-in-law. She wrote to Duff Cooper that while she was staying with Angie she had found a leatherbound book in which Bob Laycock wrote his favourite quotations from authors. Several passages from Duff's writing were among them. She explained: 'I thought the whole book very touching – It was written in very lately and the great General obviously regards it as his Bible.'[30] In another letter to Duff she told him that her son-in-law's 'beautiful Chinese eyes were aglow with enthusiastic fan-like love and admiration' for Duff's work.[31] Bob Laycock was equally fond of his mother-in-law, he always wrote to her as 'my darling Ma-in-law'.[32]

At the end of the war Freda and her family began to piece their lives back together. The Laycocks' children, Tilly and Joe, had returned from Canada in 1944. They had been away for four years and were now aged

5 and 7. At first it was hard for them to readjust; they had not seen their mother and father for years and they resented coming back to the austerity of post-war Britian.[33] Freda described them as 'radiantly beautiful' but she felt they needed some discipline after their years away from their parents. Perhaps making up for lost time, they never stopped talking day and night. Freda joked to Duff Cooper that she had suggested to Angie that she should have them taken to a psychoanalyst to have them 'impregnated with a few inhibitions'. However, she admitted that she might just be 'bitter' as, at first, they preferred their other grandmother, Lady Laycock, 'because she has a wooden leg which fascinates them – and the other day they were found hurrying off to the woodshed [...] with it to chop it up for firewood!'[34]

In 1947, Bob resigned from the army. He wanted to spend more time with his growing family. In the years immediately after the war Angie and Bob had three more children, Ben, Emma and Martha. Only in his 40s, Bob was ready for a new challenge. Freda did everything she could to help him. In 1952, she wrote to Winston Churchill asking him to consider Laycock for the new chief of police.[35] For a time he did not take on a full-time job. He accepted some non-executive appointments; he became a director of Lloyds Bank and chairman of Windsor Hospital management committee.[36] He also helped Freda with her charity work, serving as president of the Feathers Club Association.

From 1954 until 1959 Bob Laycock was Governor of Malta. He held the position during a period when tensions were high on the island. The Maltese politician Dom Mintoff, who was leader of the Labour party, was leading a campaign for full integration with Britain, while the Nationalist party wanted Malta to become an independent dominion in the Commonwealth.[37] Before going to Malta, Laycock was knighted by the queen. The posting was a new adventure for all the family. They moved into the governor's residence, St Anton Palace. When the children were home from school on holiday, there were trips in the governor's barge, a former picket boat with a cabin, and bathing in the palace's swimming pool. Angie kept a sailing boat at St Paul's Bay and Bob took up snorkelling. The Laycocks had a hectic schedule. While he grappled with the complex political situation, she relished her role as hostess. There were frequent cocktail parties and dinners for visiting guests. The Queen Mother, the Duke of Edinburgh, the Duchess of Kent and the Mountbattens all visited.[38] Each year, Freda came to stay for a month. While she was there, in the evenings after dinner, they would play her favourite card game, canasta.[39] Angie used to like filming the family on her cine-camera. Although she was by this time in her 60s, there is some film footage of Freda looking incredibly young and glamorous. She can be seen sitting on the rocks, looking out to sea, wearing big sunglasses, a scarf and shorts which show off her slender legs.[40]

The only visitors Angie was not happy to receive in Malta were the Duke and Duchess of Windsor. When they arrived in Malta aboard Loel Guinness's yacht, *Calisto*, Bob Laycock had lunch with them but Angie decided to be away.[41] Edward's callous rejection of her family still hurt.

Pempie's life also changed after the war. In 1944, she divorced her first husband, Anthony Pelissier. Carol Reed had found it impossible to remain married to his wife, Diana, when he was still in love with Pempie. As soon as regular civilian air services to America were reinstated, he visited Pempie in New York. Separation had made their love for each other even stronger and they resumed their affair. Once Pempie returned to England, Carol divorced Diana. He married Pempie in January 1948 in a civil ceremony at a registry office in Windsor. Their son Max was born later that year. Until they found a suitable house, the family lived in a flat in the same building as Freda, in Albert Hall Mansions, Kensington. Pempie gave up acting as soon as she married Carol. She became a devoted wife and mother. She spent the rest of her life supporting her husband's career and creating a happy home life for her family.[42] Freda got on very well with Carol and was very fond of him.

By the early 1950s Freda's marriage to Bobby was coming to an end. He was serially unfaithful, often with her friends. In 1954, she divorced him on the grounds of adultery. Ironically, the woman he had been having an affair with was Laura, second wife of Eric, Lord Dudley. Eric had married Laura in 1943. The granddaughter of Lord Wemyss, she was twenty years younger than him but there was an intense physical attraction between them. Laura described Eric as 'fantastically attractive' and 'all-powerful'. Many women in his social circle pursued him. However, Laura recognised that he had never got over Rosemary's death and that he was still very sad deep down.[43] Young and inexperienced, she had found Rosemary a hard act to follow. In her autobiography, she described her experience as a young bride coming to Himley Hall as being like the heroine in Daphne du Maurier's novel *Rebecca*, who was overwhelmed by the legacy of her husband's charismatic first wife. Everyone still loved Rosemary and, unlike Rebecca, she had deserved that adoration.[44]

Eric and Laura often socialised with Freda and Bobby. There was a complex dynamic between the two couples. According to Laura, Eric still loved Freda, but Laura recognised that it was not in the same way that he loved her. While Lord Dudley was infatuated with his old friend, Bobby turned his attentions to Laura. She found him good looking, but she complained that he had limited conversation.[45] Eric dismissively called him 'that Cuban motor car mechanic'.[46]

As the Dudleys' marriage deteriorated, Bobby and Freda were invited to stay more often. Inevitably, Bobby's flirtation with Laura turned into an affair. Laura explained that he had a real 'reverence for sex', treating it like going to church. He was such an 'ardent and single-minded lover' that no jokes were allowed.[47] They used to meet in London, but Laura had no intention of leaving her husband for him. Bobby told her that Freda was bored with him and that she now wanted to marry Eric.[48] It was a messy situation, and both couples were very unhappy. Freda employed private detectives to track her husband. When she found out the truth she moved Bobby out of their flat in Albert Hall Mansions. He claimed to have no money, but he managed to move into the Berkeley Hotel.[49] For several years, Freda agonised about what to do. She did not want to precipitate a row which would involve unpleasant publicity and damage everyone's reputations. Her solicitor told her that it was also possible that Laura and Eric might have a reconciliation and by acting too soon they could put everyone in a difficult position. However, remaining in limbo was not a permanent option either, so eventually both Eric and Freda decided that divorce was the only solution. Bobby wanted Laura's name kept out of court, but Freda's solicitor said that the judge would want her to give him a truthful answer and she should not say anything that was not right to protect other people.[50]

Characteristically, after the divorce, Freda was magnanimous to her ex-husband. Bobby's affair with Laura soon fizzled out; once he was available she became terribly bored with him. Despite his bad behaviour, Freda and Bobby remained friends. He sometimes went on holidays with her and occasionally they visited her family in Malta together. Unable to resist a pretty woman of any age, Bobby flirted with Freda's granddaughter Tilly.[51] However, Tilly had fallen in love with one of her father's aides-de-camp, Lieutenant Mark Agnew. They were married in April 1955; a year later their first daughter Leonie was born, making Freda a great-grandmother at the youthful age of 61.[52]

On her own again, Freda continued to live in her Victorian flat in Albert Hall Mansions, Kensington, which she filled with stylish modern furniture. When Bobby ran out of money and became ill with cancer, Freda moved him into the flat next door to her apartment. She would not have him back as a husband, but she looked after him through his final illness.[53]

After her second divorce, Freda had admirers but no lasting relationship. She remained close to Rosemary's widower, Eric Dudley, sometimes staying with him in his Bahamas home, Marion House, Nassau. Another man who fell in love with her was the politician Kenneth Lindsay. It seems that they first met when he joined the Feathers Club Association Council in 1942. They worked together on several projects for the charity and he was soon infatuated with her, writing: 'I cannot stop thinking of you because I love you.'[54] He moved to America, where he was Walker-Ames Lecturer in political science at the University of Washington. Freda's relationship with Kenneth was based on an intellectual bond. Freda had always been interested in politics and ideas. She was as supportive of Kenneth as she had been to her earlier lovers. He wrote to her thanking her for the enormous encouragement she had given him in his work. However, as in the past, her new love became dissatisfied with the level of commitment she was willing to give him. He wrote to her: 'Last night was so unsatisfactory and left me with such an unsympathetic outlook that I must write this short line. I did not know it was possible for so much rust to gather in the soul within 24 hours and by last night the corroding powers were well advanced when we met.'[55] The problem seemed to be that Freda had so many friends and family who needed her that she could not give him the undivided attention he craved.

Freda continued her charity work for the Feathers Club Association until she was in her late 60s. After the war, the charity moved into youth and community work. Their aim was to prevent children in over-crowded areas from getting into trouble which would see them end up in court. The Association's slogan was: 'It is cheaper to keep a boy and girl in a Youth Club than in an Approved School – Please Help Us to Help Them to Help Themselves.'[56] In 1952 Freda took a journalist from *The Sketch* to visit the clubs. The journalist was very impressed with the way they were run, largely by the members for themselves. The writer commented on the friendliness of the atmosphere and the 'obvious popularity' of Freda, who he reckoned could 'leave a jewel case unlocked in an unlocked car in these slum districts of London (where the police go in pairs) without the slightest worry'.[57] Mixing with the club members, Freda became streetwise. Her granddaughter Emma remembers her advising her never to bother locking her car because if someone wanted to steal something from it they would just break the window to get in.[58] Freda readily built a rapport with the young people she met. As her grandson Ben Laycock explains: 'She was the least snob-bish person you could imagine. It was always a huge pleasure when she was around. She was fun and had a great sense of humour.'[59] Perhaps an initial icebreaker with members of the youth clubs was that in her ear-lier years at house parties she is credited with inspiring the game called 'Freda', which is a cross between billiards and snooker.[60]

In the 1950s there were 2,130 members of the seven clubs, which were in some of the most deprived areas in London. They were open all day providing school meals for children, afternoon clubs for housewives and pensioners and play centres for 4- to 7-year-olds. In the evening, they ran youth clubs offering a range of activities including drama, boxing, table tennis, football, athletics and dancing. In the summer they put on camps; the boys went to Battlesbridge and the girls to Chigwell Row.

In 1958, Freda wrote to Winston Churchill thanking him for another instalment of the money from the 'Gramophone company' for his war-time speeches. She explained that the charity was expanding fast, but it was always short of funds. They had bought another hall in Paddington where they could take 300 children in the evenings. She wrote: 'It is in the environs of the Edgware Road, a rough and tough neighbourhood and just where we ought to be!!!'[61] The charity received an annual grant from the Ministry of Education, but this came nowhere near meeting the cost of the clubs, so the rest of the money had to be raised by Freda and her volunteers. She was a very hands-on chairman, who rarely missed a meeting for more than twenty years. She put on an annual jumble sale at her flat which raised £1,500. Every year she put on a dance for 700 society youngsters aged 10 to 17 to raise funds for those who were less fortunate. At one square dance at Chelsea Town Hall, the girls wore full skirts and coloured blouses while the boys were dressed in checked and tartan shirts and jeans. Henrietta Tiarks (the future Duchess of Bedford), Anna Massey (who was to become a famous actress) and the film star Vivien Leigh were there to support Freda.[62] Her grandchildren were regularly inviegled into her charity work, and they still remember attending the events she organised.[63] When he was a trendy teenager in the 1960s Freda's grandson Ben loathed going but there was 'a three-line whip' from his mother, so they all had to attend the dance. Ben was particularly annoyed because his mother made him have his hair cut and wear 'incredibly straight clothes' for the evening. 'It was hell,' he recalled.[64]

For decades, Freda had shown so much dedication to the cause that it was felt by many of her friends and colleagues that she should be honoured for her work. In 1954, Lord Willingdon, Kenneth Lindsay and Brendan Bracken approached another friend of hers, Prime Minister Winston Churchill, about her being made a Dame of the British Empire to mark the twenty-first anniversary of the foundation of the Feathers Club Association. Lord Willingdon, who was a vice-president of the clubs, explained that it would please the many members, especially the old people who were devoted to the marquesa.[65] However, although the prime minister's office considered the suggestion, nothing came of it.

In 1963 Freda's old friend Eric, Lord Dudley, tried again. He asked Winston Churchill to write to the present prime minister, Harold Macmillan, saying that she should be honoured for her work. Eric had been a vice-president of the Feathers Association for many years. He explained that he thought Freda was, in many ways, one of the outstanding women of her generation.[66] It seems that Clementine was pushing her husband to recommend their old friend too. Winston told Eric that they both admired the great work Freda had done.[67] In August 1963 Churchill wrote a letter to the prime minister setting out what Freda had achieved. Macmillan replied saying that Winston could assure Clemmie that he would bear Freda's name in mind when he was thinking about his New Year's Honours List.[68] Lord Dudley had thought that with Churchill's backing the honour would be a fait accompli.[69] However, the repercussions from the Profumo scandal affected Macmillan's self-confidence and he resigned as prime minister on health grounds in October. Although Freda certainly deserved official recognition, she never received it. It is also possible that she was offered an honour and turned it down. As her relationship with the prince showed, Freda had never pursued titles, she did the work for its own sake. Lord Dudley wrote to Winston Churchill: 'As you know, her unselfish character, she would probably refuse anything that might be offered, but yet be pleased by the gesture.'[70]

By the middle of the 1960s Freda had given up being chairwoman of the Feathers Club Association. For the next decade she occasionally attended meetings and was always given a special welcome. Her family continued their connections with the charity when Pempie became president. Freda had always been very involved with her daughters and as she grew older she also played an important role in the lives of her seven grandchildren. When her granddaughter Emma was 11 she came to live with Freda during the week because she was going to school in London. Emma recalls that her grandmother never interfered and left her to her own devices. On one occasion Emma asked if she could help her with her homework. Freda replied that she couldn't possibly as she would get it wrong. One of her wise sayings was: 'Never interfere in other people's lives. The only thing you can do for your children is fix their teeth.' She was always there to support her grandchildren, but she also encouraged them to be independent.[71]

As she got older, Freda was never lonely because people of all ages found her fun to be with. At one family gathering, she looked around the room and was surprised to see so many people there. She said: 'But I only had two children.'[72] Her grandchildren loved visiting her. They remember her as someone who they could talk to about anything.

She was totally unjudgemental and she always asked her grandchildren about what they were doing rather than wanting to talk about herself.

Freda also had many lifelong friends because she rarely fell out with anyone. She developed very close relationships with both her male and female friends. She preferred intimate lunches or dinners on her own with one friend so that they could pour their hearts out to her.[73] She introduced her grandchildren to her fascinating circle. Her grand-daughter Martha Milinaric recalls meeting Nancy Astor, who was rather formidable, and Paula Gellibrand, who was wonderful with children. Clemmie Churchill was also a great friend.

Although she was very close to her grandmother, Martha did not know that Freda had been the Prince of Wales's mistress until she was in her 20s. She read about it when Frances Donaldson's biography of the prince appeared. When Martha asked her grandmother about it she was reluctant to talk, saying it was all so long ago. She had moved on and was living her life to the full in the present. She did not seem inter-ested in the past.[74] Freda's great-niece, Lady Isabella Naylor-Leyland (Bindy's daughter), recalls her telling her about when the prince refused to return her phone calls. Freda said it was a shame, but she did not say anything derogatory about her former lover and showed no bitterness. Isabella remembers her as being very wise; she said to her: 'All those things seem so important at the time but when you get to my age, none of it matters at all.'[75]

As the years went by Freda was one of the last survivors of her glam-orous generation. Reflecting their shrinking circle, Lady Diana Cooper phoned Freda and said that as they were the only ones left perhaps they should try to see each other more. Freda was polite but honest, reply-ing that they had never really got on and she did not see any point in pretending now.[76] When Freda's grandson Max Reed saw her looking up something in a battered old address book, he offered to buy her a new one, but she told him not to bother as most of her friends were dead.[77] The Duke of Windsor had died in Paris in 1972; Freda had not seen or spoken to him for nearly four decades. However, she still wore the two rings he had given her during their long relationship. One was a beautiful ruby and white gold ring from Cartier, while the other had a message inscribed inside. They were slightly chipped after years of being worn every day, but they were a secret symbol of the past. It was only after Freda's death that her family realised they had come from the Prince of Wales.[78]

For Freda there were no regrets; there were too many people still in her life for her to dwell on the past. However, the life of her replacement, the Duchess of Windsor, was very different. She lived on, suffering from dementia, increasingly isolated and cut off in her own world. Freda was never a vindictive woman and her grandchildren say they never heard her say a bad word about Wallis. If they asked her about the woman who replaced her she refused to be drawn.[79] However, she was thrilled when Caroline Blackwood, who was writing a book on the Windsors, came to interview her and told her that she looked years younger than Wallis.[80]

As she grew older, Freda remained as elegant and charming as ever. Although she became a frail old lady, who was very tiny and almost bird-like in appearance, she still made an effort to look attractive. Her style had changed little since the 1930s and every morning she went through the same ritual, spending ages curling her hair and applying her make-up in front of the mirror.[81] She also carried on smoking, often having one cigarette on the go after another.[82] Her great-niece Lady Isabella Naylor-Leyland describes her as 'very quaint, she always wore a little bow tie under her neatly collared shirts'.[83] Another great-niece, Lucinda Lambton, recalls: 'It was like seeing someone from a different world. She had an overwhelming innate glamour, without being ostentatious. I loved her delicacy, she was ethereal and enchanting.'[84]

The last years of Freda's life were marred by the premature deaths of some of her closest family. Both Freda's daughters were widowed. First, Bob Laycock had a fatal heart attack in 1968, aged only 60. His death was a great shock to all the family, and after it Angie spent much of her time in Spain. In 1976 Pempie's husband, Carol Reed, also died of a heart attack.[85] When her sons-in-law died Freda was very strong and supported her daughters and their children.

After Pempie was widowed she bought three houses in Old Church Street, Chelsea. Freda moved in to one of them with her Filipino maid, Marcie, who had become her friend and companion. At first Freda missed her flat and humorously described her new house as 'a slum'.[86] However, it was a practical solution and as they lived next door to each other, mother and daughter saw each other all the time. Freda's niece Bindy, who had married Lord Lambton, also liked to stay close to her aunt. She lived on the King's Road close to Freda's new house.[87]

Freda, Pempie and Angie remained not just physically but emotionally very close to each other but there was some sibling rivalry and at times Freda's daughters rowed. Freda found their arguments funny. One day when they were both visiting her, Angie asked Pempie if she could use her car, which was parked outside. At first Pempie said no because she thought her sister was such an awful driver. However, after Angie got cross Pempie relented and gave her the keys. Freda and her elder daughter watched from the window as Angie tried to drive out of the parking space. As Angie reversed into the car behind, Freda laughed so much that there were tears running down her face. 'They haven't changed since they were children,' she said.[88]

In 1980 tragedy struck Angie's family when her eldest son Joe and his 8-year-old daughter Flora were killed in a boating accident. Perhaps hardest of all for Freda was when Pempie died of a brain tumour in 1982. Freda had lived through many hard times and was a philosophical person, but she did not have a strong faith. Her grandson Ben recalls her saying: 'If God exists, he's either completely inefficient or a total bastard.'[89] Freda only survived her eldest daughter by a year. While staying with Angie in Spain, she had a fall and broke her pelvis. She never fully recovered and seemed to just fade away. She died in 1983 at the age of 88. In her later years, when her grandchildren asked her about dying she told them she was not afraid, explaining: 'It was perfectly all right before I was born so I'm sure it will be all right after I'm dead.'[90]

Throughout her long life she rarely spoke and never wrote about her affair with the prince. However, after her death Freda's trusted maid, Miss McCann, handed Angie a suitcase which she had never seen before. When Angie opened it, she found hundreds of letters from the prince and Michael Herbert which tell the remarkable story of the devotion Freda had inspired. They reveal a love affair to rival Edward and Mrs Simpson's 'romance of the century'.

THELMA

THELMA

15

THE INTERNATIONAL
PLAYGIRL

When the Prince of Wales replaced Thelma with Wallis, she reacted in a very different way from Freda, retaliating by having a quick fling with Prince Aly Khan. The glamorous couple set off to Spain together in one of his fast cars. Thelma admitted that part of Aly's attraction was that he was adventurous: free from any ties he was ready to do anything, anywhere, at any time. She conceded that her actions were aimed at getting back at her former lover and she believed that Aly was aware of this.[1]

Aly was very eligible, and fully aware of his power over women. He considered himself to be the best rider and dancer and the most attractive man on the international scene. He provided just the escapism Thelma needed. Aly drove her at top speed in his sports car to Barcelona then, after a few days there, they moved on to Seville. His driving could be terrifying; his normal cruising speed was 80 miles an hour. Once, to keep a date in Paris, he drove the 600 miles from Cannes in eight hours. His friend and admirer, the songwriter and author Elsa Maxwell, often said to him that she would do anything in the world for him except get into a car when he was driving.[2]

Thelma's relationship with Aly was far more tempestuous than her more domestic experience with the Prince of Wales. Always romanticising her situation, Thelma described herself as feeling like Carmen after the moody Don José had been replaced by the glamorous matador Escamillo.[3] Unlike her affair with the prince, Thelma's liaison with Aly was based on sex. According to one of Edward's biographers, Thelma had told friends that he was a most unsatisfactory sexual partner.[4] In contrast, Aly's prowess in the bedroom was legendary. He liked to say: 'I think only of the woman's pleasure when I'm in love.'[5] According to his biographer, as a teenager he was sent to Cairo to be taught Ismak by a Persian hakim. This practice taught a man how to restrain his sexual climax indefinitely to ensure the total satisfaction of his partner.[6] It was mentioned by Richard F. Burton in his 'Terminal Essay' in his translation of *The Arabian Nights* and other sex manuals he translated.[7]

Over the next few months, Aly and Thelma jetted around the world to London, Paris and Ireland, attending every important race meeting on the continent. One of the highlights was a midnight race at Longchamp. Thelma and her twin sister, Gloria, dined with Aly, his father and his wife and the socialite Daisy Fellowes. They then went to the races in full evening dress. Most of the party were wearing hats but, never one to follow the fashion set by others, Thelma wrapped some delicate antique lace around her head and fastened it with a large black pearl pin which matched her famous necklace of black pearls. It was a memorable evening. It was dark, so the course was brightly lit. Before the racing began the corps de ballet from the Grand Opera and the Russian ballet danced on a raised platform in front of the grandstand. At nine different points along the course orchestras played. Famous racehorse owners from across Europe had come for this one night in Paris. Lord Carnarvon and Lord Derby had brought over their finest horses to race. There were six flat races, one major race and a gentleman's race in which Aly rode. He was a fearless rider who raced wearing the Ismaili colours of green and red. The only disappointment of the evening for Thelma and her sister was that Aly did not win.[8]

Thelma and Aly spent the summer together at a villa in Deauville, sunbathing on the beach, entertaining friends and gambling at the casino. Deauville was known as 'the playground of the Best People in

France'.[9] One gossip columnist dubbed it 'the queen of the Watering Places of Northern France [...] though she may be slightly morganatic'.[10] Society women from France and Britain visited the resort for the races and the glamorous social life. Mornings were spent by the sea, where the women wore a beach dress or dressing gown, but never shorts. At lunchtime they would dash back to their hotel or villa and change into white or pastel crepe dresses and large straw hats before drinking Dubonnets and having a leisurely lunch. Most afternoons there would be horseracing at the Deauville course. In the sunny paddock at the racecourse race-goers lounged in easy chairs under spreading trees.[11]

During the summer season of 1934, Thelma and Aly were the centre of attention. One gossip columnist who saw her at the casino wrote that Lady Furness had 'never looked more alluring than now. The new old-fashioned evening décolletage suits her milky skin and she quite often smiles.'[12] She was photographed at the races looking cool and elegant in a white crepe dress with a short cape jacket which showed off to perfection her brunette beauty. Showing what Thelma interpreted as a degree of commitment, Aly bought her a racehorse.[13] However, their relationship was not to last. At the end of the summer Thelma returned to America and they drifted apart. This was typical of Aly; he never finished his love affairs abruptly. Instead, he would find a new love and then go back to the previous one, or his lover before her. He was so charming and generous, women usually forgave him and accepted his womanising behaviour.[14]

As Aly's relationship with Thelma was cooling, he met his next conquest at a dinner party in Deauville. Joan Guinness was the daughter of Lord Churston and the wife of Loel Guinness, the MP for Bath. At the dinner party, Aly ignored the cool blonde for most of the evening but when there was a silence he turned to her and said, 'Darling, will you marry me?' Joan just smiled.[15] Three years older than Aly, Joan epitomised English aristocratic beauty. Although she had a 2-year-old son with Loel Guinness, she left her husband to be with Aly, and they married in the spring of 1936. At the end of the year Joan gave birth to Aly's son.[16] The marriage of Aly to a divorced woman showed that if Thelma had played her cards right, she might have been able to marry this prince. However, in her memoir Thelma confessed that she was never really in love with him.[17] She had been more in love with the Prince of Wales; Aly had just provided an exciting interlude at the end of her affair with Edward.

In Thelma's life men came and went, but the most lasting and important relationship was with her twin, Gloria. As the two sisters wrote in their memoir, they had a psychic bond and were almost like 'Siamese twins' without the physical connection.[18] While Thelma had been having her own marital adventures, Gloria had married into the super-rich Vanderbilt dynasty. Like Duke Furness, Gloria's husband Reginald Claypole Vanderbilt was much older than his stylish bride. The couple seem to have been genuinely in love, but their happiness did not last long. In 1925 Reggie died of cirrhosis of the liver, leaving Gloria with their baby daughter, Little Gloria, who was only 15 months old. By the time Reggie died he had spent much of his money. He was in debt and his widow was not entitled to the $5 million trust fund set up for his children. Little Gloria would only receive her share when she was 21, and until then her legal guardian, the New York Surrogate Court judge James Foley, was put in charge of the fund. Gloria senior was given a monthly allowance to support her daughter and herself.[19]

Just as Thelma's relationship with Aly Khan was coming to an end, Gloria was fighting for custody of her daughter in what became known as 'the trial of the century'. When her sister needed her, Thelma immediately rushed over to America to be by her side. According to the twins, Gloria contacted Thelma when she was attending a ball at Claridge's with Aly Khan. When Gloria begged Thelma to be with her, she immediately rushed to Southampton, still wearing her silver lamé evening dress, to catch *The Empress of Britain*, which was sailing to America. In fact, as so often with the twins' stories, reality does not quite match their romanticised fantasies; Thelma sailed on *The Empress of Britain* a fortnight later, on 6 October.[20] As she embarked, she told reporters: 'I want to do everything I can to stop this nonsense. I am going over to see if I can help my sister in any way possible, for she needs me with her at a time like this. I shall certainly appear in court if I am asked to do so.'[21]

Thelma stood by her sister throughout the harrowing custody battle which saw Gloria's sister-in-law, Gertrude Vanderbilt Whitney, who was known as 'the richest woman in America', and Gloria's own mother,

Mrs Morgan, turn against her. Gloria was labelled an unfit mother and her private life was torn apart in public. It was a far cry from the fairy-tale lifestyle the twins had planned for themselves. After Reggie died, Gloria senior and Little Gloria had moved to Paris where they lived with Thelma and their mother, Mrs Morgan. Thelma was called 'Aunt Toto' by her niece, who, like everyone else, could not tell her mother and aunt apart.[22] Gloria senior was a distant parent who left her daughter in the care of Mrs Morgan and the nanny, Dodo, while she partied with her sister. After Thelma married Lord Furness, Gloria started seeing a German prince, Gottfried Hohenlohe-Langenburg, who was the great-grandson of Queen Victoria. They wanted to get married and take Little Gloria to live in his castle in Germany, but Mrs Morgan did not approve. She hated Germans and was concerned because the prince had a title but not much money. She decided that her granddaughter should live in America with the Vanderbilt family. Thelma and Gloria senior believed that their mother was always ruled by money and it was this motivation which made her turn against her daughter. They thought that Mrs Morgan wanted to be guardian of her granddaughter so that she would have access to the allowance from the Vanderbilt trust fund.[23]

Problems began for Gloria senior after she returned to America with her daughter in the spring of 1932. Little Gloria's guardians had insisted that she should be brought up as an American heiress and go to school in New York. In June, the young girl had her tonsils out, and after the operation she went to convalesce at her Aunt Gertrude's Long Island estate.[24] Little Gloria stayed in the United States while Gloria senior went back to France. Mrs Morgan told Gertrude Vanderbilt Whitney about her daughter's decadent lifestyle and said that she was spending money from the trust fund on herself rather than on Little Gloria. It was at this stage that Gloria senior realised that she needed to be guardian of her daughter, so she petitioned the court. To her horror, her own mother filed a complaint with the court stating that she was an unfit mother.

When Thelma heard what had happened she went to see her mother and told her that mothers did not behave as she was doing and blacken their children's characters before the world. Mrs Morgan would not listen to her, claiming that Thelma had not been aware of the neglect that had gone on. When Thelma argued with her and said that she was on her twin's side, Mrs Morgan became angry and told her to be careful or she would take her child away from her too. Thelma replied: 'Luckily, mamma, my child has a father alive, and if there is any complaint it will come from him.'[25]

A custody battle began which was to tear the whole family apart. Mrs Vanderbilt Whitney and Mrs Morgan were on one side while all Mrs Morgan's children – Gloria senior, Thelma, Consuelo and Harry – were on the other. Little Gloria was caught in the middle. The trial began in October 1934; it became a media sensation as 10-year-old Gloria Vanderbilt was labelled the 'Poor Little Rich Girl' whose future was fought over in public. In the trial, Gloria senior was accused of spending money from the trust fund on herself instead of her daughter. She was also accused of drinking too much alcohol, partying all night and neglecting her child.[26] There were lurid stories about her sex life. It was claimed that Prince Gottfried had been seen in bed with Gloria senior and they regularly read pornographic books together. Most shocking of all, in an era when lesbianism had to be kept secret, Gloria's French maid claimed to have seen her kissing Nada, Marchioness of Milford Haven. Nada was a member of the British royal family and the sister-in-law of Lord Louis Mountbatten. The accusations were strongly refuted, but Gloria senior's reputation was ruined. As the spotlight fell on the Morgan twins' private lives, there were fears that the Prince of Wales's relationship with Thelma would be exposed, but his name was never mentioned in court.[27]

Every day, the Morgan sisters arrived arm in arm at the court dressed immaculately in neat hats with veils, chic black dresses and furs. When Thelma was called as a witness, her twin wrote admiringly of how her sister animated the proceedings by bringing warmth and colour into the courtroom. Thelma claimed that Little Gloria's childhood had been full of love from her mother. She said that she used to visit her niece in Paris once a month with Lord Furness, when he went to buy racehorses and she was buying clothes. She would bring Little Gloria dolls with trunks of clothes and her niece would rush up to her and kiss her. She described a life of luxury for the little girl; she had her own car and chauffeur and had the freedom to go anywhere she wanted. She stayed in grand houses in New York, France and England. Thelma tried to portray herself and her twin as good Catholic girls. However, under cross-examination this image was undermined when it became clear her first marriage had been to a divorced man and her second ended in divorce. At the end of her testimony, Thelma was furious at her treatment and left the court-room in a rage. When the press asked her for a statement she attacked Gertrude for trying to take her sister's only child from her.[28]

When Gloria senior gave evidence, she recalled seeing Consuelo and Thelma sitting together, their faces 'tense and very white'.[29] After fif-teen minutes on the witness stand the judge called for a short recess. Thelma and a nurse walked Gloria into the corridor where she fainted. Thelma told the waiting reporters: 'We hope for the best. We hope my sister does not collapse.'[30] In her testimony Gloria senior told the court how much she loved her daughter. As she appeared each morning on the arm of her nurse, she won public sympathy as a poor, vulnerable mother who would be destroyed by losing her only child. Thelma acted as her spokeswoman to the press, helping to create this image.[31] In her account of the trial, Gloria senior said that she felt like 'a sleep-walker' who could not sleep, think or speak. Each day after the trial when she got home she would immediately go to bed. She could not eat and so her weight dropped from 124lb to 107.[32] Thelma tried to cheer her up but even she could not repair the damage done by those hours in court. Gloria wrote that she dreaded to think how she would have coped without her two sisters.[33]

The crucial testimony came from Little Gloria herself. Manipulated by her grandmother and her nanny, she testified that she did not want to live with her mother. In a private testimony, made just to the judge, she told him that she was afraid of her parent. She also added that she did not like her aunts Thelma and Consuelo.[34] After a seven-week trial it was decided that Little Gloria should be made a ward of court until she was 21. It was stated that it would be in the best interests of the child if custody was awarded to Gertrude Vanderbilt Whitney. Gloria senior would be allowed supervised visits at weekends and some holidays.[35] She continued to receive a regular, though reduced, income from the trust fund until Little Gloria turned 21 and then it would be up to her daughter whether she was paid.

When the verdict was announced there was much sympathy for Gloria senior among her contemporaries. Her behaviour was not unusual among society women of the era; many of them left childrearing to nannies and continued to behave as if they were single.[36] Freda's involved parenting was the exception rather than the rule. As the gossip columnist in *The Bystander* candidly admitted: 'Lucky we don't live in America – some of us would soon lose our chicks.'[37]

16

THE BUSINESSWOMAN

After the case ended Gloria was so near to a nervous breakdown that Thelma said she would only go back to England for long enough to collect her son, Tony. She then returned to New York to be with her sister. Perhaps inspired by the society women who had opened shops in London, in 1935 the twins set up a fashion business together with Sonia Rosenberg. When they opened their dress shop in New York, Thelma told reporters: 'My sister and I want something to occupy our time.' Gloria added: 'We are both fond of good clothes and so we are going into that business.'[1] Paying herself $75 a week, Gloria travelled around the country promoting the dresses, which were in 'the medium price range'.[2] She wrote with pride, although not completely truthfully, that every cheque she wrote now was with money earned by herself.[3] As always, Thelma was the stronger one in the partnership. There is a film of the twins showing dresses they have designed. The same scene was shot repeatedly and with each take Gloria became more deflated while Thelma took control of the situation.[4]

When her former lover became king, Thelma made the most of the occasion to promote her business. She was photographed in a long evening dress she had designed herself, with a fur wrap, white gloves and tiara. She modelled the outfit in Philadelphia as a style suitable to wear at functions to celebrate the coronation.[5] The twins also promoted their clothes in England. In October 1936 they held a fashion show in Harrods. They presented the collection themselves, introducing the models.[6] From the start Gloria Vanderbilt-Sonia Gowns Inc. lost money. As the debts increased the suppliers began to sue. Without letting their partner Sonia Rosenberg know, they opened their own dress wholesaler called Ladyship Gowns. Miss Rosenberg sued for breach of contract. She claimed that the twins had drunk alcohol during business hours and gave clothes to their friends, pretending that these transactions were sales. Gloria and Thelma countersued. Eventually both suits were abandoned and Gloria filed for bankruptcy.[7] Both Gloria and Thelma's reputations had been damaged by the custody trial. When they decided to leave for England a gossip columnist on the *Daily News* wrote: 'Thelma Furness – the former girlfriend of royalty has lost her former glamour.'[8] Thelma was furious; she sued the newspaper and was awarded $5,000.[9]

Thelma divided her time between New York and London. When her former lover Edward VIII abdicated Thelma was shocked. She had thought that once the prince became king he would change and use his royal authority to become a dynamic and progressive monarch. Even she wondered if he had ever really wanted to be king.[10] In February 1937 she was photographed at London's newest show, *The Cochran Review's Home and Beauty* at the Adelphi Theatre. Her old rival Freda Dudley Ward was also there. They were wearing similar velvet coats and were accompanied by obscure escorts.[11] Both women were looking miserable; in their different ways they had paved the way for Wallis, the woman who had wreaked havoc in the life of their ex-lover and the monarchy.

In the months before the Second World War began Thelma was reconciled with her ex-husband Lord Furness. His marriage to his third wife, Enid, was tempestuous. Enid Cavendish was a striking beauty; her hair had turned silver at the age of 28 and this unusual feature combined with her vivid green eyes and flawless skin made her turn heads wherever she went. When Lord Furness first took her to the casino at Monte

Carlo, all gambling stopped as she entered the hall in her violet taffeta and white lace Molyneux evening dress. The Aga Khan, who was in the casino and had known her for many years, turned to her and said: 'My dear Enid, could you not be more discreet with your entrance? Next time come in black.'[12]

Duke Furness married Enid in 1933, shortly after his divorce from Thelma. They had met at the casino at Le Touquet; Duke told friends that when she came into the room he lost all concentration. As in his relationship with Thelma, he made up his mind to marry her, sending her jewels and flowers and putting his yachts, planes and Rolls-Royce at her disposal. He not only bought her the Chelsea flat she was living in, he bought the rest of the block as well.[13] Enid had been married and widowed twice before, first to Roderick Cameron and then to Frederick 'Caviar' Cavendish. Although later in life she said Lord Furness had been the husband she loved the most – as with his immense fortune she could have anything she wanted – their marriage was not happy. Enid had affairs which made Duke intensely jealous, and he reacted by hiring detectives to keep an eye on her.[14]

At first after his divorce from Thelma, Duke had been furious with his ex-wife. He could not even bear to see his stepdaughter Pat's governess, because she looked like Thelma.[15] However, as the years went by and his marriage to his new wife failed to live up to expectations, he began to relent. In 1939, Thelma took a small house near Cannes; Duke was staying at the Carlton Hotel and wanted to see her. It seems that they put the past behind them. When they met for lunch, he told her about his marital problems. She realised that he was sick and needed some form of medication. Thelma noticed that Duke was very 'jittery' and in pain but he would not say what was wrong with him. In his hotel suite he asked her to give him an injection; Thelma did not know how to do it, so he had to inject himself.[16]

While in the south of France Thelma also saw her debonair stepson, Dick, who was an officer in the Welsh Guards. Thelma and Dick had always got on well and during his visit he put on a party to celebrate her birthday. When the war began Dick was asked to report to his regiment. He travelled back to England with Thelma and Tony and stayed with them in London until he was sent back to France to fight.

Thelma's lawyer advised her to take Tony to America to be out of danger during the war. However, before she left she wanted to return to the south of France one more time so that Duke could see his son. Lord Furness had moved into a villa near Monte Carlo with Enid. He was so ill that the doctor visited him every day and his wife had hired a trained nurse to look after him. He was suffering from cirrhosis of the liver and was dependent on morphine injections.[17] When Thelma met up with her ex-husband she could not believe how frail he had become. She suggested that he should travel to America with them, but it was evident that he was too ill to move. After seeing Duke for the final time, Thelma and Tony sailed to New York where they met up with Gloria senior.[18]

In May 1940, Thelma heard that her stepson Dick had been reported missing in action at Arras. He had been covering the withdrawal of some vehicles when he heard that the Germany infantry were in a wood nearby. Immediately, Dick went off to reconnoitre with the intention of attacking the enemy. Suddenly fire was opened on him by a concealed German anti-tank gun. Several carriers were destroyed including Dick's. His fellow officers said that he charged straight at the gunner and shot him before he fell himself. An eyewitness recalled that he saw Dick spread-eagled across the top of the tank with a Bren gun in front of him. He said: 'Mr Furness must have known then the very slender chances of his returning from such a hell.'[19] Dick's body was never found, so it was unclear whether he had been killed or taken prisoner. His action had saved an entire column from destruction, and he was posthumously awarded the Victoria Cross for his extreme gallantry.[20]

When Duke heard the news he wept and wept, but he held on to the hope that his son might have been taken prisoner.[21] He could not face the thought of losing his eldest son as he had already lost his daughter Averill four years before. She had married a much older man, Andrew Rattray, who had been her father's white hunter on safaris in Africa. The oddly matched couple had fallen in love when Rattray brought two zebras over to England for her father's stables. Lord Furness had disapproved of the match and had cut his daughter off without a penny. When Averill's husband died suddenly, she never recovered from the shock. She remained in Africa, living in Rattray's bush shack. She died of heart failure in a nursing home in Nairobi aged only 27. According to some reports she had drunk herself to death.

With both his children from his first marriage dead and his own health shattered, Duke died in October 1940. Thelma was very upset when she heard the news.[22] Adding to her feeling that an era was coming to an end, the next blow came when her old home, Burrough Court, was accidentally burnt down while the Canadian Air Force were stationed there.

With the past wiped out, all Thelma had left was her son, Tony, and Gloria. She started a new life with them in Beverly Hills, California. The sisters bought a house on North Maple Drive and were soon socialising with film stars. The glamorous Morgan twins were invited out most evenings to the smartest Hollywood parties. After a late night they would sleep in until lunchtime when their maid would bring them their lunch on a tray or they would sit out on their terrace under a sun shade gossiping about their friends and eating smoked salmon followed by mangoes.[23] They would then spend a languid afternoon embroidering or knitting. If they got bored they would flick through the *Los Angeles Examiner* to the column of the famous gossip columnist, Louella Parson, which they would read to each other.[24]

Thelma and Gloria often appeared in Louella's pages. They were always good copy. When Thelma met the actor Edmund Lowe at a party, he greeted her with the old cliché: 'Where have you been all my life?' to which she replied: 'Looking for you.'[25] After splitting up from his wife, Edmund had been flitting from nightclub to nightclub but once he met Thelma he concentrated all his attention on winning her over. His car was seen most days parked in front of her house and they often dined together at local cafes.[26] Friends thought that they might marry, but instead they had an on/off affair for many years. Thelma described their relationship as one of her happiest friendships.[27] They laughed a great deal together and had a relaxed relationship. Edmund introduced Thelma to one of his passions, baseball, and she became a fan.

It was not so easy for Thelma's son Tony to adapt to life in America. After inheriting the Furness title at the age of 11 he had been dubbed the richest little boy in England. Once his mother moved him to California he got to know many of the child stars of the era including

Shirley Temple, Roddy McDowall and Elizabeth Taylor. However, with his English accent and bad health due to diabetes and poor eyesight, he never really fitted in. He seemed a lonely, isolated little boy. He was called 'his lordship' by fellow pupils at his Santa Barbara school.[28]

One summer the twins rented a house near Nissequogue on Long Island. Their children, Little Gloria and Tony Furness, joined them for their summer holiday. Little Gloria had hoped to have some time alone with her mother, but her aunt was always there beside her. Their lifestyle was as sybaritic as in California. The twins invited a group of friends to join them. They all slept in until lunchtime, then Thelma and Gloria senior would appear in matching eau de nil robes. It was stiflingly hot, so lunch was served outside on the porch. While the adults gossiped and sipped cocktails the children drank Coca-Cola in silence. After an afternoon nap the children would walk down to the beach with their nannies while the adults took even longer siestas. The highlight of the holiday was when one of the twin's friends arrived in an aeroplane and gave Tony and Little Gloria a ride. There were love affairs going on which were supposed to be hidden from the children, but Little Gloria picked up on the undertones and felt annoyed by the pretence.[29]

In the summer of 1941, Little Gloria decided to move in with her mother and aunt in Hollywood. Although she was only a teenager, Thelma and Gloria treated her as an adult. They were too preoccupied with their own affairs to bother much with what she was getting up to. She went on dates with much older film stars including George Montgomery, Ray Milland and Errol Flynn. When she got engaged to Pat DeCicco, a former actors' agent, gambler and an alleged mobster who worked for Howard Hughes, her mother and aunt were delighted. They did not bother to look into his background. Pat had been married to the actress Thelma Todd who, after their divorce, was found dead; there were rumours that her ex-husband might have killed her. Rather than considering whether the 33-year-old was a suitable match for a 17-year-old heiress, Gloria senior and Thelma concentrated on planning the wedding.[30]

The ceremony was held in December 1941 at the Old Mission Catholic Church in Santa Barbara. Afterwards a cocktail reception was hosted by Gloria senior and Thelma at their Maple Drive home. As always with the twins, there was drama. Once the bride and groom had left on honeymoon, at the end of the reception a gunman, posing as a chauffeur, tried to rob them and the eight remaining guests. Tall and lanky with a long nose and receding chin, the robber came in through the back door and said: 'This is a stick up.' He made it seem that he had a gun in his overcoat pocket.

Both Gloria and Thelma kept their cool. Gloria stood in front of her guests, who were wearing expensive jewellery, and said to him: 'You're a little bit late, most of the guests have left.' He replied: 'Yes, I know.' Thelma gave up her $1,000 'V for Victory' clips and said calmly: 'You're quite foolish to do this because the house is full of cops.' The gunman then fled without attempting to rob the other guests. The next day, when Thelma and Gloria were telling reporters about the robbery, the gunman appeared at the front door and handed a package to the maid. He demanded a receipt and then left in a hurry. The parcel contained Thelma's 'V for Victory' clips and bizarrely, a note with the phrase '*Dieu et mon droit*' (God and my right) scrawled in pencil on it, which is the motto of the British monarch.[31] Apparently, the inept robber had thought it was the patriotic thing to do to give the clips back. It seems that even when she was robbed Thelma could not escape her past with the prince.

Little Gloria's marriage to Pat DeCicco only lasted three years as he was violent. Shortly after leaving him she turned 21 and inherited her trust fund of more than $4 million. Hoping to find the closeness she had always desired with her mother, Little Gloria gave her a substantial allowance and they moved in together in an apartment in Park Avenue, New York. However, it was not long before the younger Gloria fell in love again. When she became involved with the conductor Leopold Stokowski – who at 63 was 42 years her senior – her mother did not approve. Under her new love's influence, Gloria became estranged from her mother. She stopped her allowance, believing that Thelma would be able to support her sister using her divorce settlement from Lord Furness. Once Little Gloria's divorce from Pat came through, she married Stokowski. She did not see or speak to her mother for fifteen years.[32] However, after a few years she agreed to give her mother an allowance.[33]

Thelma had her own battles to fight over money. After the Second World War ended, she sued Enid, the subseqent wife of her ex-husband Lord Furness, over a codicil that cut Tony out of his father's will. The codicil was initialled by Lord Furness in a shaky hand, but not signed, just three months before his death. Thelma claimed that Duke had not been in his right mind when he signed the codicil as he had been addicted to morphine. There was even gossip that Enid had administered a fatal dose of the drug to her husband. It was a bitter battle. Thelma produced an affidavit signed by one of Lord Furness's nurses to support her case. However, her evidence was discredited when it was revealed that the nurse had been bribed. Thelma had to write a letter of apology admitting that there was not the slightest justification for any of the allegations or insinuations made.[34] In the end Tony received a substantial out-of-court settlement, while Enid received the bulk of the Furness fortune. After the case ended, Tony used some of his inheritance to support his mother and aunt.[35]

Although there were brief relationships, neither twin remarried. The one constant in their lives was each other. When she was in her 40s, Gloria's health began to fail as she developed glaucoma. Thelma took her all over Europe and America hoping to find a treatment which would save her sister's sight.[36] When Gloria became almost completely blind, Thelma guided her with such skill that very few people realised her disability.[37] In 1947 Gloria became seriously ill after surgery. The doctors thought that she might die as she had an abscess which caused peritonitis. Thelma rushed to be with her in hospital. She could not stand the thought of losing her twin and willed her to live.[38] During the long operation on her sister, Thelma felt as though she was dying herself. When she heard it had been successful she burst into tears.

In 1950 Tony came of age. Thelma and Gloria senior celebrated his 21st birthday with him at Maxim's in Paris with a dinner for forty or fifty guests. Another proud moment was when Tony took his seat in the House of Lords. Sitting in the Peeresses' Gallery, Thelma listened with pride as he made his maiden speech.[39] Tony became a strong Catholic and considered becoming a priest. It was said he lived a celibate life after he had proposed marriage to one woman and been refused.[40]

With Thelma's son living in London, the twins were once again alone together. Repeating the patterns of their childhood, they never lived in one place for long. By the time Gloria senior was 53 she had crossed the Atlantic more than 120 times, which meant that she had spent almost two years of her life at sea.[41] In 1955 the sisters moved to Nassau and then to a small apartment in New York. In 1956 their mother, Mrs Morgan, died. After her behaviour against her daughter in the trial, it had taken a long time for the twins to forgive her, but they had been reconciled with her before her death and were by her bedside when she died. She left them both substantial sums of money in her will.[42]

Over the years money had often been in short supply for Gloria senior. She had been dependent on first the Vanderbilt trust fund and then her daughter's goodwill. In a bid to make money and keep themselves occupied, Thelma and Gloria set up a variety of short-lived businesses. In the early 1950s they got into the toy-making business, setting up a toy factory in a dreary industrial street in Hollywood. The twins only made two products. There was a cardboard penthouse for children to build, complete with a king-sized bed with a satin coverlet, freezer, television set, mirrored dressing table and shrubbery roof garden. Perhaps drawing their inspiration from what might have been, the twins' second toy was a princess doll with a real ermine-trimmed robe. The plastic novelty dolls were called 'Pooks'. Gloria painted the dolls' faces then the sisters bent over sewing machines making dresses for them which sold for 85 cents in Woolworths.[43] Justifying their new business, Thelma told reporters: 'Well everyone in the world has changed. You know with income tax and all [...] those days of sitting around and clipping coupons are gone forever. So we make toys.' She added: 'Our family and friends thought this was a joke at first. Now they know we're serious.'[44]

When the dolls failed to make their fortune, the twins pointed their entrepreneurial skills in another direction. At a party they met the chemist Dr Alexander Farkas, who in the 1920s had created a unique scent for them. When he blended two new scents for them called 'Curtain Call' for the winter and 'White Pique' for spring, they were excited by the business potential of the fragrances.[45] They marketed the scents as Parfums Jumelles (French for twins) and travelled around the country setting up outlets for their latest venture.[46] As with their previous enter-prises, it did not last long and soon went out of business.

Their next venture was in advertising. Thelma had endorsed prod-ucts twenty years before when she appeared in the Pond's Cold Cream advertisements. In 1957, both twins promoted the slimming product Ayds, which was a low-calorie vitamin- and mineral-enriched sweet. In the advert, Gloria enthused: 'I'm really astonished at the job Ayds has done helping me keep my figure slim.' Thelma agreed: 'Ayds really works. I can say that from my own experience.'[47]

Reflecting how intertwined their lives had always been, in 1958, Gloria and Thelma wrote a joint memoir called *Double Exposure*. It told their versions of their life stories. They explained that they recognised that the F. Scott Fitzgerald age in which they had grown up was over, but they were happy to adapt to the modern world. At the end of the book they wrote that if they had their lives to live over again they would probably behave in the same way and make the same mistakes.[48] However, in a later interview Thelma reconsidered this comment and added: 'I would do it all again. The only thing I would NOT do again is introduce Wallis Simpson to the Prince of Wales.'[49]

Perhaps the greatest missed opportunity in Gloria's life had been her inability to bond with her child. In 1960 Gloria senior was given a second chance when, after fifteen years of estrangement, she was reconciled with her daughter. For many years Little Gloria was fearful of her mother; she was never exactly sure why this fear developed and in retrospect she sus-pected her wariness was due to her grandmother's and nanny's influence. She had always longed to feel connected to her mother but there was always a distance.[50] The younger woman had had therapy which enabled her to come to terms with what had happened.[51] As a mature woman herself, she realised that some people should not be parents and perhaps her mother was one of those people.[52] Now she had a different perspec-tive, Gloria junior invited her mother to tea at her apartment. When she first saw her mother again she would not have recognised her. Although Gloria senior was beautifully dressed she had become a fragile figure who was 'hesitant' and nervous. Her daughter found it hard to believe that this was the woman whom she had feared all her life.[53] The first meeting went well enough for mother and daughter to arrange to meet again.

In the summer of 1961, Thelma suggested that her niece should come, with her two sons from her marriage to Stokowski, to visit them in Los Angeles. They rented cottages next to each other on the beach in Malibu for a week. It was a success and Gloria senior had a chance to spend time with her grandchildren.[54] During the next few years mother and daughter continued to meet, but they never fully opened up to each other or discussed the custody trial. After years of mutual wariness, it was too late to become close and the topic of Little Gloria's childhood was still too emotionally charged for either of them to broach it.[55]

Although the younger Gloria recognised the limitations of their relationship, she wanted to involve her mother in her life. After divorcing Stokowski in 1955, Little Gloria found true happiness when she married the author Wyatt Cooper in 1963. The following year she put on a 60th birthday party for her mother and aunt. She gave Gloria a diamond bracelet and Thelma a pair of diamond earings.[56] When she found out that she was pregnant again, she invited her mother and her aunt to stay in her house so that they could be there when the baby was born. Unfortunately, Gloria senior was too ill to go. In December 1964, she had been operated on to remove a fusiform aneurysm followed by extensive artery replacement at Los Angeles's Cedar of Lebanon Hospital. A few months later she needed further surgery and was admitted again to hospital.[57] Her daughter spoke to her on the phone a few hours after she had given birth to another son. Her mother had hoped for a granddaughter who would be 'the third Gloria', but instead she joked to her daughter that she would soon have so many sons she could start a baseball team.[58] Gloria senior died shortly afterwards; she was 60 years old. Right to the end, Thelma was by her side.

Analysing her mother's life, Gloria Vanderbilt has written that she believes the only person her mother truly loved was her twin, Thelma.[59] When considering if she was like her mother, Gloria, who became a very successful businesswoman, believes that she is more like her aunt. She wrote that while her mother was passive and remote, Thelma was more extrovert with a burning desire to live life to the full.[60]

After Gloria senior's death, her daughter remained in contact with her aunt. Many years later, Gloria told a newspaper that she found it 'astonishing' that Thelma could live without her twin because 'they really were one person'.[61] In 1970 Thelma died of a heart attack. She had been visiting her niece in New York, and dropped dead on her way to see her doctor. It was clear that she had never totally got over her relationship with the Prince of Wales; in her handbag was the now threadbare miniature teddy bear they had exchanged decades before as a way of remaining close to each other when apart.[62] In death as in life, Thelma wanted to be close to her twin; she was buried with Gloria in the Holy Cross Cemetery, Culver City, Los Angeles.

NOTES

Introduction

1 Andrew Morton. *17 Carnations: The Windsors, The Nazis and the Cover Up*. London: Michael O'Mara Books, 2015. 1–2.

2 D.J. Taylor. *Bright Young People: The Rise and Fall of a Generation 1918–1940*. London: Vintage Books, 2008. 29, 36.

3 J. Bryan III and Charles J.V. Murphy. *The Windsor Story*. London: Granada Publishing, 1981. 72.

4 James Pope-Hennessy. *Queen Mary*. London: George Allen and Unwin, 1959. 514.

5 Frances Donaldson. *A Twentieth-Century Life: A Memoir*. London: Weidenfeld and Nicolson, 1992. 219.

6 Ralph G. Martin. *The Woman He Loved: The Story of the Duke and Duchess of Windsor*. New York: Simon and Schuster, 1973. 13.

7 Duff Hart-Davis (ed.). *King's Counsellor: Abdication and War: The Diaries of Sir Alan Lascelles*. London: Weidenfeld and Nicolson, 2006. 112–13.

8 The Duchess of Windsor. *The Heart Has Its Reasons: The Story of the Abdication*. London: Tandem, 1975. 243.

9 The Duke of Windsor. *A King's Story: The Memoirs of HRH the Duke of Windsor*. London: Pan Books, 1957. 200.

10 Donaldson. *A Twentieth-Century Life*. 205.

11 Duchess of Windsor. *The Heart Has Its Reasons*. 149.

12 Philip Ziegler. *King Edward VIII: The Official Biography*. London: Fontana, 1991. 105.

13 Tommy Lascelles to Joan Lascelles. 23 November 1936. Duff Hart-Davis (ed.). *In Royal Service: Letters and Journals of Sir Alan Lascelles from 1920 to 1936*. London: Hamish Hamilton, 1989. 201.

Chapter 1

1 J.M. Barrie. 'Obituary. Lady Ednam.' 25 July 1930. *The Times*. 14.

2 In an interview with Michael Thornton on 29 May 1972 Lady Victor Paget confirmed that the Prince of Wales was present at this incident. Michael Thornton. *Royal Feud: The Queen Mother and the Duchess of Windsor*. London: Michael Joseph, 1985. 45.

3 The Duke of Sutherland. *Looking Back: The Autobiography of the Duke of Sutherland*. London: Odhams Press, 1957. 80.

4 Queen Mary to Edward, Prince of Wales. 29 July 1917. RA EDW/PRIV/MAIN/A/2080. The Royal Archives.

5 Natasha McEnroe. 'Life in a First World War Field Hospital is Depicted in a New Exhibition.' *History Today*. Vol. 64, Issue 3, March 2014.

6 20 February 1916. Edward, Prince of Wales's Diary. RA EDW/PRIV/DIARY: 1915–1917. The Royal Archives.

7 *Ibid*. 1 March 1916.

8 *Ibid*. 25 February 1916.

9 Philip Ziegler. *King Edward VIII: The Official Biography*. London: Fontana, 1991. 51.

10 25 February 1916. Edward, Prince of Wales's Diary.

11 Turtle Bunbury. *The Glorious Madness: Tales of the Irish and the Great War First-hand*. Dublin: Gill & Macmillan Ltd, 2014.

12 Queen Mary to Edward, Prince of Wales. 16 March 1916. RA EDW/PRIV/MAIN/A/1817. The Royal Archives.

13 Edward Prince of Wales to Millicent, Duchess of Sutherland. 5 March 1916. Sutherland Collection. Staffordshire Record Office. D6528-15-174-2.

14 Duke of Sutherland. *Looking Back*. 80.

15 'Mentioned in Despatches for Distinguished Service at the Front.' 17 January 1917. *The Tatler*.

16 Frances Donaldson. *Edward VIII*. London: Futura Publications, 1976. 50.

17 Desmond Fitzgerald to Edward, Prince of Wales. 9 October 1914. RA EDW/PRIV/MAIN A/1386. The Royal Archives.

18 Desmond Fitzgerald to Edward, Prince of Wales. 28 December 1914. RA EDW/PRIV/MAIN A/1444. The Royal Archives.

19 Desmond Fitzgerald to Edward, Prince of Wales. 23 June 1915. RA EDW/PRIV/MAIN A. The Royal Archives.

20 September 1915. Edward, Prince of Wales's Diary.

21 The Duke of Windsor. *A King's Story: The Memoirs of HRH the Duke of Windsor*. London: Pan Books, 1957. 124.

22 Ziegler. *King Edward VIII*. 76.

23 Sir Almeric Fitzroy. *Memoirs*. London: Hutchinson, 1925. Vol. ii. 802–3.

24 Helen Hardinge. *Loyal to Three Kings: A Memoir of Alec Hardinge, Private Secretary to the Sovereign 1920–1943*. London: William Kimber, 1967. 66.

25 Robert Vacha (ed.). *The Kaiser's Daughter: Memoirs of HRH Viktoria Luise, Duchess of Brunswick and Luneburg, Princess of Prussia*. London: W.H. Allen, 1977. 46–8.

26 Ziegler. *King Edward VIII*. 44.

27 Michael Thornton. *Royal Feud: The Queen Mother and the Duchess of Windsor*. London: Michael Joseph, 1985. 44.

Chapter 2

1   Denis Stuart. *Dear Duchess: Millicent, Duchess of Sutherland 1867–1955*. London: Victor Gollancz, 1982. 29.

2   *Ibid*. 47.

3   The Duke of Sutherland. *Looking Back: The Autobiography of the Duke of Sutherland*. London: Odhams Press, 1957. 40

4   *Ibid*. 33–5.

5   *Ibid*. 39.

6   *Ibid*. 48.

7   'Ball of the Season.' 20 June 1911. *Sheffield Daily Telegraph*.

8   'Woman's Sphere.' 2 July 1904. *The Sphere*.

9   'Princess Victoria's Birthday Party.' 26 July 1905. *The Tatler*.

10 'Debut of the Duchess of Sutherland's Daughter.' 19 May 1911. *Lichfield Mercury*.

11 Duke of Sutherland. *Looking Back*. 54.

12 'Lady Ednam's Schooldays.' 13 December 1922. *Yorkshire Evening Post*.

13 Duke of Sutherland. *Looking Back*. 54–6.

14 Richard Davenport-Hines. *Ettie: The Intimate Life and Dauntless Spirit of Lady Desborough*. London: Weidenfeld and Nicolson, 2008. 117–18.

15 Ethel Grenfell, Lady Desborough. *Pages from a Family Journal 1888–1915*. Berkshire: Eton College, 1916.

16 18 March 1902. *Mid Sussex Times*.

17 Mabell, Countess of Airlie. *Thatched with Gold: The Memoirs of Mabell, Countess of Airlie*. London: Hutchinson, 1962. 112.

18 Anne Edwards. *Matriarch: Queen Mary and the House of Windsor*. London: Rowan and Littlefield, 2015. 95–102.

19 Ralph G. Martin. *The Woman He Loved: The Story of the Duke and Duchess of Windsor*. New York: Simon and Schuster, 1973. 53.

20 The Duke of Windsor. *A King's Story: The Memoirs of HRH the Duke of Windsor*. London: Pan Books, 1957. 33.

21 *Ibid*. 49.

22 James Lees-Milne. *The Life of Reginald, 2nd Viscount Esher: The Enigmatic Edwardian*. London: Sidgwick and Jackson, 1986. 188, 214.
23 Edward, Prince of Wales to Queen Mary. 24 May 1916. RA QM/ PRIVCC09: 1916–1918. The Royal Archives.
24 Queen Mary to Edward, Prince of Wales. 10 February 1917. RA EDW/ PRIV/MAIN/A/2022. The Royal Archives.
25 Edward, Prince of Wales to Queen Mary. 2 June 1917. RA QM/PRIV/ CC09: 1916–1918. The Royal Archives.
26 Queen Mary to Edward, Prince of Wales. 8 June 1917. RA EDW/PRIV/ MAIN/A/2068. The Royal Archives.
27 Edwards. *Matriarch*. 145.
28 Countess of Airlie. *Thatched with Gold*. 112.
29 For a full description of Prince Edward's childhood see Philip Ziegler. *King Edward VIII: The Official Biography*. London: Fontana, 1991. 1–13.
30 Andrew Morton. *17 Carnations: The Windsors, the Nazis and the Cover Up*. London: Michael O'Mara Books, 2015. 8.
31 Duke of Windsor. *A King's Story*. 36.
32 Edwards. *Matriarch*. 147.
33 For a full description of Prince Edward's childhood see Ziegler. *King Edward VIII*. 1–13.

Chapter 3

1 Edward, Prince of Wales to Queen Mary. 4 September 1917. RA QM/ PRIV/CC09: 1916–1918. The Royal Archives.
2 *Ibid.*
3 Edward, Prince of Wales to Queen Mary. 12 September 1917. RA QM/ PRIV/CC09: 1916–1918. The Royal Archives.
4 Diana Cooper. *Darling Monster: The Letters of Lady Diana Cooper to her Son John Julius Norwich. 1939–1952. New York:* The Overlook Press, 2014. Accessed via Google Books.
5 Lady Victor Paget's description in her interview with Michael Thornton. *Royal Feud: The Queen Mother and the Duchess of Windsor*. London: Michael Joseph, 1985. 46.
6 22 November 1917. Lady Cynthia Asquith. *Lady Cynthia Asquith: Diaries 1915–18*. London: Hutchinson, 1968. 369.
7 Diana Cooper. *Autobiography*. London: Michael Russell, 1979. 321.
8 J.M. Barrie. 'Obituary. Lady Ednam.' 25 July 1930. *The Times*. 14.
9 Thornton. *Royal Feud: The Queen Mother and the Duchess of Windsor*. 44.
10 Lady Victor Paget, in Thornton. *Royal Feud*. 46.
11 A Correspondent. 25 July 1930. *The Times*. 14.
12 'Lady Ednam's Schooldays.' 13 December 1922. *Yorkshire Evening Post*.
13 Ettie Grenfell, Lady Desborough. *Pages from a Family Journal 1888–1915*. Berkshire: Eton College, 1916. 199.

14 'The Debutante of the Season.' 14 June 1911. *The Bystander.*

15 'The Debutante of the Season.' 14 June 1911. *The Tatler.*

16 Monica Salmond. *Bright Armour: Memories of Four Years of War.* London: Faber and Faber, 1935. 17.

17 Billy Grenfell to Ettie Lady Desborough. 31 January 1914; May 1914. Desborough. *Pages from a Family Journal.* 437.

18 Cooper. *Autobiography.* 321.

19 Cooper. *Darling Monster.*

20 Salmond. *Bright Armour.* 156–60.

21 Richard Davenport-Hines. *Ettie: The Intimate Life and Dauntless Spirit of Lady Desborough.* London: Weidenfeld and Nicolson, 2008. 216–17.

22 'Crowns, Coronets, Courtiers.' 13 December 1916. *The Sketch.*

23 Philip Ziegler. *Diana Cooper: The Biography of Lady Diana Cooper.* London: Hamish Hamilton, 1981. 81.

24 John Julius Norwich (ed.). *The Duff Cooper Diaries. 1915–1951.* London: Phoenix, 2006. 44–5.

25 *Ibid.* 47.

26 Millicent, Duchess of Sutherland to Lady Rosemary Leveson-Gower. 18 January 1917. Sutherland Collection. Staffordshire Record Office. D6578-15-175-7.

27 Duff Cooper. *Old Men Forget.* London: Faber and Faber, 2011. Accessed via Google Books.

28 2 December 1917. Norwich (ed.). *The Duff Cooper Diaries.* 61.

29 *Ibid.*

30 *Ibid.* 29 December 1917. 63.

31 Duff Hart-Davis. *King's Counsellor: Abdication and War: The Diaries of Sir Alan Lascelles.* London: Weidenfeld and Nicolson, 2006. 110.

32 Roger Powell. *Royal Sex: Mistresses and Lovers of the British Royal Family.* Stroud: Amberley Books, 2010. Accessed via Google Books.

33 1 November 1915. Edward, Prince of Wales's Diary. RA EDW/PRIV/ DIARY: 1915–1917. The Royal Archives.

34 *Ibid.* 18 April 1915.

35 *Ibid.* 5 January 1916.

36 Philip Ziegler. *King Edward VIII: The Official Biography.* London: Fontana, 1991. 91–2.

37 5 January 1916. Edward, Prince of Wales's Diary. RA EDW/PRIV/DIARY: 1915–1917. The Royal Archives.

38 *Ibid.* 17 January 1916.

39 *Ibid.* 31 January 1916.

40 *Ibid.* 7 March 1916.

41 *Ibid.* 1 February 1916.

42 *Ibid.* 7 November 1915.

43 *Ibid.* 6 December 1916.

44 *Ibid.* 10 January 1917.

45 *Ibid.* 16 Janaury 1917.

46 *Ibid.* 22 January 1917.

47 *Ibid.* 15 March 1917.

48 *Ibid.* 27 May 1917.

49 Edward, Prince of Wales to Queen Mary. 2 June 1917. RA QM/PRIV/ CC09: 1916–1918. The Royal Archives.

50 Edward, Prince of Wales to Queen Mary. 27 July 1917. RA QM/PRIV/ CC09: 1916–1918. The Royal Archives.

51 Ziegler. *King Edward VIII.* 89.

52 James Lees-Milne. *The Life of Reginald, 2nd Viscount Esher: The Enigmatic Edwardian.* London: Sidgwick and Jackson, 1986. 300.

53 18 December 1916. Edward, Prince of Wales's Diary. RA EDW/PRIV/ DIARY: 1915–1917. The Royal Archives.

54 *Ibid.* 16 December 1916.

55 *Ibid.* 1 January 1917.

56 *Ibid.* 18 December 1916.

57 Andrew Rose. *The Prince, the Princess and the Perfect Murder.* London: Coronet, 2013. 30–42.

58 *Ibid.* 59.

59 *Ibid.* 42.

60 *Ibid.* 53.

61 5 May 1917. Edward, Prince of Wales's Diary. RA EDW/PRIV/DIARY: 1915–1917. The Royal Archives.

Chapter 4

1   The Duke of Windsor. *A King's Story: The Memoirs of HRH the Duke of Windsor.* London: Pan Books, 1957. 127.

2   2 March 1918. Lady Cynthia Asquith. *Lady Cynthia Asquith: Diaries 1915–18.* London: Hutchinson, 1968. 416–17.

3   *Ibid.* 14 March 1918.

4   Lady Elizabeth Bowes-Lyon to Beryl Poignard. 22 March 1918. William Shawcross (ed.). *Counting One's Blessings: The Selected Letters of Queen Elizabeth, the Queen Mother.* London: Macmillan, 2012. 57.

5   2 March 1918. Lady Cynthia Asquith. *Lady Cynthia Asquith.* 416–17.

6   Robert Wainwright. *Sheila: The Australian Beauty Who Bewitched British Society.* London: Allen Unwin, 2014. 65.

7   Lady Victor Paget's interview with Michael Thornton. *Royal Feud: The Queen Mother and the Duchess of Windsor.* London: Michael Joseph, 1985. 46.

8   Helen Hardinge. *Loyal to Three Kings: A Memoir of Alec Hardinge, Private Secretary to the Sovereign 1920–1943.* London: William Kimber, 1967. 66.

9   Edward, Prince of Wales to Freda Dudley Ward. 19 February 1919. Rupert Godfrey (ed.). *Letters from a Prince.* London: Little, Brown, 1998. 140–1.

10 Philip Ziegler. *King Edward VIII: The Official Biography*. London: Fontana, 1991. 94.

11 Sir Robert Bruce Lockhart. *Friends, Foes and Foreigners*. London: Putnam, 1957. 211.

12 Sushila Anand. *Daisy: The Life and Loves of the Countess of Warwick*. London: Piatkus, 2008. 44.

13 Andrew Rose. *The Prince, the Princess and the Perfect Murder*. London: Coronet, 2013. 160.

14 Anand. *Daisy*. 210–15.

15 *Ibid*. 159.

16 *Ibid*. 198, 201.

17 *Ibid*. 230.

18 Queen Mary to Edward, Prince of Wales. 6 April 1917. RA EDW/PRIV/MAIN/A/2047. The Royal Archives.

19 Denis Stuart. *Dear Duchess: Millicent, Duchess of Sutherland 1867–1955*. London: Victor Gollancz, 1982. 74.

20 Thornton. *Royal Feud*. 46.

21 Wainwright. *Sheila*. 38–40.

22 *Ibid*. 41–2.

23 Lady Victor Paget, in Thornton. *Royal Feud*. 48.

24 Duke of Windsor. *A King's Story*. 125.

25 Ziegler. *King Edward VIII*. 87.

26 Queen Mary to Edward, Prince of Wales. 6 December 1918. RA EDW/PRIV/MAIN/A/2204. The Royal Archives.

27 Queen Mary to Edward, Prince of Wales. 14 December 1918. RA EDW/PRIV/MAIN/A/2207. The Royal Archives.

28 Queen Mary to Edward, Prince of Wales. 29 December 1918. RA EDW/PRIV/MAIN/A/2211. The Royal Archives.

29 Edward, Prince of Wales. 15 December 1918. RA QM/PRIV/CC09: 1916–1918. The Royal Archives.

30 Stuart. *Dear Duchess*. 1.

31 Lady Angela St Clair-Erskine. *Fore and Aft*. London: Jarrolds, 1932. 24.

32 Stuart. *Dear Duchess*. 106.

33 'Potteries Cripples' Guild Bazaar and Fete at Trentham.' 18 July 1908. *Wellington Journal*.

34 Stuart. *Dear Duchess*. 109–10.

35 The Duke of Sutherland. *Looking Back: The Autobiography of the Duke of Sutherland*. London: Odhams Press, 1957. 45–6.

36 'The Duchess of Sutherland's Garden Party.' 11 July 1899. *Pall Mall Gazette*.

37 'Hardly in Homespun at the Homespun at Home.' 22 July 1914. *The Sketch*.

38 Duke of Sutherland. *Looking Back*. 47.

39 *Ibid*. 79–80.

40 Dora M. Walker. *With the Lost Generation 1915–1919: From a VAD's Diary*. Hull: A. Brown and Sons, 1970. 18.

41 Stuart. *Dear Duchess*. 142–3.
42 Queen Mary to Edward, Prince of Wales. 22 July 1917. RA EDW/PRIV/ MAIN/A/2077. The Royal Archives.
43 Edward, Prince of Wales to Queen Mary. 27 July 1917. RA QM/PRIV/ CC09: 1916–1918. The Royal Archives.
44 Ziegler. *King Edward VIII*. 79.
45 Queen Mary to Edward, Prince of Wales. 4 April 1918. RA EDW/PRIV/ MAIN/A/2128. The Royal Archives.
46 Duke of Windsor. *A King's Story*. 127.
47 A Correspondent. 25 July 1930. *The Times*. 14.
48 *Ibid*.
49 Lady Victor Paget, in Thornton. *Royal Feud*. 47–8.
50 Hardinge. *Loyal to Three Kings*. 67.

Chapter 5
1 Frances Donaldson. *Edward VIII*. London: Futura Publications, 1976. 59.
2 J. Bryan III and Charles J.V. Murphy. *The Windsor Story*. London: Granada Publishing, 1981. 78.
3 Barbara Cartland. *We Danced All Night*. London: Arrow Books, 1977. 322.
4 Rupert Godfrey (ed.). *Letters from a Prince*. London: Little, Brown, 1998. xviii.
5 Frances Donaldson. *A Twentieth-Century Life: A Memoir*. London: Weidenfeld and Nicolson, 1992. 25.
6 Donaldson. *Edward VIII*. 59.
7 'The World of Women.' 27 January 1923. *Illustrated London News*.
8 Information from Dr Rosie Collins. 'Radcliffe-on-Trent and the First World War.'
9 Interview with Max Reed and Martha Milinaric. 10 June 2017.
10 'Local Ladies as We Know Them. No. 9. Mrs Charles Birkin.' 5 March 1931. *Nottingham Journal*.
11 Interview with Max Reed and Martha Milinaric. 10 June 2017.
12 *Ibid*.
13 29 September 1932. Kenneth Young (ed.). *The Diaries of Sir Robert Bruce Lockhart. Vol. 1. 1915–1938*. London: Macmillan, 1973. 227.
14 Interview with Max Reed and Martha Milinaric. 10 June 2017.
15 'The Rowers of Vanity Fair.' 29 March 1900. *Cambridge University Boat Club C-Spy*.
16 'Fashionable Wedding.' 9 July 1913. *Nottingham Evening Post*.
17 Sheila Loughborough. In Godfrey (ed.). *Letters from a Prince*. xviii.
18 'In Town and Out.' 5 October 1910. *The Tatler*.
19 'Treasurer's Debut.' 1 March 1910. *Globe*.
20 11 November 1922. *Hull Daily Mail*.
21 8 May 1915. *Hampshire Advertiser*.
22 'The Wife of a Very Distinguished Wet Bob Who is Doing his Bit Afloat with the Fleet.' 13 September 1916. *The Tatler*.

23 Godfrey (ed.). *Letters from a Prince.* 3.

24 Helen Hardinge. *Loyal to Three Kings: A Memoir of Alec Hardinge, Private Secretary to the Sovereign 1920–1943.* London: William Kimber, 1967. 68.

25 Godfrey (ed.). *Letters from a Prince.* 278.

26 Quoted in Anne Edwards. *Matriarch: Queen Mary and the House of Windsor.* Maryland: Rowman & Littlefield Publishers, 2014. Accessed via Google Books.

27 30 January 1924. *Dundee Courier.*

28 Edward, Prince of Wales to Freda Dudley Ward. 4 April 1918. In Godfrey (ed.). *Letters from a Prince.* 13.

29 The Duke of Windsor. *A King's Story: The Memoirs of HRH the Duke of Windsor.* London: Pan Books, 1957. 125.

30 Edward, Prince of Wales to Freda Dudley Ward. 14 April 1918. In Godfrey (ed.). *Letters from a Prince.* 18–19.

31 Edward, Prince of Wales to Freda Dudley Ward. 6 May 1918. In *ibid.* 28.

32 *Ibid.* ix.

33 *Ibid.* xix.

34 *Ibid.* 77.

35 Major Reginald Seymour to Freda Dudley Ward. 9 October 1918. In Godfrey (ed.). *Letters from a Prince.* 88.

36 Edward, Prince of Wales to Freda Dudley Ward. 11 October 1918. In *ibid.* 89.

37 Edward, Prince of Wales to Freda Dudley Ward. 16 October 1918. In *ibid.* 94.

38 Edward, Prince of Wales to Freda Dudley Ward. 3 December 1918. In *ibid.* 112.

39 Edward, Prince of Wales to Freda Dudley Ward. 15 February 1919. In *ibid.* 140

40 Edward, Prince of Wales to Freda Dudley Ward. 8 July 1918. In *ibid.* 54.

41 Edward, Prince of Wales to Freda Dudley Ward. 9 October 1918. In *ibid.* 87.

42 *Ibid.* 101.

43 Edward, Prince of Wales to Freda Dudley Ward. 2 May 1919. In *ibid.* 144.

44 Edward, Prince of Wales to Freda Dudley Ward. 2 January 1920. In *ibid.* 240–1.

45 Edward, Prince of Wales to Freda Dudley Ward. 14 January 1920. In *ibid.* 245.

46 Edward, Prince of Wales to Freda Dudley Ward. 31 August 1923. Max Reed Papers.

47 Edward, Prince of Wales to Freda Dudley Ward. 22 July 1920. In Godfrey (ed.). *Letters from a Prince.* 356.

48 Edward, Prince of Wales to Freda Dudley Ward. 22 July 1920. In *ibid.* 356.

49 Edward, Prince of Wales to Freda Dudley Ward. 28 April 1920. In *ibid.* 289

50 Duke of Windsor. *A King's Story.* 131.

51 Bryan and Murphy. *The Windsor Story.* 83–4.

52 Edward, Prince of Wales to Freda Dudley Ward. 5 December 1918. In Godfrey (ed.). *Letters from a Prince.* 114.

53 Edward, Prince of Wales to Freda Dudley Ward. 20 August 1918. In *ibid.* 70.

54 Edward, Prince of Wales to Freda Dudley Ward. 9 December 1918. In *ibid.* 116.

55 Mabell, Countess of Airlie. *Thatched with Gold: The Memoirs of Mabell, Countess of Airlie.* London: Hutchinson, 1962. 162–3.

56 Queen Mary to Edward, Prince of Wales. 31 March 1917. RA EDW/ PRIV/MAIN/A/2042. The Royal Archives.
57 Hardinge. *Loyal to Three Kings*. 30–8.
58 Queen Mary to Edward, Prince of Wales. 7 September 1918. RA EDW/ PRIV/MAIN/A/2173. The Royal Archives.
59 Edward, Prince of Wales to Queen Mary. 7 September 1918. RA QM/ PRIV/CC09: 1916–1918. The Royal Archives.
60 Edward, Prince of Wales to Queen Mary. 15 December 1918. RA QM/ PRIV/CC09: 1916–1918. The Royal Archives.
61 Queen Mary to Edward, Prince of Wales. 6 December 1918. RA EDW/ PRIV/MAIN/A/2204. The Royal Archives.
62 Duke of Windsor. *A King's Story*. 184.
63 Mabell, Countess of Airlie. *Thatched with Gold*. 128–9.
64 Hardinge. *Loyal to Three Kings*. 51.
65 Quoted in Andrew Morton. *17 Carnations: The Windsors, the Nazis and the Cover Up*. London: Michael O'Mara Books, 2015. 14.
66 Bryan and Murphy. *The Windsor Story*. 83.
67 For a full description of the '4 Dos' time together see Robert Wainwright. *Sheila: The Australian Beauty Who Bewitched British Society*. Australia: Allen and Unwin, 2014.
68 Duke of Windsor. *A King's Story*. 128.
69 'More About Mariegold.' 29 December 1920. *The Sketch*.
70 Cartland. *We Danced All Night*. 383.
71 Frances Donaldson. *Child of the Twenties*. London: Rupert Hart-Davis, 1959. 69.
72 Cartland. *We Danced All Night*. 322.
73 Donaldson. *Child of the Twenties*. 69.
74 Donaldson. *Edward VIII*. 103–5.
75 Donaldson. *Child of the Twenties*. 70–1.
76 *Ibid*. 72.
77 Donaldson. *Edward VIII*. 107.
78 Bryan and Murphy. *The Windsor Story*. 81.

Chapter 6
1 Mabell, Countess of Airlie. *Thatched with Gold: The Memoirs of Mabell, Countess of Airlie*. London: Hutchinson, 1962. 145.
2 The Duke of Windsor. *A King's Story: The Memoirs of HRH the Duke of Windsor*. London: Pan Books, 1957. 137.
3 Frances Donaldson. *Edward VIII*. London: Futura Publications, 1976. 63.
4 J. Bryan III and Charles J.V. Murphy. *The Windsor Story*. London: Granada Publishing, 1981. 78.
5 *Ibid*. 84.
6 Ralph G. Martin. *The Woman He Loved: The Story of the Duke and Duchess of Windsor*. New York: Simon and Schuster, 1973. 144.

7   *Ibid.* 144–5.
8   Lord Esher to Edward, Prince of Wales. 14 October 1921. RA EDW/PRIV/MAIN/A/2346. The Royal Archives.
9   Duke of Windsor. *A King's Story.* 60.
10 Philip Ziegler. *King Edward VIII: The Official Biography.* London: Fontana, 1991. 181.
11 *Ibid.* 110.
12 16 March 1920. A.J.P. Taylor (ed.). *Lloyd George: A Diary by Frances Stevenson.* London: Hutchinson, 1971. 206.
13 'The Camera in Society.' 7 April 1920. *The Tatler.*
14 5 July 1922. *The Sketch.*
15 'Other People's Troubles.' 20 April 1921. *The Sketch.*
16 Interview with Martha Milinaric and Max Reed. 10 June 2017.
17 'Mariegold in Society.' 19 December 1923. *The Sketch.*
18 Interview with Martha Milinaric and Max Reed. 10 June 2017.
19 Edward, Prince of Wales to Sheila, Lady Loughborough. 13 November 1921. National Records of Scotland. Rosslyn Papers. GD164/2289/41 1–5.
20 Ziegler. *King Edward VIII.* 9.
21 Bryan and Murphy. *The Windsor Story.* 86.
22 Anne Edwards. *Matriarch: Queen Mary and the House of Windsor.* London: Rowan and Littlefield, 2015. 358.
23 Bryan and Murphy. *The Windsor Story.* 86.
24 27 July 1919. Alfred Shaughnessy (ed.). *Sarah: The Letters and Diaries of a Courtier's Wife 1906–1936.* London: Peter Owen, 1989. 105–6.
25 17 November 1920. John Julius Norwich (ed.). *The Duff Cooper Diaries 1915–1951.* London: Phoenix, 2006. 136.
26 Winston Churchill to Clementine Churchill. 9 February 1921. In Mary Soames (ed.). *Speaking for Themselves: The Personal Letters of Winston and Clementine Churchill.* London: Doubleday, 1998. 227.
27 Donaldson. *Edward VIII.* 58.
28 James Lees-Milne. *The Life of Reginald, 2nd Viscount Esher: The Enigmatic Edwardian.* London: Sidgwick and Jackson, 1986. 326.
29 19 January 1931. Kenneth Young (ed.). *The Diaries of Sir Robert Bruce Lockhart. Vol. 1: 1915–1938.* London: Macmillan, 1973. 147.
30 Bryan and Murphy. *The Windsor Story.* 85.
31 Information from Dr Rosie Collins. 'Radcliffe-on-Trent and the First World War.'
32 'Local Ladies as We Know Them. No.9. Mrs Charles Birkin.' 5 March 1931. *Nottingham Journal.*
33 Interview with Dr Rosie Collins.
34 Information from Dr Rosie Collins. 'Radcliffe-on-Trent and the First World War.'
35 10 December 1925. *Nottingham Journal.*
36 2 December 1927. *Dundee Courier.*

37 'A Radcliffe Play: Mrs C. Birkin's Company at the Village Hall.' 17 January 1928. *Nottingham Journal*.
38 11 August 1919. In Shaughnessy (ed.). *Sarah*. 108.
39 Donaldson. *Edward VIII*. 62.
40 30 October 1919. In Shaughnessy (ed.). *Sarah*. 115–17.
41 Ziegler. *King Edward VIII*. 98.
42 Edward, Prince of Wales to Freda Dudley Ward. 20 October 1919. In Rupert Godfrey (ed.). *Letters from a Prince*. London: Little, Brown, 1998. 212.
43 Ziegler. *King Edward VIII*. 118.
44 Donaldson. *Edward VIII*. 71.
45 Edward, Prince of Wales to Freda Dudley Ward. 24 October 1919. In Godfrey (ed.). *Letters from a Prince*. 215.
46 Bryan and Murphy. *The Windsor Story*. 83.
47 Edward, Prince of Wales to Freda Dudley Ward. 8 September 1919. In Godfrey (ed.). *Letters from a Prince*. 184.
48 Edward, Prince of Wales to Freda Dudley Ward. 7 September 1919. In *ibid*.183.
49 Edward, Prince of Wales to Freda Dudley Ward. 24 October 1919. In *ibid*. 215.
50 Edward, Prince of Wales to Freda Dudley Ward. 7 November 1919. In *ibid*. 222.
51 Lucy Moore. *Anything Goes: A Biography of the Roaring Twenties*. London: Atlantic Books, 2008. 232–9.
52 Edward, Prince of Wales to Freda Dudley Ward. 19 March 1920. In Godfrey (ed.). *Letters from a Prince*. 257.
53 Edward, Prince of Wales to Freda Dudley Ward. 18 April 1920. In *ibid*. 279.
54 *Ibid*. 53.
55 Edward, Prince of Wales to Freda Dudley Ward. 20 March 1920. In *ibid*. 259.
56 Louis Mountbatten to the Marchioness of Milford Haven. 15 July 1920. Mountbatten Archive. Southampton University. MS62-MB6-M61.
57 Ziegler. *King Edward VIII*. 128.
58 Donaldson. *Edward VIII*. 79.
59 Joey Legh to Sarah Shaughnessy. 14 June 1920. In Shaughnessy (ed.). *Sarah*. 126.
60 Louis Mountbatten to the Marchioness of Milford Haven. 9 May 1920. Mountbatten Archive. Southampton University. MS62-MB6-M61.
61 Joey Legh to Sarah Shaughnessy. 20 June 1920. In Shaughnessy (ed.). *Sarah*. 127.
62 Sir Francis Newdigate Newdegate to Willy. 15 February 1921. Shropshire Archives. 4629/1/1921/3/1.
63 *Ibid*.
64 Edward, Prince of Wales to Lady Weigall. 17 July 1920. RA EDW/PRIV/MAIN/A/2296. The Royal Archives.
65 Sir Francis Newdigate Newdegate to Willy. 15 February 1921. Shropshire Archives. 4629/1/1921/3/1.

66 Lees-Milne. *The Life of Reginald 2nd Viscount Esher.* 331.
67 Lord Esher to Edward, Prince of Wales. 13 November 1921. RA EDW/ PRIV/MAIN/A/2360. The Royal Archives.
68 *Ibid.*
69 Edward, Prince of Wales to Freda Dudley Ward. 22 May 1920. In Godfrey (ed.). *Letters from a Prince.* 300.
70 Edward, Prince of Wales to Freda Dudley Ward. 24 June 1920. In *ibid.* 329.
71 Edward, Prince of Wales to Freda Dudley Ward. 27 June 1920. In *ibid.* 336.
72 Joey Legh to Sarah Shaughnessy. 15 June 1920. In Shaughnessy (ed.). *Sarah.* 126.
73 Louis Mountbatten to the Marchioness of Milford Haven. 15 July 1920. Mountbatten Archive. Southampton University. MS62-MB6-M61.
74 Ziegler. *King Edward VIII.* 134.
75 12 December 1920. In Norwich (ed.). *The Duff Cooper Diaries.* 137.
76 Winston Churchill to Clementine Churchill. 16 February 1921. In Soames (ed.). *Speaking for Themselves.* 230.
77 Edward, Prince of Wales to Freda Dudley Ward. 16 May 1921. Max Reed Papers.
78 Edwards. *Matriarch.* 323.
79 Ziegler. *King Edward VIII.* 104.
80 Martin. *The Woman He Loved.* 143.
81 Ziegler. *King Edward VIII.* 104.
82 'The Prince's Blow to Flunkeydom: An Unconventional Character Sketch by Hannen Swaffer.' 22 January 1921. *The Graphic.*

Chapter 7
1 Frances Donaldson. *Edward VIII.* London: Futura Publications, 1976. 108.
2 John Julius Norwich (ed.). *The Duff Cooper Diaries 1915–1951.* London: Phoenix, 2006. 30.
3 'Michael Herbert.' 27 September 1932. *The Times.*
4 'Memorial Hall.' 3 June 1938. *Western Gazette.*
5 'Imp's Jest.' 25 October 1929. *Yorkshire Post and Leeds Intelligencer.*
6 'Michael Herbert.' 27 September 1932. *The Times.*
7 Diana Cooper to Duff Cooper. 30 March 1924. In Artemis Cooper (ed.). *A Durable Fire: The Letters of Duff and Diana Cooper 1913–1950.* London: Hamish Hamilton, 1985. 177.
8 Philip Ziegler. *Diana Cooper: The Biography of Lady Diana Cooper.* London: Hamish Hamilton, 1981. 64.
9 Edward, Prince of Wales to Freda Dudley Ward. 30 November 1918. In Rupert Godfrey (ed.). *Letters from a Prince.* London: Little, Brown, 1998. 112.
10 Michael Herbert to Freda Dudley Ward. No date. Michael Herbert Letters. Wiltshire and Swindon Archives. 2057/F4/113.
11 *Ibid.*

12 *Ibid.*

13 *Ibid.*

14 *Ibid.*

15 *Ibid.*

16 *Ibid.*

17 Edward, Prince of Wales to Sheila, Lady Loughborough. 13 November 1921. Rosslyn Papers. National Records of Scotland. GD164/2289/41 1–5.

18 Edward, Prince of Wales to Freda Dudley Ward. 17 January 1922. Max Reed Papers.

19 Edward, Prince of Wales to Freda Dudley Ward. 23 November 1921. Max Reed Papers.

20 Philip Ziegler. *Mountbatten: The Official Biography.* London: Book Club Associates, 1985. 60.

21 Donaldson. *Edward VIII.* 85.

22 Philip Ziegler. *King Edward VIII: The Official Biography.* London: Fontana, 1991. 139.

23 Donaldson. *Edward VIII.* 88–9.

24 *Ibid.* 96–7.

25 Edward, Prince of Wales to Freda Dudley Ward. 23 January 1922. Max Reed Papers.

26 Edward, Prince of Wales to Freda Dudley Ward. 15 January 1922. Max Reed Papers.

27 Edward, Prince of Wales to Freda Dudley Ward. 17 January 1922. Max Reed Papers.

28 'Prince's Return from India.' 'The Letters of Evelyn.' 28 June 1922. *The Tatler.*

29 'The Jottings of Jane. Frinton Again.' 12 July 1922. *The Sketch.*

30 24 July 1924. *Cornubian and Redruth Times.*

31 Edward, Prince of Wales to Freda Dudley Ward. 28 October 1922. Max Reed Papers.

32 Edward, Prince of Wales to Freda Dudley Ward. 17 August 1922. Max Reed Papers.

33 Brendan O Cathaoir. 'An Irishman's Diary.' 27 May 1997. *The Irish Times.*

34 Edward, Prince of Wales to Freda Dudley Ward. 15 August 1922. Max Reed Papers.

35 11 November 1922. *Hampshire Advertiser.*

36 'Letter to Electors of Southampton.' 4 November 1922. *Hampshire Advertiser.*

37 18 November 1922. *Hampshire Advertiser.*

38 30 June 1923. *Hampshire Advertiser.*

39 'The Letters of Eve.' 13 April 1932. *The Tatler.*

40 Michael Thornton. *Royal Feud: The Queen Mother and the Duchess of Windsor.* London: Michael Joseph, 1985. 53.

41 Anne Edwards. *Matriarch: Queen Mary and the House of Windsor.* London: Rowan and Littlefield, 2015. 336.

42 Queen Elizabeth, the Queen Mother to Queen Elizabeth. 2 May 1988. In William Shawcross (ed.). *Counting One's Blessings: The Selected Letters of Queen Elizabeth, the Queen Mother.* London: Macmillan, 2012. 591.

43 J. Bryan III and Charles J.V. Murphy. *The Windsor Story.* London: Granada Publishing, 1981. 86.

44 Edward, Prince of Wales to Freda Dudley Ward. No date. Max Reed Papers.

45 Ralph G. Martin. *The Woman He Loved: The Story of the Duke and Duchess of Windsor.* New York: Simon and Schuster, 1973. 146.

46 Bryan and Murphy. *The Windsor Story.* 86.

47 Michael Herbert to Freda Dudley Ward. 21 August 1923. Martha Milinaric Papers.

48 Ziegler. *King Edward VIII.* 100.

49 Anne Sebba. *That Woman: The Life of Wallis Simpson Duchess of Windsor.* London: Weidenfeld and Nicolson, 2011. 139.

50 Lucy Moore. *Anything Goes: A Biography of the Roaring Twenties.* London: Atlantic Books, 2008. 216.

CHAPTER 8

1 Edward, Prince of Wales to Freda Dudley Ward. 27 October 1921. Max Reed Papers.

2 Edward, Prince of Wales to Freda Dudley Ward. 2 January 1920. Rupert Godfrey (ed.). *Letters from a Prince.* London: Little, Brown, 1998. 241.

3 27 February 1924. *The Bystander.*

4 7 March 1916. Edward, Prince of Wales's Diary. RA EDW/PRIV/DIARY: 1915–1917. The Royal Archives.

5 *Ibid.* 19 May 1916.

6 Edward, Prince of Wales to Freda Dudley Ward. 3 August 1921. Max Reed Papers.

7 Interview with Michael Thornton. Michael Thornton. *Royal Feud: The Queen Mother and the Duchess of Windsor.* London: Michael Joseph, 1985. 45.

8 J. Bryan III and Charles J.V. Murphy. *The Windsor Story.* London: Granada Publishing, 1981. 96.

9 Edward James. *Swans Reflecting Elephants: My Early Years.* London: Weidenfeld and Nicolson, 1982. 4.

10 *Ibid.* 21.

11 Louis Mountbatten to the Marchioness of Milford Haven. 28 December 1919. Mountbatten Papers. Southampton University. MS62-MB6-M60.

12 Frances Donaldson. *Child of the Twenties.* London: Rupert Hart-Davis, 1959. 81–2.

13 Bryan and Murphy. *The Windsor Story.* 90.

14 Philip Ziegler. *Mountbatten: The Official Biography.* London: Book Club Associates, 1985. 59–60.

15 Duff Hart-Davis (ed.). *In Royal Service: Letters and Journals of Sir Alan Lascelles from 1920 to 1936.* London: Hamish Hamilton, 1989. 12.

16 The Duke of Windsor. *A King's Story: The Memoirs of HRH the Duke of Windsor.* London: Pan Books, 1957. 33.

17 *Ibid.* 191.

18 Hart-Davis (ed.). *In Royal Service.* 13.

19 18 January 1922. *The Tatler.*

20 Louis Mountbatten to the Marchioness of Milford Haven. 28 December 1919. Mountbatten Papers. Southampton University. MS62-MB6-M60.

21 'Lady Rider Thrown.' 24 January 1925. *Warwick and Warwickshire Advertiser.*

22 'From Hunting to Shop-Keeping.' 29 August 1925. *Illustrated Sporting and Dramatic News.*

23 'Echoes from Town.' 14 April 1925. *Nottingham Evening Post.*

24 Bryan and Murphy. *The Windsor Story.* 90.

25 Edward, Prince of Wales to Freda Dudley Ward. 10 March 1923. Max Reed Papers.

26 Edward, Prince of Wales to Freda Dudley Ward. 18 July 1923. Max Reed Papers.

27 Edward, Prince of Wales to Freda Dudley Ward. 6 April 1923. Max Reed Papers.

28 Edward, Prince of Wales to Freda Dudley Ward. 10 April 1923. Max Reed Papers.

29 Edward, Prince of Wales to Freda Dudley Ward. 30 May 1923. Max Reed Papers.

30 Edward, Prince of Wales to Freda Dudley Ward. 2 August 1923. Max Reed Papers.

31 Edward, Prince of Wales to Freda Dudley Ward. 31 August 1923. Max Reed Papers.

32 'Our London Letter.' 31 August 1923. *Dundee Courier.*

33 Edward, Prince of Wales to Freda Dudley Ward. 31 August 1923. Max Reed Papers.

34 For the full story of the Maggy Alibert affair see Andrew Rose. *The Prince, the Princess and the Perfect Murder.* London: Coronet, 2013.

35 Edward, Prince of Wales to Freda Dudley Ward. 10 September 1923. Max Reed Papers.

36 Ziegler. *King Edward VIII.* 148.

37 Edward, Prince of Wales to Freda Dudley Ward. 13 September 1923. Max Reed Papers

38 Edward, Prince of Wales to Freda Dudley Ward. 22 November 1923. Max Reed Papers.

39 Diana Cooper. *Autobiography.* London: Michael Russell, 1979. 348.

40 *Ibid.* 349.

41 *Ibid.*

42 24 July 1924. In John Julius Norwich (ed.). *The Duff Cooper Diaries 1915–1951.* London: Phoenix, 2006. 201.

43 Ziegler. *King Edward VIII.* 162.

44 Hart-Davis (ed.). *In Royal Service.* 17.

45 Joey Legh to Sarah Legh. 20 July 1925. In Alfred Shaughnessy (ed.). *Sarah: The Letters and Diaries of a Courtier's Wife 1906–1936.* London: Peter Owen, 1989. 139.

46 Joey Legh to Sarah Legh. 20 July 1925. 3 August 1925. In *ibid.* 139–40.

47 Duff Hart-Davis. *King's Counsellor: Abdication and War: The Diaries of Sir Alan Lascelles.* London: Weidenfeld and Nicolson, 2006. 109.

48 Michael Herbert to Freda Dudley Ward. 11 November 1924. Martha Milinaric Papers.

49 Michael Herbert to Freda Dudley Ward. 10 December 1924. Martha Milinaric Papers.

50 Bryan and Murphy. *The Windsor Story.* 86.

51 Michael Herbert to Freda Dudley Ward. December 1924. Martha Milinaric Papers.

52 Michael Herbert to Lady Victor Paget. No date. Martha Milinaric Papers.

53 18 February 1925. *The Tatler.*

54 Interview with Dr Rosie Collins.

55 6 February 1925. *Nottingham Journal.*

56 Edward, Prince of Wales to Freda Dudley Ward. 23 August 1923. Max Reed Papers.

57 Duke of Windsor. *A King's Story.* 198–9.

58 Ziegler. *King Edward VIII.* 173.

59 Mabell, Countess of Airlie. *Thatched with Gold: The Memoirs of Mabell, Countess of Airlie.* London: Hutchinson, 1962. 167, 198.

60 Christopher Warwick. *George and Marina: Duke and Duchess of Kent.* London: Albert Bridge Books, 2016. 45.

61 Duke of Windsor. *A King's Story.* 199.

62 Winston Churchill to Clementine Churchill. 22 October 1927. In Mary Soames (ed.). *Speaking for Themselves: The Personal Letters of Winston and Clementine Churchill.* London: Doubleday, 1998. 313–14.

63 16 July 1925. *Dundee Courier.*

64 22 July 1925. *The Sketch.*

65 7 July 1925. *Dundee Courier.*

66 'Echoes from Town.' 24 May 1926. *Nottingham Evening Post.*

67 Lady Angela St Clair-Erskine. *Fore and Aft.* London: Jarrolds, 1932. 37.

68 'Perthshire Laird Dead.' 8 August 1927. *Dundee Courier.*

69 11 April 1927. *Dundee Evening Telegraph.*

70 'Sir Stuart Coats' Daughter-in-law.' 12 April 1928. *Dundee Evening Telegraph.*

71 'Hunting With the Prince.' 8 November 1927. *The Scotsman.*

72 Bryan and Murphy. *The Windsor Story.* 91.

73 10 March 1928. *Aberdeen Press and Journal.*

74 Michael Herbert to Freda Dudley Ward. 5 January 1927. Martha Milinaric Papers.

75 Michael Herbert to Freda Dudley Ward. 6 September 1928. Martha Milinaric Papers.
76 Michael Herbert to Freda Dudley Ward. 13 November 1928. Martha Milinaric Papers.
77 25 February 1929. *Yorkshire Post and Leeds Intelligencer.*
78 3 February 1929. *Port Arthur News.*
79 Michael Herbert to Freda Dudley Ward. 25 January 1929. Martha Milinaric Papers.
80 6 September 1929. In Kenneth Young (ed.). *The Diaries of Sir Robert Bruce Lockhart. Vol. 1: 1915–1938.* London: Macmillan, 1973. 106.
81 Hart-Davis. *King's Counsellor.* 104.
82 Edward, Prince of Wales to Freda Dudley Ward. No date. Max Reed Papers.
83 Hart-Davis (ed.). *In Royal Service.* 74.
84 Ziegler. *King Edward VIII.* 193.
85 Hart-Davis (ed.). *In Royal Service.* 74–6.
86 Edward, Prince of Wales to Freda Dudley Ward. 28 September 1928. Max Reed Papers.
87 James Fox. *White Mischief.* London: Vintage, 1998. 2.
88 *Ibid.* 49.
89 Isak Dinesen to Ingeborg Dinesen. 11 November 1928. Isak Dinesen. *Letters from Africa 1914–1931: The Private Story Behind Karen Blixen's Great Memoir Out of Africa.* London: Weidenfeld and Nicolson, 1981. 387.
90 Isak Dinesen to Ingeborg Dinesen. 30 September 1928. *Ibid.* 384.
91 Fox. *White Mischief.* 26, 34.
92 *Ibid.* 34.
93 *Ibid.* 25–7.
94 Mary S. Lowell. *Straight on Till Morning: The Life of Beryl Markham.* London: Abacus, 2014. 87.
95 Hart-Davis. *King's Counsellor.* 105.
96 Ziegler. *King Edward VIII.* 190–3.
97 Hart-Davis. *King's Counsellor.* xii.
98 *Ibid.* 105.
99 Warwick. *George and Marina.* 57.
100 *Ibid.* 64.
101 *Ibid.* 64–5.
102 Ziegler. *King Edward VIII.* 200.
103 Edward, Prince of Wales to Freda Dudley Ward. No date. Max Reed Papers.
104 Edward, Prince of Wales to Freda Dudley Ward. No date. Max Reed Papers.
105 Michael Herbert to Freda Dudley Ward. No date. Martha Milinaric Papers.
106 Edward, Prince of Wales to Freda Dudley Ward. No date. Max Reed Papers.

Chapter 9

1   Gloria Vanderbilt and Thelma Furness. *Double Exposure: A Twin Autobiography.* London: Frederick Muller, 1958. 178.
2   Gloria Morgan Vanderbilt and Palma Wayne. *Without Prejudice.* New York: E.P. Dutton, 1936. 14.
3   Vanderbilt and Furness. *Double Exposure.* 50.
4   *Ibid.* 3.
5   Vanderbilt and Wayne. *Without Prejudice.* 75.
6   *Ibid.* 63.
7   Gloria Vanderbilt. *Woman to Woman.* New York: Doubleday and Co., 1979. 177.
8   Vanderbilt and Furness. *Double Exposure.* 17–18.
9   *Ibid.* 21–3.
10 *Ibid.* 34–9.
11 Barbara Goldsmith. *Little Gloria ... Happy at Last.* London: Pan Books, 1981. 42.
12 Vanderbilt and Furness. *Double Exposure.* 57.
13 Lucy Moore. *Anything Goes: A Biography of the Roaring Twenties.* London: Atlantic Books, 2008. 11.
14 Donald L. Miller. *Supreme City: How Jazz Age Manhattan Gave Birth to Modern America.* New York: Simon and Schuster, 2015. 69–71, 115–18.
15 Vanderbilt and Wayne. *Without Prejudice.* 78.
16 Moore. *Anything Goes.* 65.
17 *Ibid.* 65–7.
18 Goldsmith. *Little Gloria ... Happy at Last.* 43.
19 Miller. *Supreme City.* 349.
20 Vanderbilt and Furness. *Double Exposure.* 60.
21 Quoted in *ibid.* 121–2.
22 *Ibid.* 59.
23 *Ibid.* 71.
24 *Ibid.* 75–6.
25 Moore. *Anything Goes.* 97.
26 *Ibid.* 80.
27 Vanderbilt and Furness. *Double Exposure.* 118.
28 Moore. *Anything Goes.* 82.
29 Eileen Whitfield. *Pickford: The Woman Who Made Hollywood.* Kentucky: The University Press of Kentucky, 2007. 218.
30 Moore. *Anything Goes.* 95.
31 Whitfield. *Pickford.* 228.
32 Moore. *Anything Goes.* 82.
33 Vanderbilt and Furness. *Double Exposure.* 117.
34 Peter Ackroyd. *Charlie Chaplin.* London: Vintage Books, 2015. 138–9.
35 Vanderbilt and Furness. *Double Exposure.* 117.

36 Mary S. Lovell. *Straight on Till Morning: The Life of Beryl Markham*. London: Abacus, 2014. 129.
37 Barbara Cartland. *We Danced All Night*. London: Arrow Books, 1977. 309.
38 'Death of Lady Furness. Sudden Relapse on a Yacht off Cadiz.' 28 February 1921. *Sheffield Independent*.
39 Lovell. *Straight on Till Morning*. 129.
40 Vanderbilt and Furness. *Double Exposure*. 127.
41 *Ibid*. 133.
42 Goldsmith. *Little Gloria … Happy at Last*. 97.
43 *Ibid*. 97.
44 Vanderbilt and Furness. *Double Exposure*. 168.
45 Vanderbilt and Wayne. *Without Prejudice*. 144.
46 Vanderbilt and Furness. *Double Exposure*. 191.
47 Pat Cavendish O'Neill. *A Lion in the Bedroom*. Johannesburg and Cape Town: Jonathan Ball Publishers, 2004. 40–1.
48 *Ibid*. 41.
49 *Ibid*. 40.
50 *Ibid*. 45.
51 Vanderbilt and Wayne. *Without Prejudice*. 174–5.
52 Frances Donaldson. *Child of the Twenties*. London: Rupert Hart-Davis, 1959. 132–3.
53 Vanderbilt and Furness. *Double Exposure*. 224.
54 Gloria Vanderbilt. *Once Upon a Time: A True Story By Gloria Vanderbilt*. London: Chatto and Windus, 1985. 28.
55 Frances Donaldson. *Child of the Twenties*. London: Rupert Hart-Davis, 1959. 132–3.
56 Ackroyd. *Charlie Chaplin*. 138.
57 Vanderbilt and Furness. *Double Exposure*. 219–20.
58 *Ibid*. 222.
59 *Ibid*. 223–4.
60 Ralph G. Martin. *The Woman He Loved: The Story of the Duke and Duchess of Windsor*. New York: Simon and Schuster, 1973. 147.
61 'The Letters of Evelyn.' 15 December 1926. *The Tatler*.
62 'Melton Hunt Ball.' 13 January 1928. *Nottingham Journal*.
63 Cavendish O'Neill. *A Lion in the Bedroom*. 73–4.
64 Richard Fawkes. 'Obituary: Viscount Furness.' 11 May 1995. *The Independent*.
65 Vanderbilt and Furness. *Double Exposure*. 226.
66 *Ibid*. 226–7.
67 *Ibid*. 261.
68 Cartland. *We Danced All Night*. 337.
69 Martin. *The Woman He Loved*. New York: Simon and Schuster, 1973. 147.
70 Vanderbilt and Furness. *Double Exposure*. 261.
71 Anna Sebba. *That Woman: The Life of Wallis Simpson, Duchess of Windsor*. London: Weidenfeld and Nicolson, 2011. 84.

72 Goldsmith. *Little Gloria … Happy at Last.* 138–9.
73 Vanderbilt and Furness. *Double Exposure.* 262.
74 Lovell. *Straight on Till Morning.* 82.
75 Vanderbilt and Furness. *Double Exposure.* 265–6.
76 *Ibid.* 269.
77 *Ibid.* 265.
78 *Ibid.* 267–8.
79 Edward, Prince of Wales to Freda Dudley Ward. 5 February 1930. Max Reed Papers.
80 Edward, Prince of Wales to Freda Dudley Ward. 31 February 1930. Max Reed Papers.
81 Edward, Prince of Wales to Freda Dudley Ward. 29 May 1930. Max Reed Papers.
82 Robert Wainwright. *Sheila: The Australian Beauty Who Bewitched British Society.* Australia: Allen and Unwin, 2014. 272.
83 Anne Edwards. *Matriarch: Queen Mary and the House of Windsor.* London: Rowan and Littlefield, 2015. 362.
84 Frances Donaldson. *Edward VIII.* London: Futura Publications, 1976. 109.
85 12 September 1931. Kenneth Young (ed.). *The Diaries of Sir Robert Bruce Lockhart. Vol. 1: 1915–1938.* London: Macmillan, 1973. 185.
86 Vanderbilt and Furness. *Double Exposure.* 271.
87 8 October 1931. In Young (ed.). *The Diaries of Sir Robert Bruce Lockart. Vol. 1: 1915–1938.* 190.
88 Anna Thomasson. *A Curious Friendship: The Story of a Blue-Stocking and a Bright Young Thing.* Basingstoke: Pan Macmillan, 2015. Accessed via Google Books.
89 24 November 1931. *Portsmouth Evening News.*
90 It seems that rather than being a real girlfriend of Duddie's, as in so many divorce cases at the time, Lilian was employed to provide the necessary evidence of infidelity. It is possible Miss Gallifent was an actress. In 1916 Nellie Gallifent was a 'dainty comedienne' and singer of sentimental songs, who performed at Blackpool pier. Perhaps she could not make it as an entertainer so she used her acting skills in other ways. There is no further record of Lilian in Duddie's life and Miss Gallifent went on to marry Ralph Altson in Kensington three years later.
91 Sebba. *That Woman.* 139.
92 'Divorce'. 19 June 1930. *Yorkshire Post and Leeds Intelligencer.*
93 Michael Herbert to Freda Dudley Ward. No date. Martha Milinaric Papers.
94 Edward, Prince of Wales to Freda Dudley Ward. No date. Max Reed Papers.
95 Freda Dudley Ward to Duff Cooper. 2 October 1932. Duff Cooper Papers. Churchill Archives Centre, Churchill College, Cambridge University. DUFC 12021 (4).
96 'Mr Michael Herbert's £500,000 Will.' 6 January 1933. *Warminster and Westbury Journal.*
97 23 June 1939. *Western Gazette.*

98 Philip Ziegler. *King Edward VIII: The Official Biography.* London: Fontana, 1991. 199.

99 *Ibid.* 206.

100 Andrew Morton. *17 Carnations: The Windsors, the Nazis and the Cover Up.* London: Michael O'Mara Books, 2015. 28.

101 Robert Vacha (ed.). *The Kaiser's Daughter: Memoirs of HRH Viktoria Luise, Duchess of Brunswick and Luneberg, Princess of Prussia.* London: W.H. Allen, 1977. 188.

102 Memorandum by Lord Wigram. 3 March 1932. RA PS/PSO/GVI/C/019/269. The Royal Archives.

103 Memorandum by Lord Wigram. 4 March 1932. RA PS/PSO/GVI/C/019/270. The Royal Archives.

104 Ziegler. *King Edward VIII.* 198.

105 Goldsmith. *Little Gloria ... Happy at Last.* 144.

106 8 October 1931. In Young (ed.). *The Diaries of Sir Robert Bruce Lockart. Vol. 1: 1915–1938.* 190.

107 Ziegler. *King Edward VIII.* 219.

108 Martin. *The Woman He Loved.* 159.

109 Robert Rhodes James (ed.). *'Chips': The Diaries of Sir Henry Channon.* London: Weidenfeld and Nicolson, 1993. 50.

110 J. Bryan III and Charles J.V. Murphy. *The Windsor Story.* London: Granada Publishing, 1981. 125.

111 'Biarritz Asides.' 6 September 1933. *The Sketch.*

112 *Ibid.*

113 'Biarritz Asides.' 13 September 1933. *The Sketch.*

114 'Prince of Wales Lourdes Visit.' 27 November 1931. *Edinburgh Evening News.*

115 Vanderbilt and Furness. *Double Exposure.* 273.

116 Sebba. *That Woman.* 94.

117 Vanderbilt and Furness. *Double Exposure.* 282.

118 Goldsmith. *Little Gloria ... Happy at Last.* 141.

119 The Duchess of Windsor. *The Heart Has its Reasons: The Story of the Abdication.* London: Tandem, 1975. 191–2.

120 *Ibid.* 194–5.

121 Vanderbilt and Wayne. *Without Prejudice.* 176.

122 Vanderbilt and Furness. *Double Exposure.* 269.

123 Bryan and Murphy. *The Windsor Story.* 103.

124 Vanderbilt and Furness. *Double Exposure.* 269.

125 *Ibid.* 279.

126 Goldsmith. *Little Gloria ... Happy at Last.* 137.

127 Bryan and Murphy. *The Windsor Story.* 109.

Chapter 10

1 The Duchess of Windsor. *The Heart Has its Reasons: The Story of the Abdication.* London: Tandem, 1975. 153, 169.
2 Gloria Vanderbilt and Thelma Furness. *Double Exposure: A Twin Autobiography.* London: Frederick Muller, 1958. 274.
3 *Ibid.* 274–5.
4 The Duke of Windsor. *A King's Story: The Memoirs of HRH the Duke of Windsor.* London: Pan Books, 1957. 248.
5 Philip Ziegler. *King Edward VIII: The Official Biography.* London: Fontana, 1991. 227.
6 Duchess of Windsor. *The Heart Has its Reasons.* 176–7.
7 Wallis Simpson to Aunt Bessie. 13 January 1931. In Michael Bloch (ed.). *Wallis and Edward. Letters 1931–37: The Intimate Correspondence of the Duke and Duchess of Windsor.* London: Weidenfeld and Nicolson, 1986. 24.
8 Duchess of Windsor. *The Heart Has its Reasons.* 177–84.
9 Ziegler. *King Edward VIII.* 227.
10 Duchess of Windsor. *The Heart Has its Reasons.* 177–84.
11 Barbara Goldsmith. *Little Gloria … Happy at Last.* London: Pan Books, 1981. 149.
12 'The Prince and I.' 20 June 1954. *American Weekly.* Quoted in *ibid.* 149.
13 Duchess of Windsor. *The Heart Has its Reasons.* 185–6.
14 *Ibid.* 187–8.
15 Helen Hardinge. *Loyal to Three Kings: A Memoir of Alec Hardinge, Private Secretary to the Sovereign 1920–1943.* London: William Kimber, 1967. 73.
16 Duchess of Windsor. *The Heart Has its Reasons.* 204.
17 Anne Sebba. *That Woman: The Life of Wallis Simpson, Duchess of Windsor.* London: Weidenfeld and Nicolson, 2011. 93–4.
18 Wallis Simpson to Aunt Bessie. 29 January 1933. In Bloch (ed.). *Wallis and Edward. Letters 1931–37.* 65.
19 Vanderbilt and Furness. *Double Exposure.* 274.
20 Duchess of Windsor. *The Heart Has its Reasons.* 200.
21 Sebba. *That Woman.* 93.
22 'Popular Rendez-Vous and their Patrons.' 8 January 1935. *The Bystander.*
23 Duchess of Windsor. *The Heart Has its Reasons.* 202.
24 'Viscount Furness Divorced.' 23 January 1933. *Gloucestershire Echo.*
25 Pat Cavendish O'Neill. *A Lion in the Bedroom.* Johannesburg and Cape Town: Jonathan Ball, 2004. 74.
26 Vanderbilt and Furness. *Double Exposure.* 286.
27 Duke of Windsor. *A King's Story.* 251.
28 *Ibid.* 251.
29 Vanderbilt and Furness. *Double Exposure.* 286.
30 'Cholly Knickerbocker.' September 1937. *The American.* Quoted in Goldsmith. *Little Gloria … Happy at Last.* 236.
31 Barclay Beckman. 31 March 1946. *The Mirror.* Quoted in *ibid.* 142.

32 'What Every Woman Wants to Know.' 30 May 1934. *The Sketch*.
33 Robert Wainwright. *Sheila: The Australian Beauty Who Bewitched British Society*. Sydney: Allen and Unwin, 2014. 241–2.
34 Pond's advert. 26 January 1934.
35 Vanderbilt and Furness. *Double Exposure*. 291.
36 *Ibid*.
37 Wallis Simpson to Aunt Bessie. 12 February 1934. In Bloch (ed.). *Wallis and Edward. Letters 1931–37*. 87.
38 Duchess of Windsor. *The Heart Has its Reasons*. 150.
39 Duke of Windsor. *A King's Story*. 249.
40 *Ibid*. 250.
41 'Royal Obsession.' 27 March 1975. *Kenosha News*.
42 Wallis Simpson to Aunt Bessie. 18 February 1934. In Bloch (ed.). *Wallis and Edward. Letters 1931–37*. 89.
43 Frances Donaldson. *Edward VIII*. London: Futura Publications, 1976. 169–70.
44 Wallis Simpson to Aunt Bessie. 18 February 1934. In Bloch (ed.). *Wallis and Edward. Letters 1931–37*. 89.
45 Mary S. Lovell. *The Riviera Set*. London: Little, Brown, 2016. 238.
46 *Ibid*. 251.
47 Elsa Maxwell. *I Married the World*. London: William Heinemann, 1955. 236.
48 Ralph G. Martin. *The Woman He Loved: The Story of the Duke and Duchess of Windsor*. New York: Simon and Schuster, 1973. 159.
49 Leonard Slater. *Aly: A Biography*. New York: Random House, 1964. 8.
50 Maxwell. *I Married the World*. 236–8.
51 Vanderbilt and Furness. *Double Exposure*. 294–5.
52 Slater. *Aly*. 7.
53 Martin. *The Woman He Loved*. 159.
54 Vanderbilt and Furness. *Double Exposure*. 296.
55 Duchess of Windsor. *The Heart Has its Reasons*. 206–7.
56 Vanderbilt and Furness. *Double Exposure*. 297–8.
57 Ziegler. *King Edward VIII*. 229.
58 5 November 1936. Robert Rhodes James (ed.). *'Chips': The Diaries of Sir Henry Channon*. London: Weidenfeld and Nicolson, 1993. 76.
59 Bloch (ed.). *Wallis and Edward. Letters 1931–37*. 109.
60 Vanderbilt and Furness. *Double Exposure*. 298.
61 Martin. *The Woman He Loved*. 163.
62 Wallis Simpson to Aunt Bessie. 15 April 1934. In Bloch (ed.). *Wallis and Edward. Letters 1931–37*. 92.
63 Quoted in Eve Brown. *Champagne Cholly*. New York: E.P. Dutton, 1947. 235.
64 Frances Donaldson. *Edward VIII*. London: Futura Publications, 1976. 142.
65 Wallis Simpson to Aunt Bessie. 25 April 1934. In Bloch (ed.). *Wallis and Edward. Letters 1931–37*. 93.
66 J. Bryan III and Charles J.V. Murphy. *The Windsor Story*. London: Granada Publishing, 1981. 120.

67 20 February 1934. *The Bystander.*

68 Anne Edwards. *Matriarch: Queen Mary and the House of Windsor.* London: Rowan and Littlefield, 2015. 367.

69 14 May 1935. In Rhodes James (ed.). *'Chips'.* 33.

70 28 July 1935. In *ibid.* 39.

71 Bryan and Murphy. *The Windsor Story.* 118.

72 14 May 1935. In Rhodes James (ed.). *'Chips'.* 33.

73 Bryan and Murphy. *The Windsor Story.* 120.

74 14 May 1935. In Rhodes James (ed.). *'Chips'.* 33.

75 20 January 1937. In Susan Lowndes (ed.). *Diaries and Letters of Marie Belloc Lowndes 1911–1947.* London: Chatto and Windus, 1971. 142.

76 16 June 1935. In Rhodes James (ed.). *'Chips'.* 36.

77 Wainwright. *Sheila.* 274.

78 Ziegler. *King Edward VIII.* 235.

79 28 July 1935. In Rhodes James (ed.). *'Chips'.* 39–40.

80 13 January 1935. In Nigel Nicolson (ed.). *Harold Nicolson: Diaries and Letters 1907–1964.* London: Phoenix, 2005. 154.

81 January 1936. In John Julius Norwich (ed.). *The Duff Cooper Diaries 1915–1951.* London: Phoenix, 2006. 228.

82 Philip Ziegler. *Diana Cooper.* London: Hamish Hamilton, 1981. 177–8.

83 I do not go into that debate in detail here. It can be found in the many biographies of the Duke and Duchess of Windsor.

84 27 May 1935. In Kenneth Young (ed.). *The Diaries of Sir Robert Bruce Lockhart. Vol. 1: 1915–1938.* London: Macmillan, 1973. 321.

85 Whitsuntide 1935. In Rhodes James (ed.). *'Chips'.* 35.

86 Michael Thornton. 'Did Mrs Simpson Ever Truly Love the King Who Gave Up His Throne for Her?' 8 April 2017. *Daily Mail.* 56.

87 Anne Sebba. *That Woman.* 126–7.

88 Donaldson. *Edward VIII.* 169.

HAPTER *11*

1 'This Morning's Gossip.' 27 February 1919. *Leeds Mercury.*

2 'The Letters of Eve.' 19 March 1919. *The Tatler.*

3 Edward, Prince of Wales to Freda Dudley Ward. 15 May 1918. In Rupert Godfrey (ed.). *Letters from a Prince.* London: Little, Brown, 1998. 32.

4 Edward, Prince of Wales to Freda Dudley Ward. 19 February 1919. In *ibid.* 140–1.

5 Rosemary Ednam to Millicent, Duchess of Sutherland. 9 March 1919. Letter in the possession of the Earl of Dudley. Quoted in Michael Thornton. *Royal Feud: The Queen Mother and the Duchess of Windsor.* London: Michael Joseph, 1985. 48.

6 'Engaged to Viscount Ednam: Lady Rosemary Leveson-Gower.' 22 February 1919. *Illustrated London News.*

7   19 February 1919. *The Tatler.*

8   'Undergrads Fined.' 19 June 1914. *Diss Express.*

9   Eric, Viscount Ednam to Rosemary Leveson-Gower. 18 May 1918. Dudley Archives and Local History Service. DE/15/1/7/1.

10 Tommy, Lady Rosslyn to Eric, Viscount Ednam. No Date. Dudley Archives and Local History Service. DE/15/1/6/48.

11 *Ibid.*

12 Lady Rosemary Leveson-Gower to Eric, Viscount Ednam. No date. Dudley Archives and Local History Service. DE/15/1/6/63.

13 'Engaged to Viscount Ednam: Lady Rosemary Leveson-Gower.' 22 February 1919. *Illustrated London News.*

14 Philip Ziegler. *King Edward VIII: The Official Biography.* London: Fontana, 1991. 37.

15 Edward, Prince of Wales to Freda Dudley Ward. 19 February 1919. In Godfrey (ed.). *Letters from a Prince.* 141.

16 Eric, Viscount Ednam to Rosemary, Viscountess Ednam. 8 January 1920. Dudley Archives and Local History Service. DE/15/1/7/3.

17 Eric, Viscount Ednam to Rosemary, Viscountess Ednam. 19 January 1920. Dudley Archives and Local History Service. DE/15/1/7/4.

18 Edward, Prince of Wales to Rosemary, Viscountess Ednam. 23 February 1920. Dudley Archives and Local History Service. DE/15/1/7/5.

19 'Men and Women of Today: Former Home of Whistler.' 18 March 1930. *Dundee Courier.*

20 Eric, Viscount Ednam to Rosemary, Viscountess Ednam. 26 July 1921. Dudley Archives and Local History Service. DE/15/1/7/8.

21 'Men and Women of Today.' 20 October 1929. *Dundee Courier.*

22 Eric, Viscount Ednam to Rosemary, Viscountess Ednam. Undated. Dudley Archives and Local History Service. DE/15/1/7/14.

23 Rosemary Ednam to Duff Cooper. No Date. Duff Cooper Papers. Churchill Archives Centre, Churchill College, Cambridge University. DUFC12/029.

24 Billy to Rosemary, Viscountess Ednam. 21 April 1927. Dudley Archives and Local History Service. DE/15/1/7/11.

25 Denis Stuart. *Dear Duchess: Millicent, Duchess of Sutherland 1867–1955.* London: Victor Gollancz, 1982. 144–6.

26 'The Third Time.' 30 October 1919. *Yorkshire Evening Post.*

27 Stuart. *Dear Duchess.* 146–7.

28 *Ibid.* 158.

29 Eric, Viscount Ednam to Rosemary, Viscountess Ednam. 26 July 1921. Dudley Archives and Local History Service. DE/15/1/7/8.

30 Rosemary Ednam to Eric Ednam, Undated. Dudley Archives and Local History Service. DE/15/1/6/65.

31 Naomi Levine. *Politics, Religion and Love: The Story of H.H. Asquith, Venetia Stanley and Edwin Montagu.* New York: New York University Press, 1991. Accessed via Google Books.

32 Eric, Viscount Ednam to Rosemary, Viscountess Ednam. 5 March 1923. Dudley Archives and Local History Service. DE/15/1/7/9.

33 29 April 1924. *Dundee Courier.*

34 Duff Cooper to Lady Diana Cooper. 30 July 1926–3 August 1926. Duff Cooper Papers. Churchill Archives Centre, Churchill College, Cambridge University. DUFC 01006004.

35 Enid to Eric, Viscount Ednam. 28 March 1926. Dudley Archives and Local History Service. DE/15/1/6/57.

36 Anonymous. 'Eulogic or Romantic Notes on "Rose".' 4 November 1926. Dudley Archives and Local History Service. DE/15/6/2 (1).

37 Hugo Vickers. *Behind Closed Doors: The Tragic Untold Story of the Duchess of Windsor.* London: Arrow, 2012. 266.

38 'The Dancing Prince.' 7 March 1924. *Leeds Mercury.*

39 'Mariegold in Society.' 9 July 1924. *The Sketch.*

40 'A Resident Landlord.' 30 November 1937. *The Bystander.*

41 The Duke of Sutherland. *Looking Back: The Autobiography of the Duke of Sutherland.* London: Odhams Press, 1957. 165.

42 'Living the Pampered Life.' 25 May 1929. *The Graphic.*

43 'Mariegold in Society.' 20 November 1929. *The Sketch.*

44 Edward, Prince of Wales to Freda Dudley Ward. Undated. Max Reed Papers.

45 'The Duke's Private Film.' 19 May 1923. *Dundee Courier.*

46 Duke of Sutherland. *Looking Back.* 89–92.

47 *Ibid.* 157.

48 Robert Wainwright. *Sheila: The Australian Beauty Who Bewitched British Society.* Sydney: Allen and Unwin, 2014. 164–5.

49 Duff Cooper to Diana Cooper. 29 January 1927. In Artemis Cooper (ed.). *A Durable Fire: The Letters of Duff and Diana Cooper 1913–1950.* London: Hamish Hamilton, 1985. 249.

Chapter 12

1   'Masked Women at Hornsey.' 7 November 1921. *Pall Mall Gazette.*

2   'Men and Women of Today: Lord and Lady Ednam.' 29 November 1921. *Dundee Courier.*

3   'Hornsey Canvassing.' 8 November 1921. *Pall Mall Gazette.*

4   Rosemary Ednam to Eric Ednam, Undated. Dudley Archives and Local History Service. DE/15/1/6/65.

5   'Lord Ednam's Debut.' 1 April 1922. *Faringdon Advertiser.*

6   Sushila Anand. *Daisy: The Life and Loves of the Countess of Warwick.* London: Piatkus, 2008. 244–51.

7   'Rosemary Ednam Speech to Conservatives: Notes for a Speech Given to Worcestershire Conservatives before General Election 1924.' Dudley Archives and Local History Service. DE/12/1/6 (1).

8   Diana Cooper. *Autobiography*. London: Michael Russell, 1979. 275–8.
9   'The Letters of Evelyn.' 5 November 1924. *The Sketch*.
10 Philip Ziegler. *King Edward VIII: The Official Biography*. London: Fontana, 1991. 183.
11 'Lady Ednam Re-Elected President.' 20 October 1928. *Staffordshire Advertiser*.
12 'Lady Ednam's Visit.' 26 October 1929. *Staffordshire Advertiser*.
13 'Cripples' Aid Society.' 30 January 1932. *Staffordshire Advertiser*.
14 J.M. Barrie. 'Obituary: Lady Ednam.' 25 July 1930. *The Times*.
15 Quoted in the Duke of Sutherland. *Looking Back: The Autobiography of the Duke of Sutherland*. London: Odhams Press, 1957. 167.
16 'A Woman's Letter: The Tweed Look.' 6 October 1928. *The Graphic*.
17 Clementine Churchill to Winston Churchill. 16 February 1924. In Mary Soames (ed.). *Speaking for Themselves: The Personal Letters of Winston and Clementine Churchill*. London: Doubleday, 1998. 276.
18 'Ripples from the Riviera.' 6 February 1924. *The Sketch*.
19 'One Stunt Too Dizzy for Chicago's Diving Countess. How Lord Beatty's Dare-devil Wife Tried to Swim the Hellespont as Byron Did and Almost Met the Fate that Overtook Leander.' 17 October 1924. *Hamilton Evening Journal*.
20 Cooper. *Autobiography*. 321.
21 'Lord A. Leveson-Gower.' 7 June 1921. *Aberdeen Press and Journal*.
22 7 August 1930. In Kenneth Young (ed.). *The Diaries of Sir Robert Bruce Lockhart. Vol. 1: 1915–1938*. London: Macmillan, 1973. 124.
23 'Viscount Ednam's Son Fatally Injured.' 10 December 1929. *The Scotsman*.
24 'Tragic Death of Viscount's Son.' 11 December 1929. *Nottingham Evening Post*.
25 'Miniature Bicycle in Collision.' 10 December 1929. *Aberdeen Press and Journal*.
26 'A Tragic Happening.' 11 December 1929. *Hartlepool Northern Daily Mail*.
27 *Ibid*.
28 Rosemary Ednam to Duff Cooper. No Date. Duff Cooper Papers. Churchill Archives Centre, Churchill College, Cambridge University. DUFC 12 029 (4).
29 Rosemary Ednam to Elizabeth, Marchioness of Salisbury. December 1929. Hatfield House Archive.
30 Duke of Sutherland. *Looking Back*. 166.
31 *Ibid*.
32 Michael Thornton. *Royal Feud: The Queen Mother and the Duchess of Windsor*. London: Michael Joseph, 1985. 48.
33 Elsa Maxwell. *I Married the World*. London: William Heinemann, 1955. 183.
34 Alfred Shaughnessy (ed.). *Sarah: The Letters and Diaries of a Courtier's Wife 1906–1936*. London: Peter Owen, 1989. 152.
35 Barbara Cartland. *We Danced All Night*. London: Arrow Books, 1977. 105–6.
36 'Four Passengers and Two Pilots Dashed to Death.' 25 July 1930. *Western Gazette*.

37 'Plane Blown to Pieces.' 22 July 1930. *Sheffield Independent*.
38 Cartland. *We Danced All Night*. 108.
39 'Air Disaster.' 25 July 1930. *Gloucester Citizen*.
40 'Search Parties Organised.' 22 July 1930. *Dundee Courier*.
41 26 January 1935. In Robert Rhodes James (ed.). *'Chips': The Diaries of Sir Henry Channon*. London: Weidenfeld and Nicolson, 1993. 23.
42 'Society's Tribute.' 26 July 1930. *Sheffield Independent*.
43 Cartland. *We Danced All Night*. 107.
44 'With Love E.P.' 26 July 1930. *Leeds Mercury*.
45 Diana Cooper. *Darling Monster: The Letters of Lady Diana Cooper to her Son John Julius Norwich, 1939–1952*. New York: The Overlook Press, 2014. Accessed via Google Books.
46 'With Love E.P.' 26 July 1930. *Leeds Mercury*.
47 Duff Cooper. Quoted in Denis Stuart. *Dear Duchess: Millicent, Duchess of Sutherland 1867–1955*. London: Victor Gollancz, 1982. 167.
48 William Cooke. *Wings Over Meir*. Stroud: Amberley, 2010. Accessed via Google Books.
49 Edward, Prince of Wales to Millicent, Duchess of Sutherland. No date. Sutherland Collection. Staffordshire Records Office. D6528-15-174-3.
50 Duke of Sutherland. *Looking Back*. 174.
51 Cooke. *Wings Over Meir*.

Chapter 13

1 J. Bryan III and Charles J.V. Murphy. *The Windsor Story*. London: Granada Publishing, 1981. 78.
2 Martha Milinaric photograph collection.
3 Interview with Martha Milinaric and Max Reed. 10 June 2017.
4 Hugo Vickers. *Behind Closed Doors: The Tragic Untold Story of the Duchess of Windsor*. London: Arrow, 2012. 266.
5 Philip Ziegler. *Mountbatten: The Official Biography*. London: Book Club Associates, 1985. 95.
6 Bryan and Murphy. *The Windsor Story*. 87.
7 *Ibid*. 86.
8 Ralph G. Martin. *The Woman He Loved: The Story of the Duke and Duchess of Windsor*. New York: Simon and Schuster, 1973. 150.
9 Philip Ziegler. *King Edward VIII: The Official Biography*. London: Fontana, 1991. 185–6.
10 The Duke of Windsor. *A King's Story: The Memoirs of HRH the Duke of Windsor*. London: Pan Books, 1957. 213.
11 *Ibid*. 243–4.
12 Ziegler. *King Edward VIII*. 215.
13 *Ibid*. 215–16.
14 Frances Donaldson. *Edward VIII*. London: Futura Publications, 1976. 133.

15 *Ibid.* 134.
16 'Feathers Club.' 15 December 1933. *Dundee Courier.*
17 Ziegler. *King Edward VIII.* 217.
18 'Duke of Kent Tour of London Community Centres.' 20 January 1937. *Nottingham Journal.*
19 'Italian's Plea.' 15 January 1936. *Sunderland Daily Echo and Shipping Gazette.*
20 Interview with Lady Isabella Naylor-Leyland. 23 October 2017.
21 *Ibid.*
22 Interview with Martha Milinaric and Max Reed. 10 June 2017.
23 9 May 1934. *The Sketch.*
24 11 September 1934. In Kenneth Young (ed.). *The Diaries of Sir Robert Bruce Lockhart. Vol. 1: 1915–1938.* London: Macmillan, 1973. 305.
25 Brendan Bracken to Winston S. Churchill. 30 July 1935. Churchill Archive Centre, Churchill College, Cambridge University. Char2/236/149.
26 Winston S. Churchill to Sir Kingsley Wood. 1 August 1935. Churchill Archive Centre, Churchill College, Cambridge University. Char2/236/150.
27 14 September 1934. Diana Cooper. *Autobiography.* London: Michael Russell, 1979. 391.
28 Lord Moran. *Winston Churchill: The Struggle for Survival 1940–1965.* London: Constable, 1966. 746.
29 Laura, Duchess of Marlborough. *Laughter from a Cloud.* London: Weidenfeld and Nicolson, 1980. 103.
30 Denis Stuart. *Dear Duchess: Millicent, Duchess of Sutherland 1867–1955.* London: Victor Gollancz, 1982. 168.
31 Millicent, Duchess of Sutherland, to Eric, Viscount Ednam. 21 March 1934. Dudley Archives and Local History Service. DE/15/1/6/115.
32 26 January 1935. In Robert Rhodes James (ed.). *'Chips': The Diaries of Sir Henry Channon.* London: Weidenfeld and Nicolson, 1993. 23.
33 Bryan and Murphy. *The Windsor Story.* 82.
34 Edward, Prince of Wales to Freda Dudley Ward. 15 April 1931. Max Reed Papers.
35 Wallis Simpson to Aunt Bessie. 14 April 1936. In Michael Bloch (ed.). *Wallis and Edward. Letters 1931–1937: The Intimate Correspondence of the Duke and Duchess of Windsor.* London: Weidenfeld and Nicolson, 1986. 171.
36 'Celebrities in Cameo: The Marquis de Casa Maury.' 11 December 1935. *The Bystander.*
37 Robert Wainwright. *Sheila: The Australian Beauty Who Bewitched British Society.* Sydney: Allen and Unwin, 2014. 304.
38 'Miss Paula Gellibrand.' 20 December 1932. *Leeds Mercury.*
39 Cecil Beaton. *The Glass of Fashion: A Personal History of Fifty Years of Changing Tastes and the People Who Have Inspired Them.* New York: Rizzoli Ex Libris, 2014. 176.

40 'Mrs Dudley Ward to Marry.' 13 October 1937. *Gloucestershire Echo.*
41 'Featured: The Style Moderne in the London House of the Marquise de Casa Maury.' 16 August 1930. *The Sphere.*
42 'Celebrities in Cameo: The Marquis de Casa Maury.' 11 December 1935. *The Bystander.*
43 'At the Pictures.' 13 December 1946. *The Tatler.*
44 'The Curzon Cinema.' 10 March 1934. *Illustrated London News.*
45 'The Cinema.' 29 March 1939. *The Tatler.*
46 'The Curzon Cinema.' 6 March 1934. *The Bystander.*
47 'Grand Cinema – The Curzon Out-Mayfairs Covent Garden.' 13 March 1934. *The Bystander.*
48 'Postponed by Penelope.' 26 July 1934. *Leeds Mercury.*
49 'A New Star.' 5 April 1935. *Derby Daily Telegraph.*
50 13 November 1935. *The Tatler.*
51 'Moscow Nights.' 8 November 1935. *Western Morning News.*
52 'A Divine Time Altogether.' 4 September 1935. *The Bystander.*
53 Richard Mead. *Commando General: The Life of Major General Sir Robert Laycock KCMG CB DSO.* Barnsley: Pen and Sword Military, 2016. 32.
54 27 November 1934. *The Bystander.*
55 'Seats Reserved for Workless Novel Feature at Society Wedding.' 25 January 1934. *Gloucester Citizen.*
56 Bryan and Murphy. *The Windsor Story.* 120.
57 Wallis Simpson to Aunt Bessie. 9 February 1936. In Bloch (ed.). *Wallis and Edward: Letters 1931–1937.* 159–60.
58 *Ibid.* 192–4.
59 27 October 1937. *The Sketch.*
60 25 October 1937. *Nottingham Journal.*
61 Interview with Martha Milinaric and Max Reed. 10 June 2017.
62 Andrew Morton. *17 Carnations.* 130.
63 Quoted in Andrew Morton. 134.
64 'Good Points in the Lighting and Heating of a New London House.' September 1938. *The Ideal Home.* 164–70.
65 Freda Dudley Ward to Duff Cooper. Undated. Duff Cooper Papers. Churchill Archives Centre, Churchill College, Cambridge. DUFC 12021 (31).
66 'Panorama.' 21 April 1937. *The Tatler.*
67 'The Paris.' 25 April 1939. *Western Mail.*
68 Duchess of Marlborough. *Laughter from a Cloud.* 138.
69 Nicholas Wapshott. *The Man Between: A Biography of Carol Reed.* London: Chatto and Windus, 1990. 146–67.

Chapter 14

1 Freda, Marquesa de Casa Maury to Winston S. Churchill. 11 November 1940. Churchill Archive Centre, Churchill College Cambridge University. Char 20/10/35.
2 'Minutes of the Feathers Clubs.' October 1941. The Feathers Assocation Archive.
3 'First Feathers Club. Annual Report. January to December 1940.' Martha Milinaric Papers.
4 Freda Dudley Ward to Duff Cooper. 20 January 1944. Duff Cooper Papers. Churchill Archives Centre. DUFC 12021 (10).
5 'Winston Churchill.' The Ditchley Foundation. Ditchley.co.uk.
6 11 January 1941. In John Colville. *The Fringes of Power: Downing Street Diaries 1939–1955*. London: Hodder and Stoughton, 1985. 332–4.
7 12 January 1941. In *ibid*. 334–5.
8 Freda Dudley Ward to Winston S. Churchill. 13 February 1941. Churchill Archives Centre, Churchill College, Cambridge University. Char 2/417.
9 Winston S. Churchill to Freda Dudley Ward. 22 April 1941. Churchill Archives Centre, Churchill College, Cambridge University. Char 2/417.
10 Freda Dudley Ward to Duff Cooper. 14 May 1944 . Duff Cooper Papers. Churchill Archives Centre. DUFC 12021 (16).
11 Duff Cooper to Freda Dudley Ward. 24 October 1941. Martha Milinaric Papers.
12 Freda Dudley Ward to Duff Cooper. 24 December 1943. Duff Cooper Papers. Churchill Archives Centre, Churchill College, Cambridge. DUFC 12021 (5).
13 Freda Dudley Ward to Duff Cooper. 25 February 1944. Duff Cooper Papers. Churchill Archives Centre. DUFC 12021 (5).
14 Freda Dudley Ward to Duff Cooper. 14 May 1944. Duff Cooper Papers. Churchill Archives Centre. DUFC 12021 (16).
15 Richard Mead. *Commando General: The Life of Major General Sir Robert Laycock KCMG CB DSO*. Barnsley: Pen and Sword Military, 2016. 43.
16 Freda Dudley Ward to Duff Cooper. Undated. Duff Cooper Papers. Churchill Archives Centre. DUFC 12021 (31).
17 *Ibid*.
18 Andrew Morton. *17 Carnations*. 178.
19 *Ibid*. 181.
20 This book is not about Edward's life with Wallis. For further information about the Windsors' behaviour in the war there are many excellent biographies – see Philip Ziegler, Frances Donaldson, Anne Sebba and Andrew Morton.
21 Mead. *Commando General*. 204.
22 *Ibid*. x–xi.
23 Robert Langton. 'The Wartime Raid that Shamed Mountbatten.' 20 August 2012. *The Daily Express*.

24 Philip Ziegler. *Mountbatten: The Official Biography*. London: Book Club Associates, 1985. 186–91.

25 *Ibid.* 194–6.

26 Mead. *Commando General*. viii.

27 *Ibid.* 129.

28 *Ibid.* x–xi.

29 *Ibid.* 183.

30 Freda Dudley Ward to Duff Cooper. 20 January 1944. Duff Cooper Papers. Churchill Archives Centre. DUFC 12021 (10).

31 Freda Dudley Ward to Duff Cooper. 5 August 1944. Duff Cooper Papers. Churchill Archives Centre. DUFC 12021 (26).

32 Robert Laycock to Freda Dudley Ward. Martha Milinaric Papers.

33 Interview with Ben Laycock. 22 November 2017.

34 Freda Dudley Ward to Duff Cooper. 14 May 1944. Duff Cooper Papers. Churchill Archives Centre. DUFC 12021 (16).

35 Freda Dudley Ward to Winston S. Churchill. 15 December 1952. Churchill Archives Centre. Chur2/182A-B.

36 Mead. *Commando General*. 184.

37 *Ibid.* 188.

38 *Ibid.* 187.

39 *Ibid.* 193.

40 Interview with Ben Laycock. 22 November 2017.

41 Mead. *Commando General*. 193.

42 Nicholas Wapshott. *The Man Between: A Biography of Carol Reed*. London: Chatto and Windus, 1990. 188–92.

43 Laura, Duchess of Marlborough. *Laughter from a Cloud*. London: Weidenfeld and Nicolson, 1980. 33.

44 *Ibid.* 46–7.

45 *Ibid.* 103.

46 *Ibid.* 135.

47 *Ibid.*

48 *Ibid.* 132.

49 *Ibid.* 134.

50 Freda's solicitor to Freda Dudley Ward. May 1952. Martha Milinaric Papers.

51 Interview with Martha Milinaric and Max Reed. 10 June 2017.

52 Mead. *Commando General*. 192.

53 Interview with Martha Milinaric and Max Reed. 10 June 2017.

54 Kenneth Lindsay to Freda Dudley Ward. Undated possibly 1955. Martha Milinaric Papers.

55 *Ibid.*

56 The Feathers Club Association Literature. Churchill Archives Centre.

57 'Our Motley Notes.' 2 July 1952. *The Sketch*.

58 Interview with Emma Temple. 2 January 2018.

59 Interview with Ben Laycock. 22 November 2017.

60 Interview with Ned, Lord Lambton. 14 November 2017.
61 Freda Dudley Ward to Winston S. Churchill. 18 March 1958. Churchill Archives Centre. Chur2/521 A–B.
62 'Jennifer's Social Journal.' 21 January 1953. *The Tatler.*
63 Interview with Martha Milinaric and Max Reed. 10 June 2017.
64 Interview with Ben Laycock. 22 November 2017.
65 Lord Willingdon to Winston S. Churchill. 9 November 1954. Churchill Archives Centre. Chur2/187.
66 Eric Ednam, Lord Dudley to Winston S. Churchill. 31 July 1963. Churchill Archives Centre. Chur2/521 A–B.
67 Winston S. Churchill to Eric Ednam, Lord Dudley. 3 August 1963. Churchill Archives Centre. Chur2/521 A–B.
68 Prime Minister's Office to Winston S. Churchill. 15 August 1963. Churchill Archive Centre. Chur2/521A–B.
69 Eric Ednam, Lord Dudley to Winston S. Churchill. 8 August 1963. Churchill Archives Centre. Chur2/521/A–B.
70 Eric Ednam, Lord Dudley to Winston S. Churchill. 31 July 1963. Churchill Archives Centre. Chur2/521/A–B.
71 Interview with Emma Temple. 2 January 2018.
72 Interview with Ben Laycock. 22 November 2017.
73 Interview with Emma Temple. 2 January 2018.
74 Interview with Martha Milinaric and Max Reed. 10 June 2017.
75 Interview with Lady Isabella Naylor-Leyland. 23 October 2017.
76 Interview with Emma Temple. 2 January 2018.
77 Interview with Max Reed. 10 June 2017.
78 Interview with Emma Temple. 2 January 2018.
79 Interview with Ben Laycock. 22 November 2017.
80 Interview with Martha Milinaric. 29 March 2017.
81 Interview with Emma Temple. 2 January 2018.
82 Interview with Ben Laycock. 22 November 2017.
83 Lady Isabella Naylor-Leyland to the Feathers Club Association. No date. Feathers Club Association Archive.
84 Interview with Lady Lucinda Worsthorne. 21 November 2017.
85 Wapshott. *The Man Between.* 341.
86 Interview with Emma Temple. 2 January 2018.
87 Interview with Ned, Lord Lambton. 14 November 2017.
88 Interview with Ben Laycock. 22 November 2017.
89 *Ibid.*
90 Interview with Emma Temple. 2 January 2018.

Chapter 15

1 Gloria Vanderbilt and Thelma Furness. *Double Exposure: A Twin Autobiography.* London: Frederick Muller, 1958. 325.
2 Elsa Maxwell. *The Celebrity Circus.* London: W.H. Allen, 1964. 29.
3 Vanderbilt and Furness. *Double Exposure.* 326.
4 Ralph G. Martin. *The Woman He Loved: The Story of the Duke and Duchess of Windsor.* New York: Simon and Schuster, 1973. 165.
5 Leonard Slater. *Aly: A Biography.* New York: Random House, 1964. 4.
6 *Ibid.* 139.
7 Mary S. Lovell. *The Riviera Set.* London: Little, Brown, 2016. 257–8.
8 Gloria Morgan Vanderbilt and Palma Wayne. *Without Prejudice.* New York: E.P. Dutton, 1936. 264–5.
9 'Deauville Asides.' 5 September 1934. *The Sketch.*
10 'Goings Out and Goings On.' 21 August 1934. *The Bystander.*
11 'Deauville Asides.' 5 September 1934. *The Sketch.*
12 *Ibid.*
13 Vanderbilt and Furness. *Double Exposure.* 327.
14 Slater. *Aly: A Biography.* 9–10.
15 *Ibid.* 91.
16 Michael Bloch (ed.). *Wallis and Edward Letters 1931–1937: The Intimate Correspondence of the Duke and Duchess of Windsor.* London: Weidenfeld and Nicolson, 1986. 116.
17 Vanderbilt and Furness. *Double Exposure.* 327.
18 *Ibid.* xii.
19 Anderson Cooper and Gloria Vanderbilt. *The Rainbow Come and Goes: A Mother and Son on Life, Love and Loss.* New York: HarperCollins, 2016. 29.
20 Barbara Goldsmith. *Little Gloria … Happy at Last.* London: Pan Books, 1981. 21.
21 'The Vanderbilt Case.' 6 October 1934. *Gloucestershire Echo.*
22 Gloria Vanderbilt. *Once Upon a Time: A True Story by Gloria Vanderbilt.* London: Chatto and Windus, 1985. 7.
23 Goldsmith. *Little Gloria … Happy at Last.* 457.
24 *Ibid.* 6.
25 Vanderbilt and Wayne. *Without Prejudice.* 245.
26 Goldsmith. *Little Gloria … Happy at Last.* ix.
27 *Ibid.* 448.
28 *Ibid.* 406–10.
29 Vanderbilt and Wayne. *Without Prejudice.* 316.
30 Goldsmith. *Little Gloria … Happy at Last.* 428.
31 *Ibid.* 437.
32 *Ibid.* 428.
33 Vanderbilt and Wayne. *Without Prejudice.* 248.
34 Goldsmith. *Little Gloria … Happy at Last.* 384–6.
35 Cooper and Vanderbilt. *The Rainbow Come and Goes.* 79.

36 Goldsmith. *Little Gloria ... Happy at Last*. xii.
37 'Listen.' 18 December 1934. *The Bystander.*

Chapter 16

1   30 January 1935. *Hartlepool Northern Daily Mail.*
2   Barbara Goldsmith. *Little Gloria ... Happy at Last*. London: Pan Books, 1981. 511.
3   Gloria Morgan Vanderbilt and Palma Wayne. *Without Prejudice*. New York: E.P. Dutton, 1936. 337.
4   Goldsmith. *Little Gloria ... Happy at Last*. xiv.
5   'Peeress Designs Coronation Garb.' 24 November 1936. *Del Rio Evening News.*
6   7 October 1936. *The Tatler.*
7   Goldsmith. *Little Gloria ... Happy at Last*. 512.
8   2 June 1937. *Daily News*. Quoted in *ibid.* 511.
9   Goldsmith. *Little Gloria ... Happy at Last*. 511.
10 Gloria Vanderbilt and Thelma Furness. *Double Exposure: A Twin Autobiography*. London: Frederick Muller, 1958. 328.
11 'Coronation Review.' 10 February 1937. *The Tatler.*
12 Pat Cavendish O'Neill. *A Lion in the Bedroom*. Johannesburg and Cape Town: Jonathan Ball Publishers, 2004. 16–17.
13 *Ibid.* 38.
14 *Ibid.* 21–4.
15 *Ibid.* 42.
16 Vanderbilt and Furness. *Double Exposure*. 304–5.
17 Cavendish O'Neill. *A Lion in the Bedroom*. 117.
18 Vanderbilt and Furness. *Double Exposure*. 308–9.
19 'Extreme Gallantry of Guards' Officer.' 8 April 1941. *Western Mail.*
20 Vanderbilt and Furness. *Double Exposure*. 309–10.
21 Cavendish O'Neill. *A Lion in the Bedroom*. 73.
22 Vanderbilt and Furness. *Double Exposure*. 310.
23 Anderson Cooper and Gloria Vanderbilt. *The Rainbow Comes and Goes: A Mother and Son on Life, Love and Loss*. New York: HarperCollins, 2016. 114–20.
24 Gloria Vanderbilt. *Once Upon a Time: A True Story by Gloria Vanderbilt*. London: Chatto and Windus, 1985. 295.
25 Vanderbilt and Furness. *Double Exposure*. 313.
26 29 April 1941. *Charleston Gazette.*
27 Vanderbilt and Furness. *Double Exposure*. 313.
28 Richard Fawkes. 'Obituary: Viscount Furness.' 11 May 1995. *The Independent.*
29 Vanderbilt. *Once Upon a Time*. 133–40.
30 Cooper and Vanderbilt. *The Rainbow Comes and Goes*. 131–40.
31 'Hold Up Follows Gloria's Wedding: Stick Up Man Robs Mrs Vanderbilt and her Sister, Lady Thelma Furness.' 30 December 1941. *Hanover Evening Sun.*

32 Cooper and Vanderbilt. *The Rainbow Comes and Goes.* 152–5.

33 Goldsmith. *Little Gloria … Happy at Last.* 515.

34 Cavendish O'Neill. *A Lion in the Bedroom.* 135–6, 157.

35 Goldsmith. *Little Gloria … Happy at Last.* 515.

36 *Ibid.*

37 *Ibid.* 517.

38 Vanderbilt and Furness. *Double Exposure.* 342.

39 *Ibid.* 347.

40 Richard Fawkes. 'Obituary: Viscount Furness.' 11 May 1995. *The Independent.*

41 Goldsmith. *Little Gloria … Happy at Last.* xiii.

42 Cooper and Vanderbilt. *The Rainbow Comes and Goes.* 84.

43 Goldsmith. *Little Gloria … Happy at Last.* 515.

44 'Socialite Morgan Twins, Beauties of the 20s and 30s Now Make Dolls.' 8 June 1953. *Brazil Daily Times.*

45 Goldsmith. *Little Gloria … Happy at Last.* 517.

46 Vanderbilt and Furness. *Double Exposure.* 350.

47 'How the Stars Stay Slim.' 12 May 1957. *Corpus Christ Caller Times.*

48 Vanderbilt and Furness. *Double Exposure.* 351.

49 16 March 1959. *Daily Herald.* Quoted in Ralph G. Martin. *The Woman He Loved: The Story of the Duke and Duchess of Windsor.* New York: Simon and Schuster, 1973. 159.

50 Cooper and Vanderbilt. *The Rainbow Comes and Goes.* 39.

51 *Ibid.* 17–18.

52 *Ibid.* 94.

53 *Ibid.* 208–9.

54 *Ibid.* 211.

55 *Ibid.* 209–11.

56 Goldsmith. *Little Gloria … Happy at Last.* 517.

57 *Ibid.*

58 Cooper and Vanderbilt. *The Rainbow Comes and Goes.* 214.

59 *Ibid.* 94.

60 *Ibid.* 217.

61 'Vanderbilt Puts Life in Order in Autobiography.' 14 June 1985. *Fort Walton Beach Playground Daily News.*

62 Dominick Dunne. *Fatal Charms and Other Tales of Today.* New York: Crown Publishers, 1987. 162.

SELECT BIBLIOGRAPHY

Ackroyd, Peter, *Charlie Chaplin* (London: Vintage Books, 2015).

Airlie, Mabell, Countess of, *Thatched with Gold: The Memoirs of Mabell, Countess of Airlie* (London: Hutchinson, 1962).

Anand, Sushila, *Daisy: The Life and Loves of the Countess of Warwick* (London: Piatkus, 2008).

Asquith, Lady Cynthia, *Diaries: 1915–18* (London: Hutchinson, 1968).

Beaton, Cecil, *The Glass of Fashion: A Personal History of Fifty Years of Changing Tastes and the People Who Have Inspired Them* (New York: Rizzoli Ex Libris, 2014).

Bloch, Michael (ed.), *Wallis and Edward. Letters 1931–1937: The Intimate Correspondence of the Duke and Duchess of Windsor* (London: Weidenfeld and Nicolson, 1986).

Brown, Eve, *Champagne Cholly* (New York: E.P. Dutton, 1947).

Bryan III, J. and Charles J.V. Murphy, *The Windsor Story* (London: Granada Publishing, 1981).

Bunbury, Turtle, *The Glorious Madness: Tales of the Irish and the Great War: First Hand* (Dublin: Gill & Macmillan Ltd, 2014).

Cartland, Barbara, *I Search for Rainbows* (London: Hutchinson, 1967).

——, *We Danced All Night* (London: Arrow Books, 1977).

Cavendish O'Neill, Pat, *A Lion in the Bedroom* (Johannesburg and Cape Town: Jonathan Ball, 2004).

Colville, John, *The Fringes of Power: Downing Street Diaries 1939–1955* (London: Hodder and Stoughton, 1985).

Cooke, William, *Wings Over Meir* (Stroud: Amberley, 2010).

Cooper, Anderson and Gloria Vanderbilt, *The Rainbow Comes and Goes: A Mother and Son on Life, Love and Loss* (New York: HarperCollins, 2016).

Cooper, Artemis (ed.), *A Durable Fire: The Letters of Duff and Diana Cooper 1913–1950* (London: Hamish Hamilton, 1985).

Cooper, Diana, *Autobiography* (London: Michael Russell, 1979).

——, *Darling Monster: The Letters of Lady Diana Cooper to her Son John Julius Norwich* (London: Chatto and Windus, 2013).

——, *Autobiography: The Rainbow Comes and Goes, The Light of Common Day and Trumpets from the Steep* (London: Faber and Faber, 2014).

Cooper, Duff, *Old Men Forget* (London: Faber and Faber, 2011).

Davenport-Hines, Richard, *Ettie: The Intimate Life and Dauntless Spirit of Lady Desborough* (London: Weidenfeld and Nicolson, 2008).

Dinesen, Isak, *Letters from Africa 1914–1931: The Private Story Behind Karen Blixen's Great Memoir Out of Africa* (London: Weidenfeld and Nicolson, 1981).

Donaldson, Frances, *Child of the Twenties* (London: Rupert Hart-Davis, 1959).

——, *Edward VIII* (London: Futura Publications, 1976).

——, *A Twentieth-Century Life: A Memoir* (London: Weidenfeld and Nicolson, 1992).

Dunne, Dominick, *Fatal Charms and Other Tales of Today* (New York: Crown Publishers, 1987).

Edwards, Anne, *Matriarch: Queen Mary and the House of Windsor* (London: Rowan and Littlefield, 2015).

Fitzroy, Sir Almeric, *Memoirs* (London: Hutchinson, 1925).

Fox, James, *White Mischief* (London: Vintage, 1998).

Godfrey, Rupert (ed.), *Letters from a Prince* (London: Little, Brown, 1998).

Goldsmith, Barbara, *Little Gloria … Happy at Last* (London: Pan Books, 1981).

Grenfell, Ethel Anne Priscilla, *Pages from a Family Journal 1888–1915* (Eton College: Privately Printed Spottiswoode, Ballantyne and Co. Ltd, 1916).

Hardinge, Helen, *Loyal to Three Kings: A Memoir of Alec Hardinge, Private Secretary to the Sovereign 1920–1943* (London: William Kimber, 1967).

Hart-Davis, Duff (ed.), *In Royal Service: Letters and Journals of Sir Alan Lascelles from 1920 to 1936* (London: Hamish Hamilton, 1989).

——, *King's Counsellor: Abdication and War: The Diaries of Sir Alan Lascelles* (London: Weidenfeld and Nicolson, 2006).

Hatch, Alden, *The Mountbattens* (London: W.H. Allen, 1966).

James, Edward, *Swans Reflecting Elephants: My Early Years* (London: Weidenfeld and Nicolson, 1982).

Lees-Milne, James, *The Life of Reginald, 2nd Viscount Esher: The Enigmatic Edwardian* (London: Sidgwick and Jackson, 1986).

Levine, Naomi, *Politics, Religion and Love: The Story of H.H. Asquith, Venetia Stanley and Edwin Montagu* (New York: New York University Press, 1991).

Lockhart, Sir Robert Bruce, *Friends, Foes and Foreigners* (London: Putnam, 1957).

Lovell, Mary S., *Straight on Till Morning: The Life of Beryl Markham* (London: Abacus, 2014).

——, *The Riviera Set* (London: Little, Brown, 2016).

Lowndes, Susan (ed.), *Diaries and Letters of Marie Belloc Lowndes 1911–1947* (London: Chatto and Windus, 1971).

MacDonald, Lyn, *The Roses of No Man's Land: Nurses on the Western Front* (London: Penguin Books, 2013).

McEnroe, Natasha and Tig Thomas (eds), *The Hospital in the Oatfield: The Art of Nursing in the First World War* (London: Florence Nightingale Museum, 2014).

MacKenzie, Compton, *The Windsor Tapestry* (London: Rich and Cowan Ltd, 1938).

Marlborough, Laura, Duchess of, *Laughter from a Cloud* (London: Weidenfeld and Nicolson, 1980).

Martin, Ralph G., *The Woman He Loved: The Story of the Duke and Duchess of Windsor* (New York: Simon and Schuster, 1973).

Maxwell, Elsa, *I Married the World* (London: William Heinemann, 1955).

——, *The Celebrity Circus* (London: W.H. Allen, 1964).

Mead, Richard, *Commando General: The Life of Major-General Sir Robert Laycock KCMG CB DSO* (Barnsley: Pen and Sword Military, 2016).

Miller, Donald L., *Supreme City: How Jazz Age Manhattan Gave Birth to Modern America* (New York: Simon and Schuster, 2015).

Moore, Lucy, *Anything Goes: A Biography of the Roaring Twenties* (London: Atlantic Books, 2008).

Moran, Lord, *Winston Churchill: The Struggle For Survival, 1940–1965* (London: Constable, 1966).

Morton, Andrew, *17 Carnations: The Windsors, The Nazis and the Cover Up* (London: Michael O'Mara Books, 2015).

Nicolson, Nigel (ed.), *Harold Nicolson: Diaries and Letters 1907–1964* (London: Phoenix Paperback, 2005).

Norwich, John Julius (ed.), *The Duff Cooper Diaries 1915–1951* (London: Phoenix, 2006).

Petropoulos, Jonathan, *Royals and the Reich: The Princes Von Hessen in Nazi Germany* (Oxford: Oxford University Press, 2006).

Pope-Hennessy, James, *Queen Mary* (London: George Allen and Unwin, 1959).

Rhodes James, Robert (ed.), *'Chips': The Diaries of Sir Henry Channon* (London: Weidenfeld and Nicolson, 1993).

Rose, Andrew, *The Prince, the Princess and the Perfect Murder* (London: Coronet, 2013).

St Clair-Erskine, Lady Angela, *Fore and Aft* (London: Jarrolds, 1932).

Salmond, Monica, *Bright Armour: Memories of Four Years of War* (London: Faber and Faber, 1935).

Sebba, Anne, *That Woman: The Life of Wallis Simpson, Duchess of Windsor* (London: Weidenfeld and Nicolson, 2011).

Shaughnessy, Alfred (ed.), *Sarah: The Letters and Diaries of a Courtier's Wife 1906–1936* (London: Peter Owen, 1989).

Shawcross, William (ed.), *Queen Elizabeth, The Queen Mother: The Official Biography* (London: Pan Macmillan, 2010).

——, *Counting One's Blessings: The Selected Letters of Queen Elizabeth, the Queen Mother* (London: Macmillan, 2012).

Slater, Leonard, *Aly: A Biography* (New York: Random House, 1964).

Smith, Adrian, *Mountbatten: Apprentice War Lord 1900–1943* (London: I.B. Tauris, 2010).

Soames, Mary (ed.), *Speaking for Themselves: The Personal Letters of Winston and Clementine Churchill* (London: Doubleday, 1998).

Stuart, Denis, *Dear Duchess: Millicent, Duchess of Sutherland 1867–1955* (London: Victor Gollancz, 1982).

Sutherland, Duke of, *Looking Back: The Autobiography of the Duke of Sutherland* (London: Odhams Press, 1957).

Sutherland, Millicent, *Six Weeks at the War* (Chicago: A.C. McClurg and Co., 1915).

Taylor, A.J.P. (ed.), *Lloyd Geroge: A Diary By Frances Stevenson* (London: Hutchinson, 1971).

Taylor, D.J., *Bright Young People: The Rise and Fall of a Generation 1918–1940* (London: Vintage Books, 2008).

Thomasson, Anna, *A Curious Friendship: The Story of a Blue-Stocking and a Bright Young Thing* (London: Pan Macmillan, 2015).

Thornton, Michael, *Royal Feud: The Queen Mother and the Duchess of Windsor* (London: Michael Joseph, 1985).

Vacha, Robert (ed.), *The Kaiser's Daughter: Memoirs of HRH Viktoria Luise, Duchess of Brunswick and Luneburg, Princess of Prussia* (London: W.H. Allen, 1977).

Vanderbilt, Gloria, *Woman to Woman* (New York: Doubleday and Co., 1979).

——, *Once upon a Time: A True Story by Gloria Vanderbilt* (London: Chatto and Windus, 1985).

Vanderbilt, Gloria and Thelma, Lady Furness, *Double Exposure: A Twin Autobiography* (London: Frederick Muller, 1958).

Vanderbilt, Gloria and Palma Wayne, *Without Prejudice* (New York: E.P. Dutton, 1936).

Vickers, Hugo, *Cecil Beaton: The Authorised Biography* (London: Weidenfeld and Nicolson, 2002).

——, *Behind Closed Doors: The Tragic Untold Story of the Duchess of Windsor* (London: Arrow, 2012).

Wainwright, Robert, *Sheila: The Australian Beauty Who Bewitched British Society* (Sydney: Allen and Unwin, 2014).

Walker, Dora, *With the Lost Generation 1915–1919: From a VAD's Diary* (Hull: A. Brown and Sons, 1970).

Wapshott, Nicholas, *The Man Between: A Biography of Carol Reed* (London: Chatto and Windus, 1990).

Warwick, Christopher, *George and Marina, Duke and Duchess of Kent* (London: Albert Bridge Books, 2016).

Whitfield, Eileen, *Pickford: The Woman Who Made Hollywood* (Kentucky: University Press of Kentucky, 2007).

Windsor, Duchess of, *The Heart Has Its Reasons: The Story of the Abdication* (London: Tandem, 1975).

Windsor, Duke of, *A King's Story: The Memoirs of HRH the Duke of Windsor* (London: Pan Books, 1957).

Young, Kenneth (ed.), *The Diaries of Sir Robert Bruce Lockhart. Vol. 1: 1915–1938* (London: Macmillan, 1973).

Ziegler, Philip, *Diana Cooper: The Biography of Lady Diana Cooper* (London: Hamish Hamilton, 1981).

——, *Mountbatten: The Official Biography* (London: Book Club Associates, 1985).

——, *The Diaries of Lord Louis Mountbatten 1920–1922: Tours with the Prince of Wales* (London: HarperCollins, 1987).

——, *King Edward VIII: The Official Biography* (London: Fontana, 1991).

INDEX

If you enjoyed this title from
The History Press …

978 0 7509 6829 4